Comprehensive Computer Learning

Microsoft Office 2010

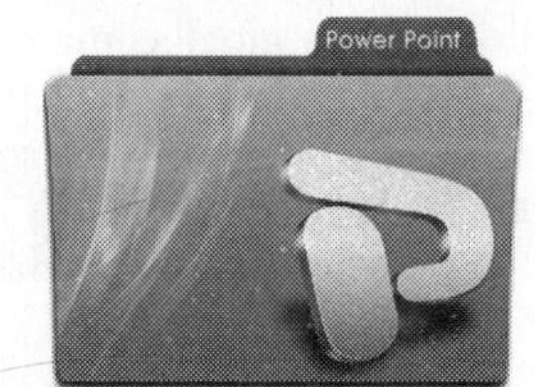

by

Bittu Kumar

Published by:

F-2/16, Ansari road, Daryaganj, New Delhi-110002
☎ 23240026, 23240027
✉ info@vspublishers.com • 🌐 www.vspublishers.com

Online Brandstore: amazon.in/vspublishers

Regional Office : Hyderabad
5-1-707/1, Brij Bhawan (Beside Central Bank of India Lane)
Bank Street, Koti, Hyderabad - 500 095
☎ 040-24737290
✉ vspublishershyd@gmail.com

Follow us on:   

BUY OUR BOOKS FROM: AMAZON FLIPKART

ISBN 978-93-505701-5-9
New Edition

DISCLAIMER

While every attempt has been made to provide accurate and timely information in this book, neither the author nor the publisher assumes any responsibility for errors, unintended omissions or commissions detected therein. The author and publisher makes no representation or warranty with respect to the comprehensiveness or completeness of the contents provided.

All matters included have been simplified under professional guidance for general information only, without any warranty for applicability on an individual. Any mention of an organization or a website in the book, by way of citation or as a source of additional information, doesn't imply the endorsement of the content either by the author or the publisher. It is possible that websites cited may have changed or removed between the time of editing and publishing the book.

Results from using the expert opinion in this book will be totally dependent on individual circumstances and factors beyond the control of the author and the publisher.

It makes sense to elicit advice from well informed sources before implementing the ideas given in the book. The reader assumes full responsibility for the consequences arising out from reading this book.

For proper guidance, it is advisable to read the book under the watchful eyes of parents/guardian. The buyer of this book assumes all responsibility for the use of given materials and information.

Printed at : Param Offsetters, Okhla, New Delhi–110020

Dedication

Dedicated To
Nirankari Baba Hardev Singh Ji Maharaj

Acknowledgements

I am highly thankful to M/S V&S Publishers, India for its valuable support throughout the making of this Book.

Mr. Dibya Jyoti Bora assisted all the time during the project development, I would like to give my heartiest thanks to him.

I would like to acknowledge the support getting from my family headed by Mr. Devendra Kumar while developing the book.

Mr. Sahil Gupta, Director, V&S Publishers should be acknowledged for allocation of resources.

At last, Nirankari Baba Hardev Singh Ji Maharaj, who provided Energy & Thoughts to develop this Project.

Publisher's Note

After successfully publishing youth-oriented books and getting commendable appreciation from students, teachers and parents alike, V&S Publishers is venturing into the arena of student and job-oriented books with a series of computer books on various important subjects for readers of all ages. Written and presented in lucid language and simple terms, without any computer jargon, these books are an easy-to-follow manual for readers. For the convenience of readers the information is set out in an easy to understand, step-by-step format, with clear illustrations and detailed explanations to accompany each action. Besides, every book is accompanied by an interactive video tutorials on Youtube for better understanding of the readers.

Today we live in a world of computers. The present scenario is that computers are used in every field be it education, business, trade and commerce, home and hobby, or even our ordinary day-to-day life. The importance of computers is an undeniable fact in today's world. In fact, we can't think of a world without computers.

Realising this indisputable fact, we are coming up with the series of **"Comprehensive Computer Learning (CCL)"** books. The series currently includes –

1. Comprehensive Computer Learning (CCL)
2. Comprehensive Computer Learning – A Youngsters' Guide
3. Comprehensive Computer Learning – Microsoft Office 2010
4. Comprehensive Computer Learning – Desktop Publishing (DTP)
5. Comprehensive Computer Learning – Adobe Photoshop

Key features of these books:

- ❑ Written in simple and lucid language
- ❑ Presented in step-by-step, easy-to-understand format with detailed explanations with appropriate images & screenshots, charts & tables
- ❑ Useful tips and notes given in every chapter as additional information
- ❑ Accompanied by interactive video tutorials on Youtube for better understanding

This book **"Comprehensive Computer Learning – Microsoft Office 2010"** has been written keeping in mind the needs of layman. MS Office with its new look & feel in its 2010 version is becoming more popular at offices & home and the book explains the basics of the same in some detail.

While every effort has been made to minimise printing and other errors, it may be possible that a few might have managed to escape the wakeful eyes. We would like to request the readers to bring these errors to our notice so that we can rectify the same in subsequent editions.

Preface

This book is for the users of Office 2010 who want to learn the program without wasting time and efforts. Not only look in this book to find out how the different programs in the Office Suite work & how to learn them, look in this book to find out how you can get your work done better and faster with these programs. Here we will discuss basic and advanced concepts of MS Office.

What Makes this Book Different

You are holding in your hands a computer book designed to make mastering the Office programs as easy and comfortable as possible. Besides the fact that this book is easy to read, it's different from other books about Office. Read on to see why.

What do you need

- ❑ Latest Edition of Microsoft office 2010
- ❑ Windows operating system: All people who have the Windows operating system installed on their computers are invited to read this book. It serves for people who have Windows 7, Windows Vista, Windows XP, and Windows NT.
- ❑ Basic Knowledge of English

What will you get

After a comprehensive reading of this book you will be able to do a variety of jobs. And you will notice that now you can do all office-related works.

– Bittu Kumar

Contents

Common Office Tools

Installing MS Office 2010

In this Chapter you will learn

- How to Install Microsoft-Office 2010 on your Computer.
- Step-by-step guide of installing Microsoft Office 2010 on your Computer.

The Most Important thing is installing the Microsoft Office on your Systems First. You can do it by purchasing a genuine copy of Microsoft Office from nearest software outlet, or simply download it from the Microsoft's official website. Here we are discussing setup instructions for Microsoft Office Professional Plus 2010.

After buying CD/Downloading files, follow these Instructions:

✓ Go to the File directory where the Microsoft office setup is.

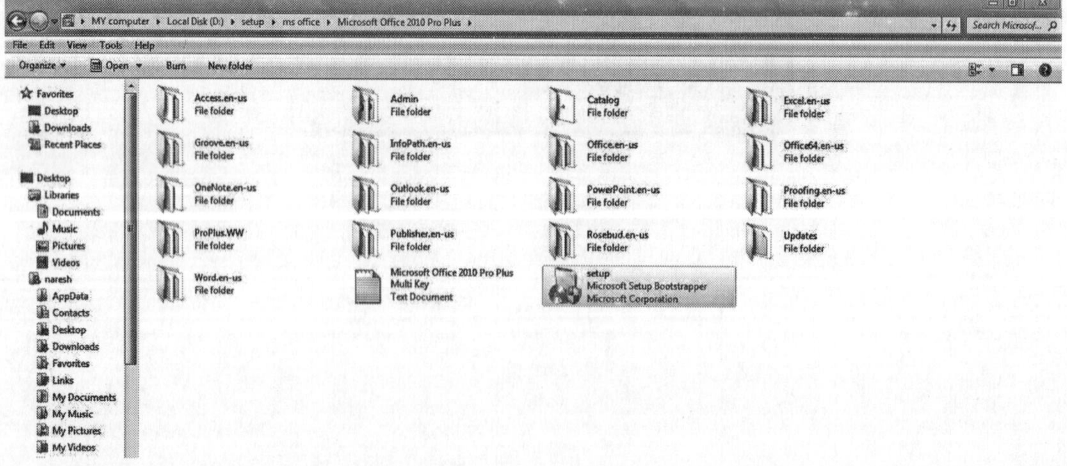

✓ Now click on Setup.exe and click on yes (In the case you are using Windows 7 or Vista).

✓ After sometime, the following dialog box will appear on your computer, Click "Install Now".

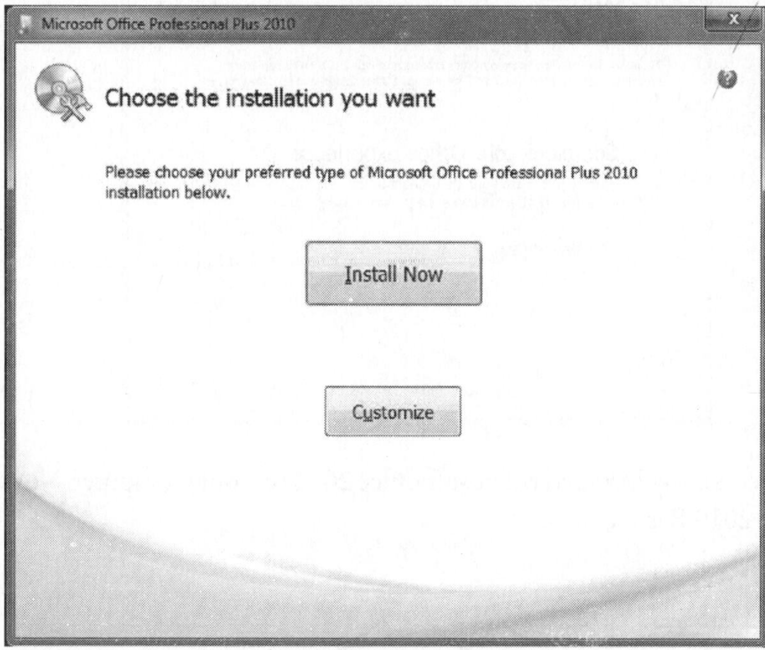

✓ The following box will appear on clicking "Install Now", wait for a few minutes and let Microsoft office 2011 be installed on your system.

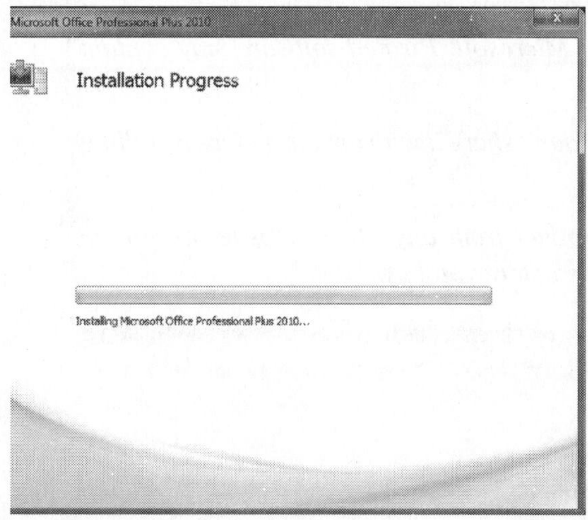

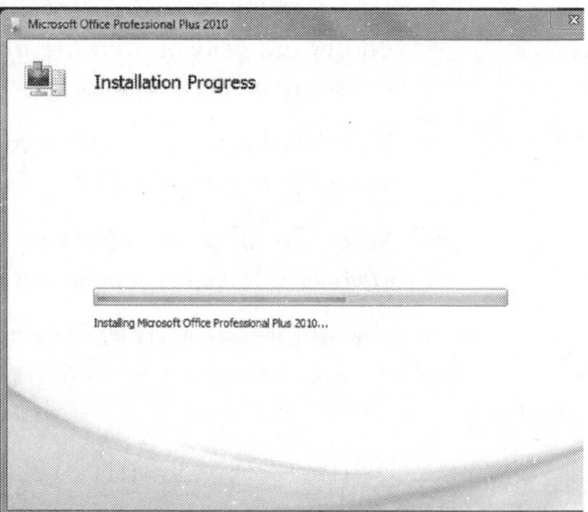

✓ Then Click "Close" and Cheers; you are done!

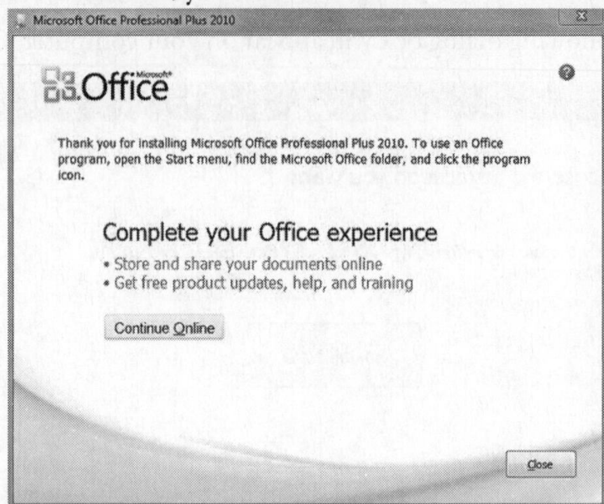

Now you have successfully Installed Microsoft office 2010 on your Computer. Now we shall begin Microsoft Office 2010 Basic Course

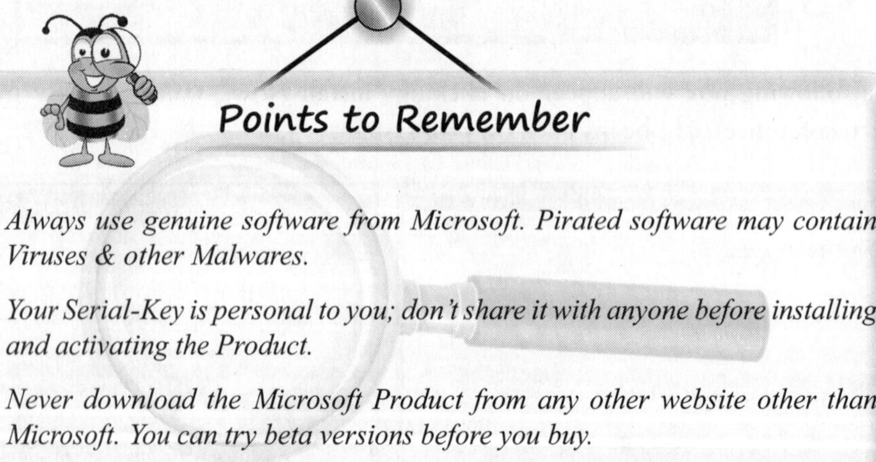

Points to Remember

- *Always use genuine software from Microsoft. Pirated software may contain Viruses & other Malwares.*
- *Your Serial-Key is personal to you; don't share it with anyone before installing and activating the Product.*
- *Never download the Microsoft Product from any other website other than Microsoft. You can try beta versions before you buy.*

Introduction to MS Office

In this chapter you will learn

- Introduction to different Microsoft Office programs
- Basic Information on the Graphical-User Interference
- Using different tabs in office Programs
- Creating, Saving & Editing your work
- Saving File in the earlier versions of Microsoft Office
- Encrypting the documents

Office 2010, sometimes called the Microsoft Office Suite, is a collection of computer programs. Why is it called Office? I think, because the people who developed it wanted to make software for completing tasks that need doing in a typical office. When you hear someone talk about "Office" or the "Office Software," they're talking about several different programs:

- **Word:** A word processor for writing letters, reports, and so on. A Word file is called a document.
- **Outlook:** A personal information manager, scheduler, and e-mailer.
- **PowerPoint:** A means of creating slide presentations to give in front of audiences. A PowerPoint file is called a presentation, or sometimes a slide show.
- **Excel:** A Part of office for performing numerical analyses. An Excel file is called a workbook.
- **Access:** A database management program.
- **Publisher:** A means of creating desktop-publishing files — pamphlets, notices, newsletters, and even books!

If you're new to Office, don't study so many different computer programs. The programs have much in common. You find the same commands throughout Office. For example, the method of choosing fonts is the same in Word, Outlook, PowerPoint, Excel, Access, and Publisher. Creating diagrams and charts works the same way in Word, PowerPoint, and Excel.

Starting an Office Program

Unless you start an Office program, you can't create a document, construct a worksheet, or make a database. Learn how you can do that.

✓ Click the Start button, choose All Programs → Microsoft Office, and then choose the program's name on the submenu.

User Interface in Microsoft Office

Interface, also called the user interface, is a computer term that describes how a software program presents itself to the people who use it.

Introduction to the GUI

❑ File tab

In the upper-left corner of the window is the File tab, Go to the File tab to find commands for creating, opening, and saving files, as well as doing other file-management tasks. Notice

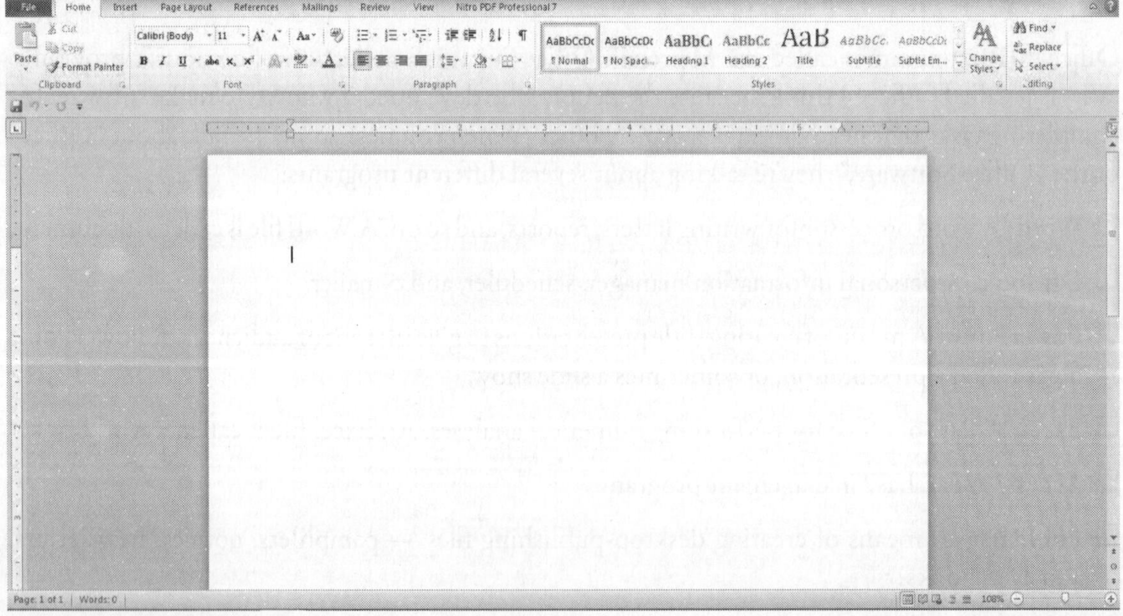

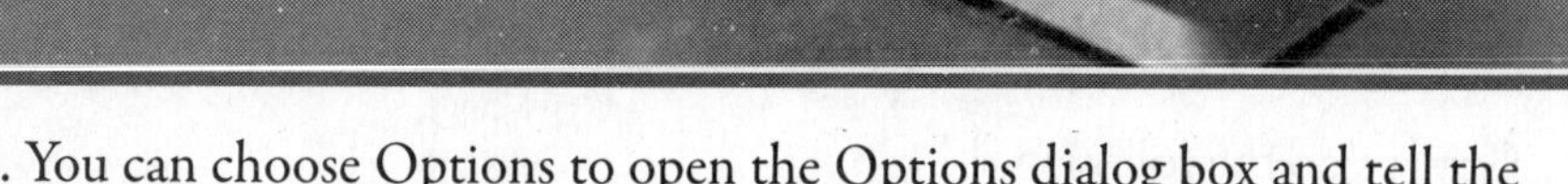

the Options command. You can choose Options to open the Options dialog box and tell the program you are working in how you want it to work.

The Ribbon and its tabs

Across the top of the screen is the Ribbon, an assortment of different tabs; click a tab to undertake a task. For example, click the Home tab to format text; click the Insert tab to insert a table or chart.

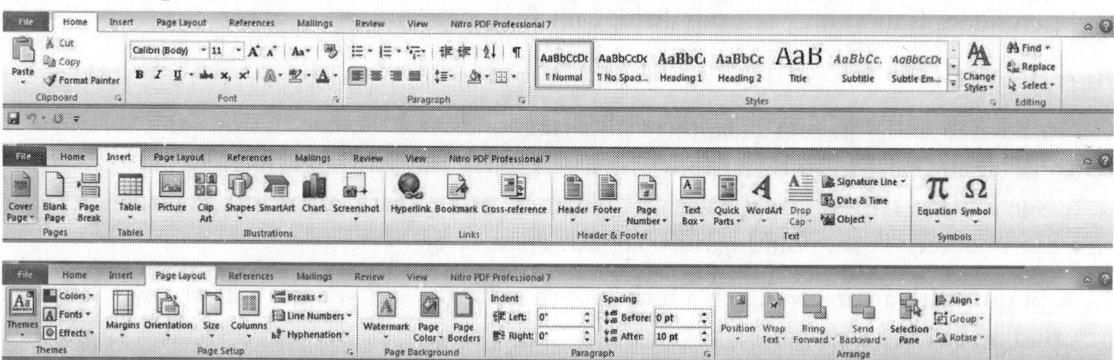

Your first step when you start a new task is to click a tab on the Ribbon. Knowing which tab to click takes a while, but the names of tabs — Home, Insert, View, and so on — hint as to which commands you find while you visit a tab.

To make the Ribbon disappear and get more room to view items on-screen, click the Minimize the Ribbon button (or press Ctrl+F1). This button is located on the right side of the Ribbon, to the left of the Help button. You can also right-click the Ribbon and choose Minimize the Ribbon on the shortcut menu, or double-click a tab on the Ribbon. To see the Ribbon again, click the Minimize the Ribbon button, press Ctrl+F1, double-click a Ribbon tab or right-click a tab name or the Quick Access toolbar and deselect Minimize the Ribbon on the shortcut menu. While the Ribbon is minimized, you can click a tab name to display a tab.

The Description of a tab

Groups

Commands on each tab are organized into groups. The names of these groups appear below the buttons and galleries on tabs. For example, the Home tab in Word is organized into several groups, including the Clipboard, Font, Paragraph, Styles.

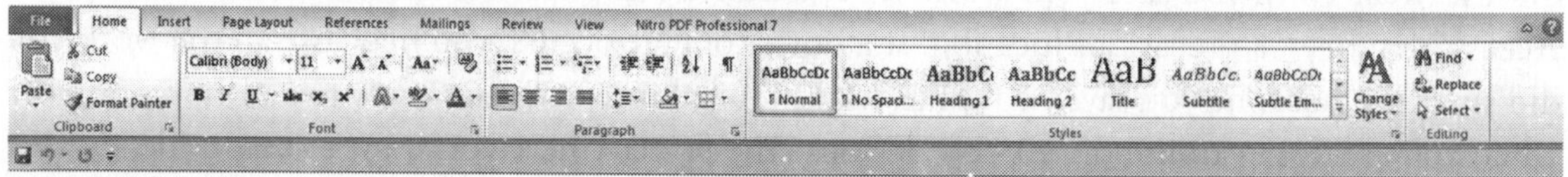

Groups do the following:

- ❑ Groups tell you what the buttons and galleries above their names are used for. On the Home tab in Word, for example, the buttons in the Font group are for formatting text. Read group names to help find the command you need.
- ❑ Many groups have a group button that you can click to open a dialog box or task pane (officially, Microsoft calls these little buttons dialog launcher).

Buttons

Go to any tab and you find buttons of all shapes and sizes. Square buttons and rectangular buttons; big and small buttons, buttons with labels and buttons without labels. Is there any rhyme or reason to these button shapes and sizes? No, there isn't. What matters isn't a button's shape or size, but whether a down-pointingarrow appears on its face:

- ❑ A button with an arrow: Click a button with an arrow and you get a drop-down list with options you can select.
- ❑ A button without an arrow: Click a button without an arrow and you complete an action of some kind.
- ❑ A hybrid button with an arrow: Some buttons serve a dual purpose as a button and a drop-down list. By clicking the symbol on the top half of the button, you complete an action; by clicking the arrow on the bottom half of the button, you open a drop-down list. On the Home tab, for example, clicking the top half of the Paste button pastes what is on the Clipboard into your file, but clicking the bottom half of the button opens a drop-down list with Paste options.

Keyboard Shortcuts

People who like to give commands by pressing keyboard shortcuts may well ask, "Is there keyboard shortcuts in Office?" The answer is: Yes, Office has shortcuts. For example, you can press Ctrl+B to boldface text and Ctrl+U tounderline text. Office offers Alt+key shortcuts as well.

Saving Your Files

Soon after you create a file, be sure to save it. And save your file from time to time while you work on it as well. Until you save your work, it rests in the computer's electronic memory (**R**andom Access Memory), a precarious location. If a power outage occurs, you may lose all the work you did since the last time you saved your file. Make it a habit to save files every five Minutes or so or when you are doing an important task. Choose the folder where you want to save a file, declare

where you want to save files by default, save files for use in 97–2003 editions of Office, and handle files that were saved automatically after a computer failure.

To save a file:

✓ Click the Save button (you find it on the Quick Access toolbar).

✓ Press Ctrl+S.

✓ Go to the File tab and choose Save. 

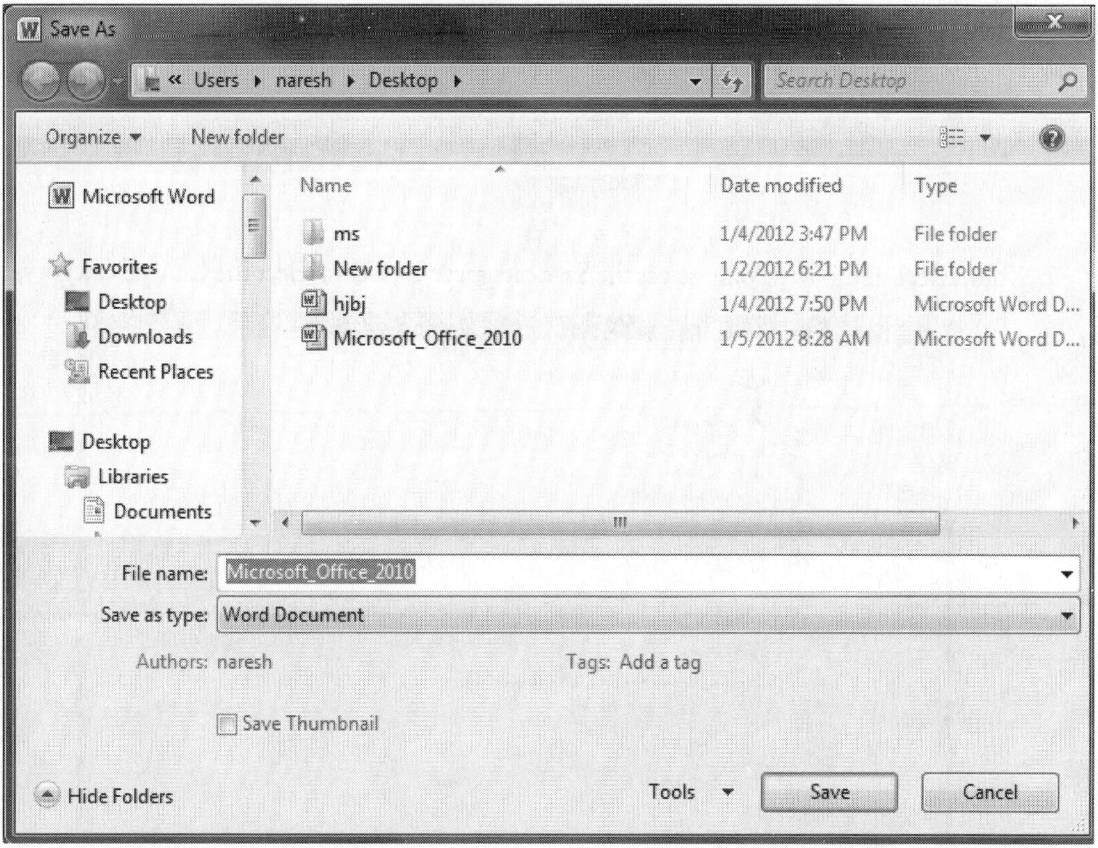

Where you like to save files

To direct Office to the folder you like best and make it appear first in the Save As and Open dialog boxes, follow these steps:

✓ In Word, Excel, PowerPoint, or Access, go to the File tab and choose Options.

You see the Options dialog box.

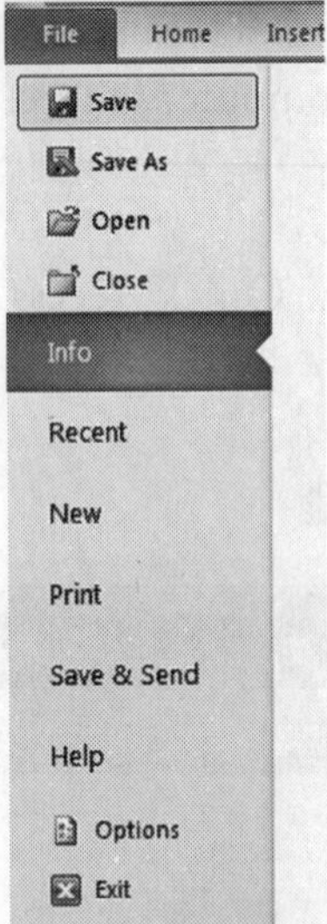

✓ In Word, Excel, and PowerPoint, select the Save category; in Access, select the General category.

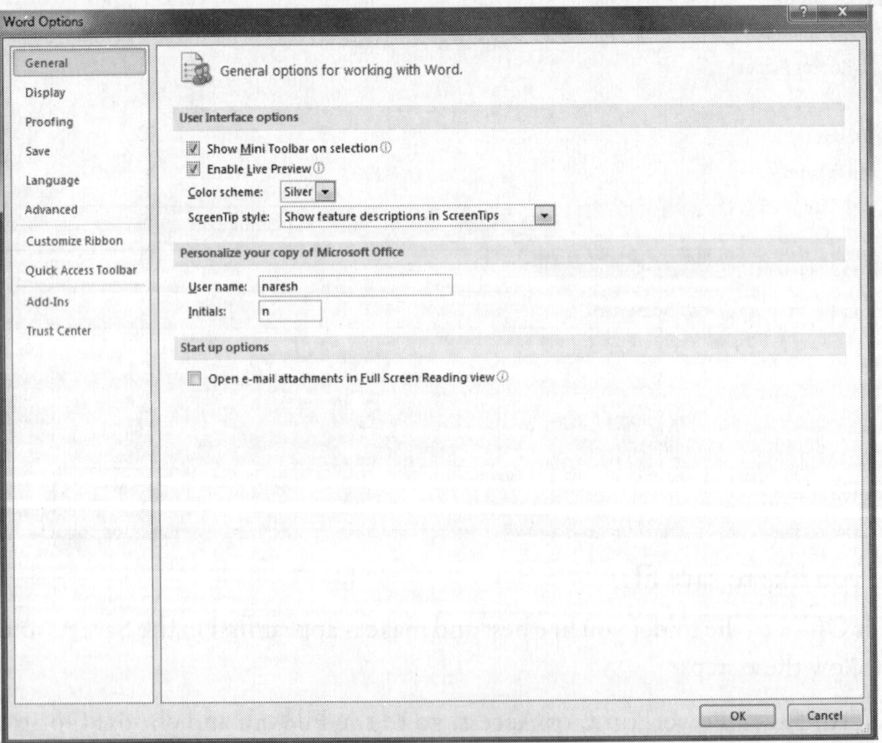

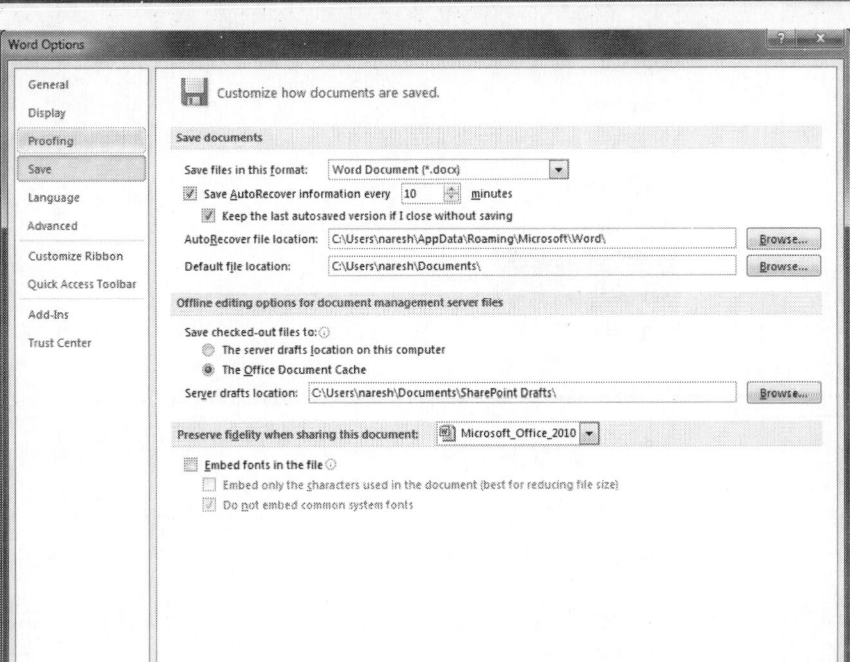

Saving a file in word

Saving files for use in earlier versions of an Office program

Before you pass along a file to a user who has Office 2003, XP, 2000, or 97, save your document in these versions so that the other person can open it. People with versions of Office prior to version 2010 and 2007 cannot open your Office files unless you save your files for earlier versions of Office.

Program	**2010, 2007**	**97–2003**
Access	.accdb	.mlb
Excel	.xlsx	.xls
PowerPoint	.pptx	.ppt
Publisher	.pub	.pub
Word	.docx	.doc

Saving a file for use in Office 97–2003

Follow these steps to save a file so that someone with Office 97, 2000, XP, or2003 can open it:

✓ Go to the File tab.

✓ Choose Save & Send.

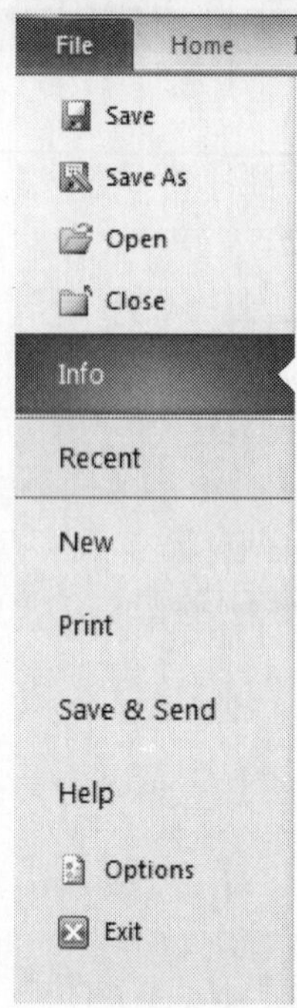

✓ You see the Share window.

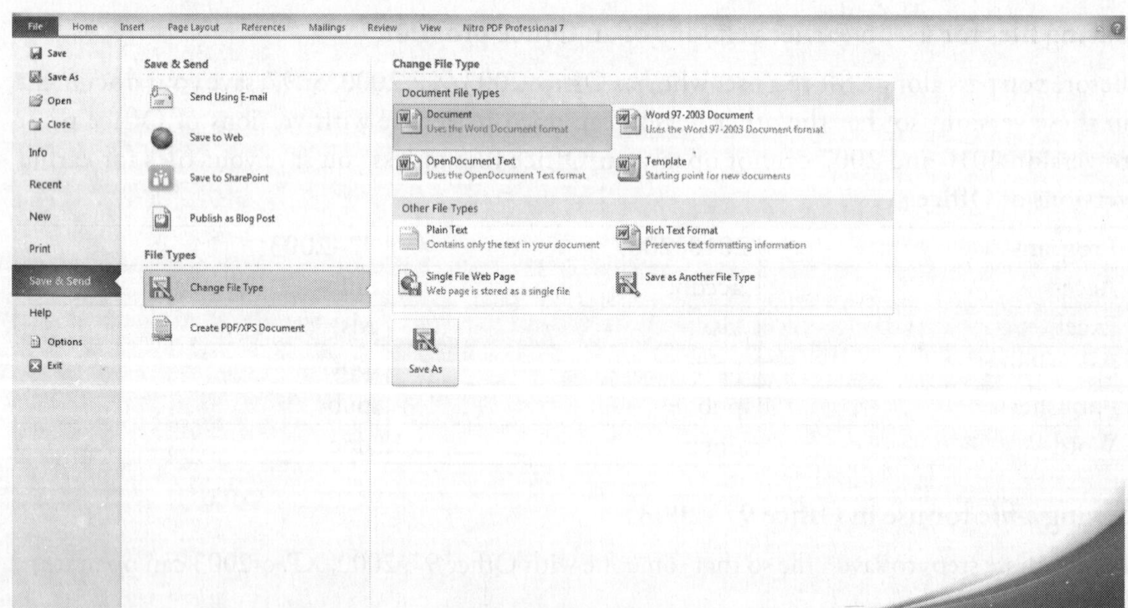

✓ Under File Types, choose Change File Type and then choose 97–2003 option for saving files.

The Save As dialog box opens.

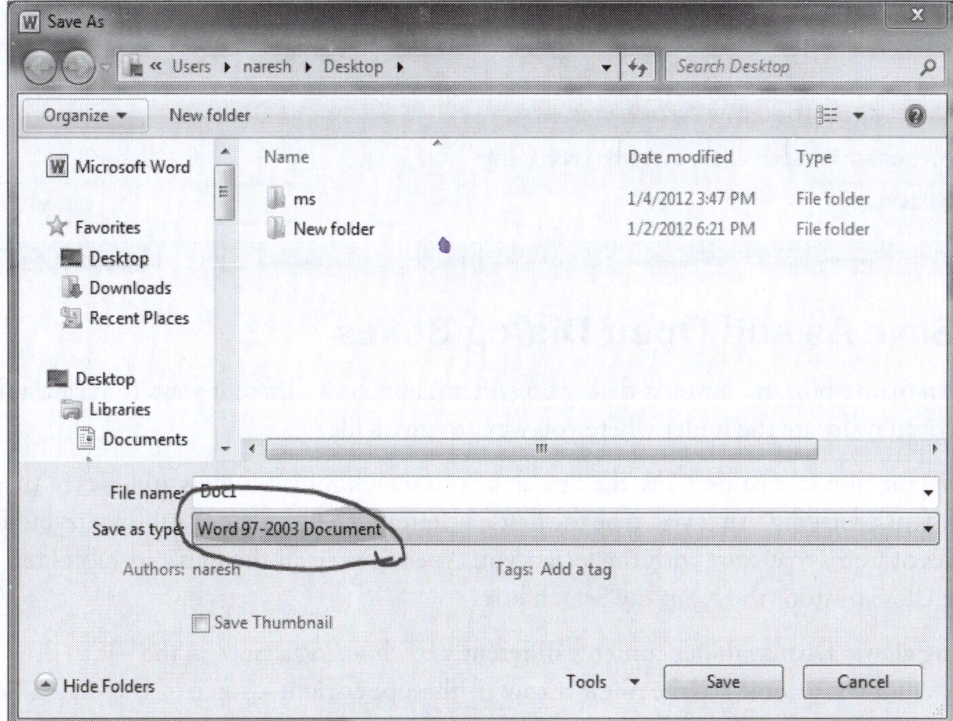

✓ Enter a new name for the file, if necessary.

✓ Click the Save button.

Saving Auto Recovery information

To insure against data loss due to computer and power failures, Office saves files on its own every ten minutes. These files are saved in an Auto Recovery file. You can try to recover some of the work you lost by getting it from the Auto Recovery file.

Convert Earlier Version of word to 2010

Compatibility Mode

Some new features are disabled to prevent problems when working with previous versions of Office. Converting this file will enable these features, but may result in layout changes.

Go to File → Convert→ Click "Okay"

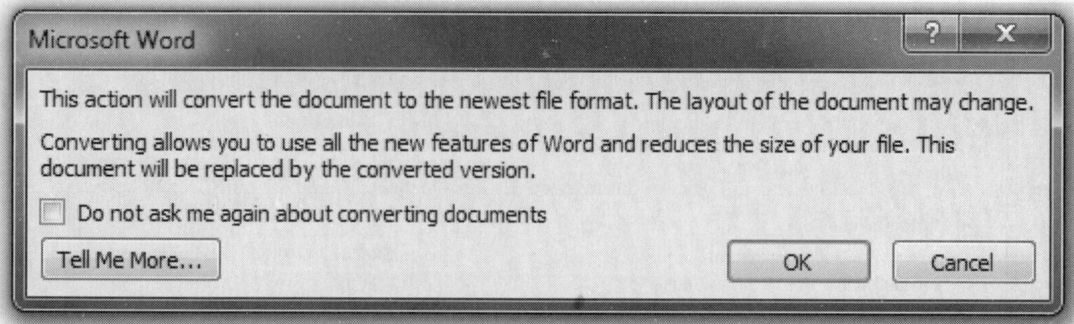

The Save As and Open Dialog Boxes

The Open dialog box and Save As dialog box offer a bunch of different ways to locate a file you want to open or locate the folder where you want to save a file.

Searching for files in a folder: Use the Search box to search for subfolders and files in the folder you is currently viewing. After you type the first few letters of a file name or subfolder, you see only the names of items that start with the letters you typed. To see all the files and subfolders again, click the Close button (the X) in the Search box.

Changing views: Display folder contents differently by choosing a view on the Views drop-down list (in Windows 7, look for the View arrow in the upper-right corner of the dialog box). In Details view, you see how large files are and when they were last edited.

Creating a new folder: Click the New Folder button to create a new subfolder for storing files. Select the folder that your new folder will be subordinate to and click the New Folder button. Then type a name forthe saved file.

Navigate to different folders: Click the Folders bar (in the lower-left corner of the dialog box) to open the Navigation pane and look for folders or presentations on a different drive, network location, or folder on your computer.

Opening a file

- ✓ On the File tab, choose Open (or press Ctrl+O).
- ✓ Locate and select the file you want to open.
- ✓ Click the Open button.

✓ Your file opens. You can also double-click a filename to open a file.

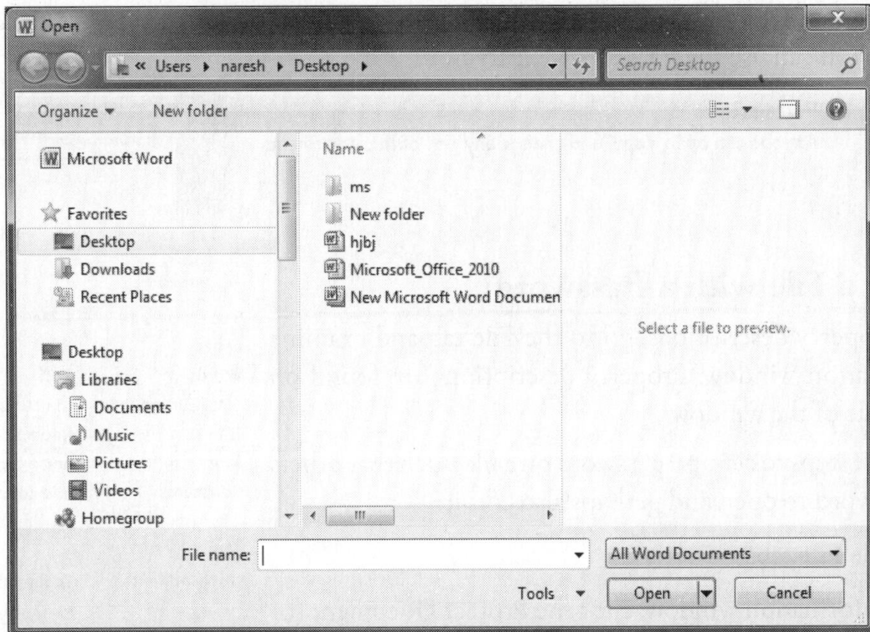

✓ If you have recently accessed the file you can use recent button in file tab.

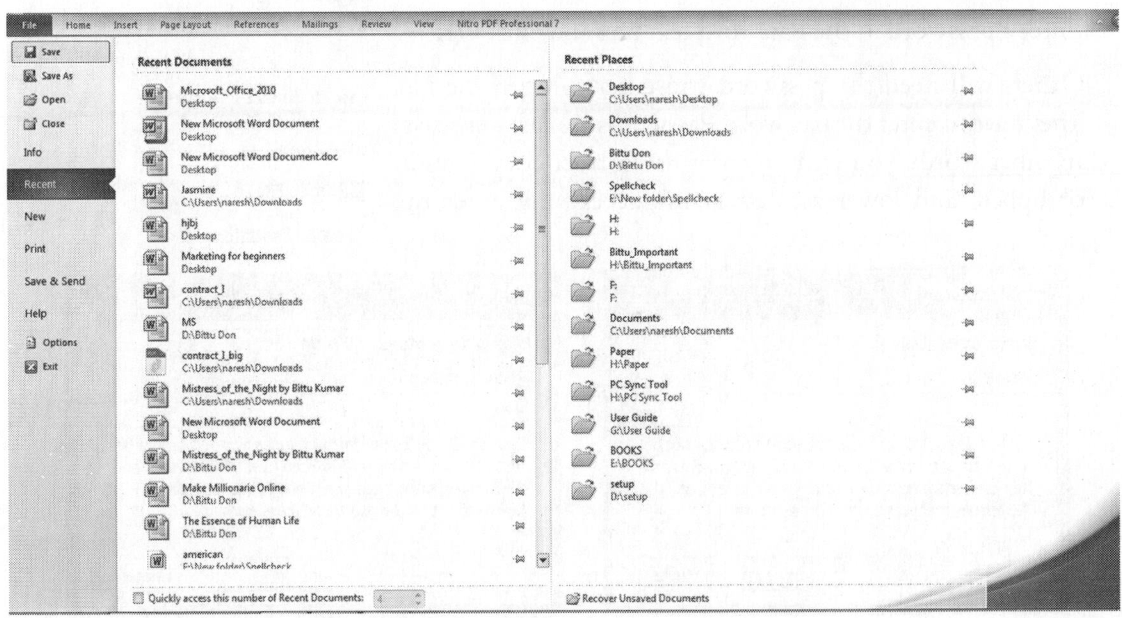

File Properties

Properties are a means of describing a file. If you manage more files, you owe it to yourself to record properties. You can use them later to identify files.

Permissions

Anyone can open, copy, and change any part of this document.

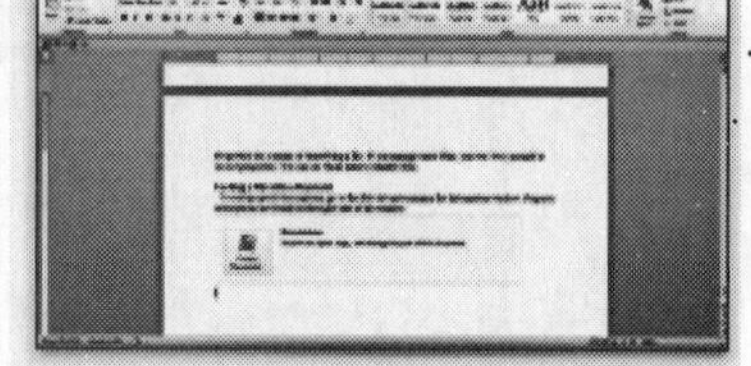

Locking a File with a Password

To read property descriptions, go to the File tab and examine the Information window. Property descriptions are found on the right side of the window.

Follow these steps to clamp a password on a file, such that others need apassword to open and perhaps also edit it:

- ✓ Go to the File tab.
- ✓ In the Information window, click the Protect Document (or Workbook) button, and choose Encrypt with Password on the drop-down list.
- ✓ Enter a password in the Password text box and click OK.

  Others will need the password you enter to open the file. They have to enter the password.Passwords are case-sensitive. In other words, you have to enter the correct combination of upper- and lowercase letters to successfully enter the

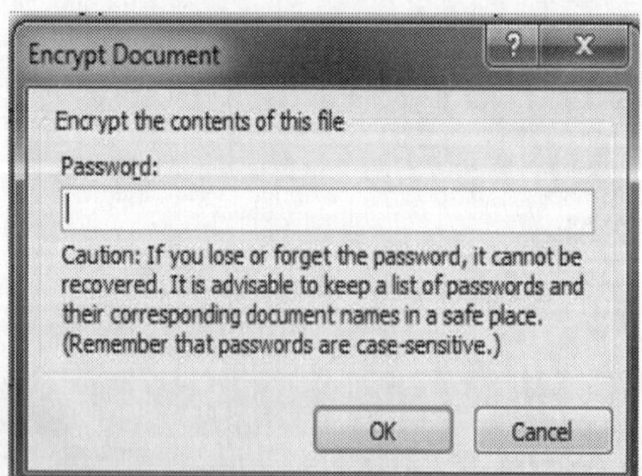

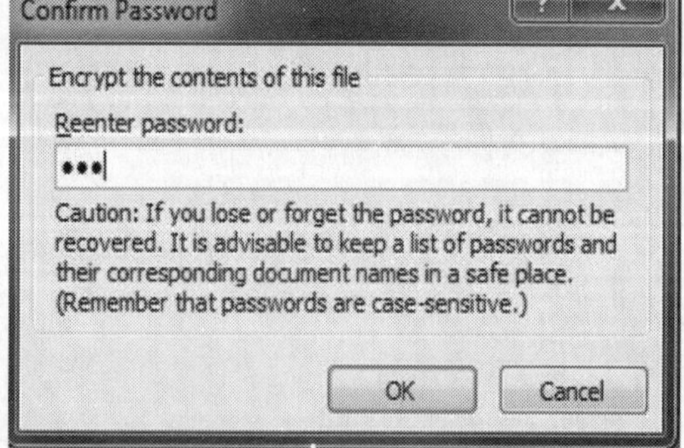

password. If the password is Apple (with an uppercase A), mentoring apple (with a lowercase a) is deemed the wrong passwordand doesn't open the file.

- ✓ In the Confirm Password dialog box, enter the password again.
- ✓ Click OK.

The Information window informs you that a password is required to open the file.

Removing Password

Follow these steps to remove a password from a file:

- ✓ Open the file that needs its password removed.
- ✓ Go to the File tab and in the Information window, click the Protect Document button, and choose Encrypt with Password.
- ✓ Delete the password and click OK.

Points to Remember

- ☞ Always save your files with custom names, so that you can easily index your files. Using default names for multiple files will waste your time in finding out which file you need to edit once you have closed the file.
- ☞ To keep the file size minimum save the file in 2010 format, it will save your disk space.
- ☞ Always keep your files in the Custom directory other than Primary Hard disk (This will help in you safeguarding your files against any system faliures). In other words never save your important files in C: / (C:/ here stands for primary directory, the primary directory may vary for different users)
- ☞ The Passwords are Case Sensitive; there is no way to recover forgotten passwords so confirm twice that you can remember it.
- ☞ Never use any foreign software for extracting/removing the password, it will harm your computer.
- ☞ If you are running your Computer in frequent power-cut environment, please save your file frequently to save your hard work in editing the file.
- ☞ Use Keyboard shortcuts to save your time.

- Use variety of names for saving your file, for example if you write essay on Independence day, your system will give your document a default name of "New Microsoft word Document X.docx (X~ some number), you can save your file as "Independence day.docx" to remember the file if you need further editing after quitting.
- Never save your file at insecure places (Web directory, etc.) where a hacker can easily access it.
- Make sure that you have an updated Anti-Malware protection enabled on your system.
- Please scan the documents with your Anti-Malware software before opening them. Most probably the Files downloaded from Internet contains some spywares, adware, Trojan horses & some other harmful programs.
- Never edit any document having other extensions than discussed in the chapter, it can corrupt the file. (For example if you open .pdf files with MS Word & Edit it, this will corrupt its contents.)

Formatting Text

In this chapter you will learn

- Ways to select different elements of the file or document
- Formatting font styles and other Elements
- Changing the size, colour, opacity of the elements in the file or document
- Using Symbols & formulae in the file or document
- Finding and replacing data in the file or document
- Creating Links to files & websites

Selecting text

Before you can perform any activity to any text you have to select it.

To Select	Do This
A word	Double-click the word.
A few words	Drag over the words.
A paragraph	Triple-click inside the paragraph
A block of text	Click the start of the text, hold down the Shift key, and click the end of the text. In Word you can also click the start of the text, press F8, and click at the end of the text.
All text	Press Ctrl+A.

Moving and Copying text

- ✓ **Dragging and Dropping:** Move the mouse over the text and then click and drag the text to a new location. Drag means to hold down the mouse button while you move the pointer on-screen. If you want to copy rather than move the text, hold down the Ctrl key while you drag.
- ✓ **Dragging and Dropping with the right mouse button**: Drag the text while holding down the right, not the left, mouse button. After you release the right mouse button, a shortcut menu appears with Move Here and Copy Here options. Choose an option to move or copy the text.
- ✓ **Using the Clipboard**: Move or copy the text to the Clipboard by clicking the Cut or Copy button, pressing Ctrl+X or Ctrl+C, or right-clicking and choosing Cut or Copy on the shortcut menu. The text is moved or copied to an electronic holding tank called the Clipboard. Paste the text by clicking the Paste button, pressing Ctrl+V, or right-clicking and choosing Paste. You can find the Paste, Cut, and Copy buttons on the Hometab.

Deleting text

To delete a bunch of text, select the text you want to delete and press the Delete key.

Changing the Look of Text

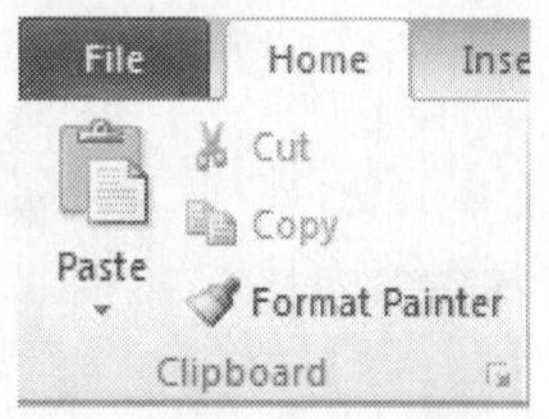

What text looks like is determined by its font, the size of the letters, the colour of the letters, and whether text effects or font styles such as italic or boldface are in the text. The text's appearance really matters in Word, PowerPoint, and Publisher because files you create in those programs are meant to be read by all and sundry. Even in Excel, Access, and Outlook messages, font choices matter because the choices you make determine whether your work is easy to read and understand.

A font is a collection of letters, numbers, and symbols in a particular typeface, including all italic and boldface variations of the letters, numbers, and symbols.

Choosing fonts for text

- ✓ **Mini-toolbar:** Move the pointer over the selected text. You see the mini toolbar. Move the pointer over this toolbar and choose a font in the Font drop-down list.
- ✓ **Shortcut menu:** Right-click the selected text and choose a new font on the shortcut menu.
- ✓ **Font drop-down list:** On the Home tab, open the Font drop-down list and choose a font.
- ✓ **Font dialog box:** On the Home tab, click the Font group button. You see the Font dialog box. select a font and click OK.

Changing the font size of text

- ✓ Font size is measured in points; a point is 1/72 of an inch.
- ✓ **Mini-toolbar:** Move the pointer over the text, and when you see the mini toolbar, move the pointer over the toolbar and choose a font size on the Font.
- ✓ **Shortcut menu:** Right-click the text and choose a new font size on the shortcut menu.
- ✓ **Font Size drop-down list:** On the Home tab, open the Font Size dropdown list and choose a font. You can live-preview font sizes this way.
- ✓ **Font dialog box:** On the Home tab, click the Font group button, and in the Font dialog box, choose a font size and click OK.
- ✓ **Increase Font Size and Decrease Font Size buttons:** Click these buttons (or press Ctrl+] or Ctrl+[) to increase or decrease the point size by the next interval on the Font Size drop-down list.

Applying font styles to text

- ❑ **Regular:** This style is just Office's way of denoting an absence of any font style.
- ❑ **Italic:** You can also italicize titles to make them a little more elegant. (Ctrl+I)

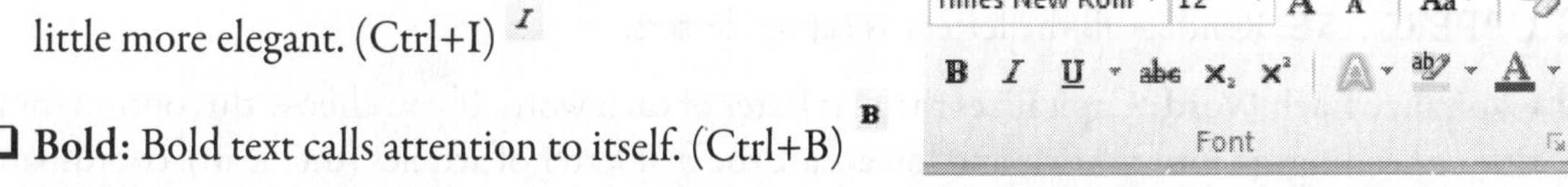

- ❑ **Bold:** Bold text calls attention to itself. (Ctrl+B)
- ❑ **Underline:** Underlined text also calls attention to itself, but use underlining sparingly. Later in this chapter, "Underlining text" discusses all the ways to underline text.
- ❑ **Strikethrough and double strikethrough:** By convention, strikethrough is used to show where passages are struck from a contract or other important document.
- ❑ **Subscript:** A subscripted letter is lowered in the text. In the chemical formula below, the 2 is lowered to show that two atoms of hydrogen are needed along with one atom of oxygen to form a molecule of water: H_2O. (Press Ctrl+=.)
- ❑ **Superscript:** A superscripted letter or number is one that is raised in the text. Superscript is used in mathematical and scientific formulas, in ordinal numbers (1st, 2nd , 3rd), and to mark footnotes. In the theory of relativity, the 2 is superscripted: $E = mc^2$. (Press Ctrl+Shift+plus sign.)

Changing the colour of text

✓ On the mini-toolbar, open the drop-down list on the Font Colour button and choose a colour.

✓ Right-click, open the drop-down list on the Font Colour button, and choose a colour on the shortcut menu.

✓ On the Home tab, open the drop-down list on the Font Colour button and choose a colour.

✓ On the Home tab, click the Font group button to open the Font dialog box, open the Font Colour drop-down list, and choose a colour. The Font Colour drop-down list offers theme colours and standard colours. You are well advised to choose a theme colour. These colours are deemed theme colours because they jive with the theme you choose for your file.

Changing Case

To change case in Word and PowerPoint, all you have to do is select the text, go to the Home tab, click the Change Case button, and choose an option on the drop-down list:

❑ **Sentence case:** Renders the letters in sentence case.

❑ **lowercase:** Makes all the letters lowercase.

❑ **UPPERCASE:** Renders all the letters as capital letters.

❑ **Capitalize Each Word:** Capitalizes the first letter of each word. If you choose this option for a title or heading, go into the title and lower case the first letter of articles (the, a, an), coordinate conjunctions (and, or, for, nor), and prepositions unless they're the first or last word in the title.

❑ **TOGGLE CASE:** Choose this option if you accidentally enter letters with the Caps Lock key pressed.

Entering Symbols and Foreign Characters

✓ On the Insert tab, click the Symbol button. (You may have to click the Symbols button first, depending on the size of your screen)

✓ If you're looking to insert a symbol, not a foreign character, choose Webdings or Wingdings 1, 2, or 3 in the Font drop-down list.

✓ Webdings and Wingdings fonts offer all kinds of weird and wacky symbols.

✓ Select a symbol or foreign character.

✓ Click the Insert button to enter the symbol and then click Close to close the dialog box.

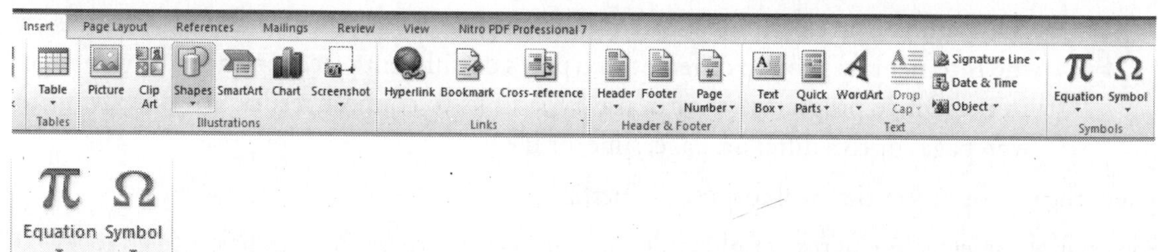

Finding and Replacing Text

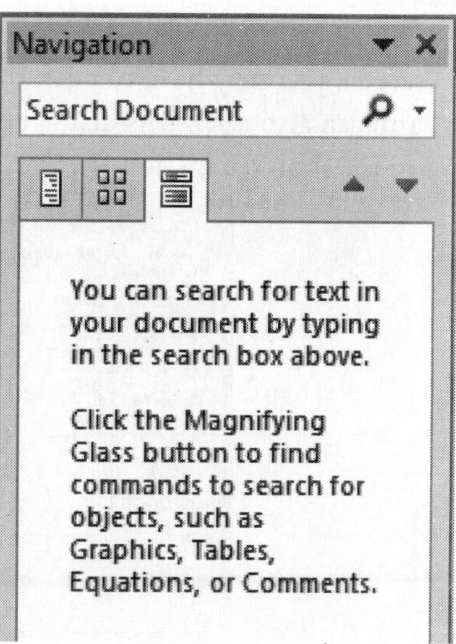

✓ Press Ctrl+F or go to the Home tab and click the Find button. (In Excel, click the Find & Select button and choose Find on the dropdown list.)

✓ Enter the word or phrase in the Find What or Search Documenttext box.

After you enter the word or phrase in Word, the Navigation pane lists each instance of the term you're looking for and the term is highlighted in your document wherever it is found. You can click an instance of the search term in the Navigation pane to scroll to a location in your document where the search term is located. You can also remove the word using replace.

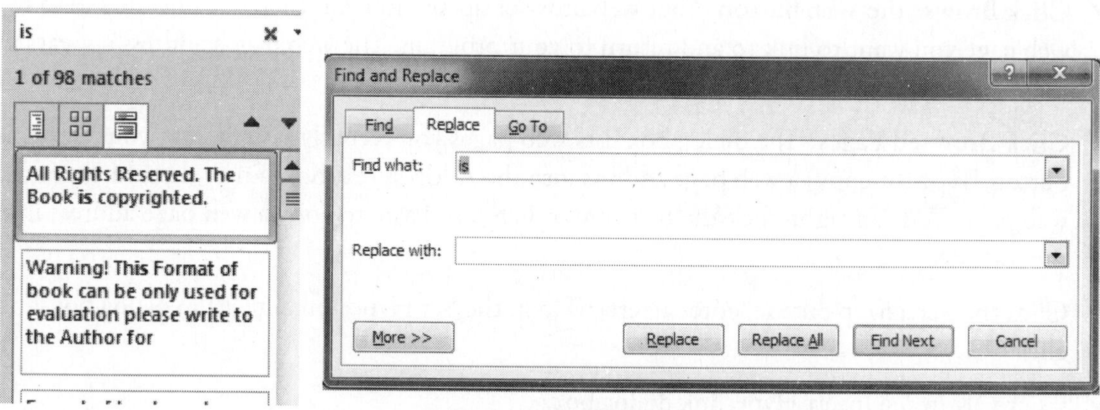

Finding and Replacing text

Creating Hyperlinks

A hyperlink is an electronic shortcut from one place to another. Clicking hyperlinks on the Internet takes you to different web pages or different places on the same web page. In the Office programs, you can use hyperlinks to connect readers to your favourite web pages or to a different page, slide, or file.

Select the text or object that will form the hyperlink.

For example, select a line of text or phrase if you want viewers to be able to click it to go to a web page.

- ✓ On the Insert tab, click the Hyperlink button (or press Ctrl+K). Depending on the size of your screen, you may have to click the Links button before you can get to the Hyperlink button. You can also open this dialog box by right-clicking an object or text and choosing Hyperlink on the shortcut menu

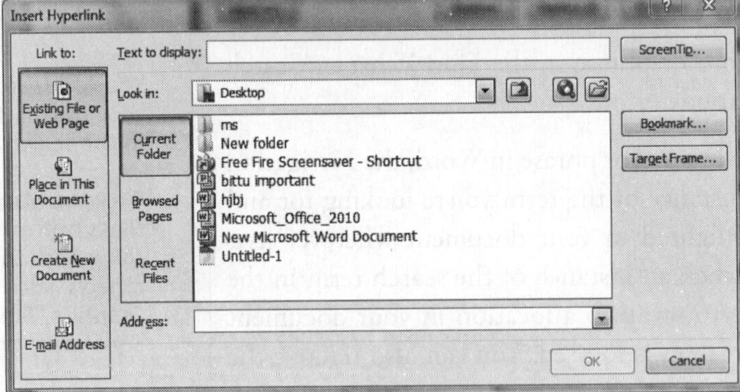

Creating Hyperlink

- ✓ **Click Browse the Web button:** Your web browser opens after you click this button. Go to the web page you want to link to and return to your program. The web page's address appears in the Address text box.
- ✓ **Click Browsed Pages:** The dialog box lists web pages you recently visited after you click this button, Type (or copy) a web page address into the Address text box: Enter the address of the web page. You can right-click the text box and choose Paste to copy a web page address into the text box.
- ✓ Click the ScreenTip button, enter a ScreenTip in the Set HyperlinkScreenTip dialog box, and click OK.
- ✓ Click OK in the Insert Hyperlink dialog box.

Creating a hyperlink to another place in your file

Follow these steps to create a hyperlink to another place in your file:

- ✓ Select the text or object that will form the hyperlink.
- ✓ On the Insert tab, click the Hyperlink button (or press Ctrl+K). You see the Insert Hyperlink dialog box. Another way to open this dialog box is to right-click and choose Hyperlink in the shortcut menu.
- ✓ Under Link To, select Place in This Document. What you see in the dialog box depends on which program you're working in.
- ✓ Select the target of the hyperlink. Click the ScreenTip button.
- ✓ You see the Set Hyperlink ScreenTip dialog box.
- ✓ Enter a ScreenTip and click OK. When viewers move their pointers over the link, they see the words you enter. Enter a description of where the hyperlink takes you.

Creating an e-mail hyperlink

- ✓ An e-mail hyperlink is one that opens an e-mail program. These links are sometimes found on web pages so that anyone visiting a web page can conveniently send an e-mail message to the person who manages the web page. When you click an e-mail hyperlink, your default e-mail program opens. And If the person who set up the link was thorough about it, the e-mail message is already addressed and given a subject line.
- ✓ Select the words or object that will constitute the link.
- ✓ On the Insert tab, click the Hyperlink button (or press Ctrl+K). The Insert Hyperlink dialog box appears.
- ✓ Under Link To, click E-Mail Address. Text boxes appear for entering an e-mail address and a subject message.
- ✓ Enter your e-mail address and a subject for the messages that others will send you. Office inserts the word mail to: before your e-mail address as you enter it.
- ✓ Click OK.

Repairing and removing hyperlinks

- ✓ **Repairing a link:** Select a target in your file or a web page and click OK.
- ✓ **Removing a link:** Click the Remove Link button. You can also remove a hyperlink by right-clicking the link and choosing Remove.

Points to Remember

- Practice selecting skills at your best before creating custom documents
- While hyperlinking, double check that the directory exits
- While hyperlinking make sure that you don't hyperlink your files present at sensitive locations

Get more from Office

In this chapter you will learn

- Tracking changes to a document or file
- Accessibility options in Microsoft office 2010
- Using language Tools

Undoing and Repeating Commands

Undo allows you to reverse actions you regret doing, and the Repeat repeats a previous action without you have to choose the same commands all over again. All is not lost if you make a big blunder because Office has a marvelous little tool called the Undo command. This command "Remembers" your previous editorial and formatting changes. As long as you catch your error in time, you can undo your mistake.

✓ Click the Undo button on the Quick Access toolbar (or press Ctrl+Z) to undo your most recent change. If you made your error and went on to do something else before you caught it, open the drop-down list on the Undo button.

✓ Click Redo to redo the change.

Zooming

You can find these controls in the lower-right corner of the window and on the View tab

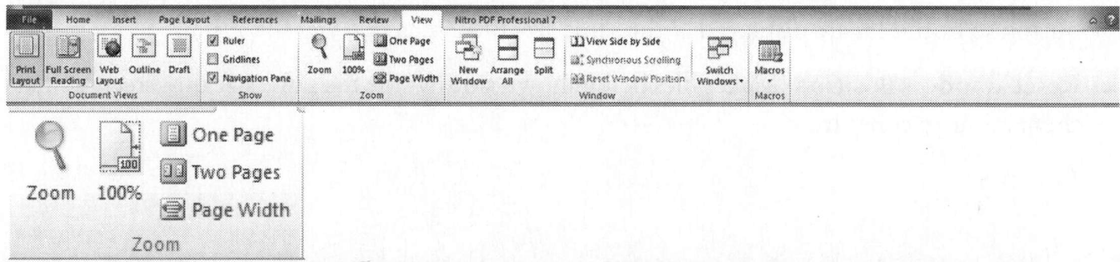

- **Zoom dialog box:** Click the Zoom button on the View tab or the Zoom box (the % listing) to display the Zoom dialog box; you can select an option button or enter a Percent measurement.
- **Zoom button:** Click the Zoom In or Zoom Out button on the Zoom slider to zoom in or out in 10-percent increments.
- **Zoom slider:** Drag the Zoom slider left to shrink or right to enlarge what is on your screen.
- **Mouse wheel:** If your mouse has a wheel, you can hold down the Ctrl key and spin the wheel to quickly zoom in or out.

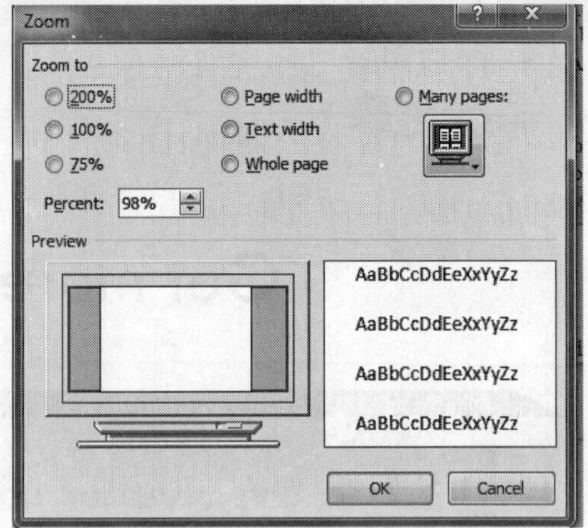

Zooming text

Viewing a File through more than One Window

- **New Window:** Opens another window on your file, so that you can view two places simultaneously in the same file. To go back and forth between windows, click a taskbar button or click the Switch Windows button and choose a window name on the drop-down list. Click window's Close button when you're finished looking at it.

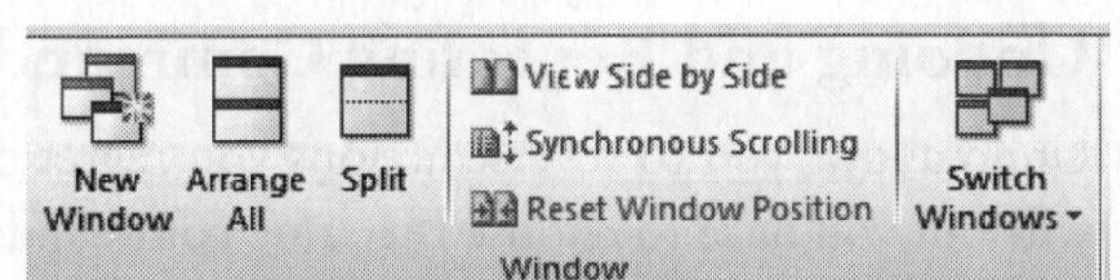

Viewing a file through more than one window

- **Arrange All:** Arranges open windows side by side on-screen.
- **Switch Windows:** Opens a drop-down list with open windows so that you can travel between windows.
- **View Side by Side:** Displays files side by side so that you can compare and contrast them.
- **Synchronous Scrolling:** Permits you to scroll two files at the same rate so that you can proofread one against the other. To use this command, start by clicking the View Side by Side button. After you click the Synchronous Scrolling button, click the Reset Window Position button so both files are displayed at the same size on-screen.
- **Reset Window Position:** Makes files being shown side by side the same size on-screen to make them easier to compare.

Opening AutoCorrect dialog box

Office corrects common spelling errors and turns punctuation mark combinations into symbols as part of its AutoCorrect feature. To see which typos are corrected and which punctuation marks are turned into symbols, open the AutoCorrect dialog box by following these steps:

- ✓ On the File tab, choose Options.
- ✓ You see the Options dialog box.
- ✓ Go to the Proofing category.
- ✓ Click the AutoCorrect Options button.
- ✓ The AutoCorrect dialog box opens.
- ✓ Click the AutoCorrect tab.
- ✓ AutoCorrect tab lists words that are corrected automatically. Scroll down the Replace list and have a look around. Go ahead and make yourself at home.

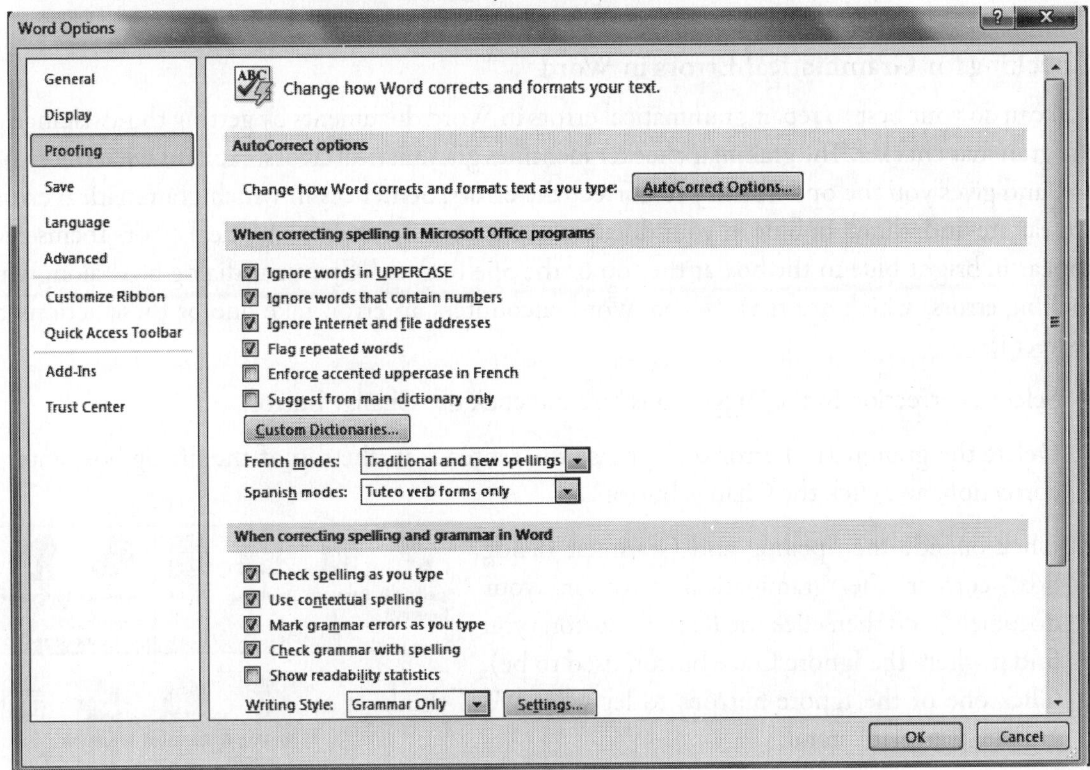

Auto correct dialog box

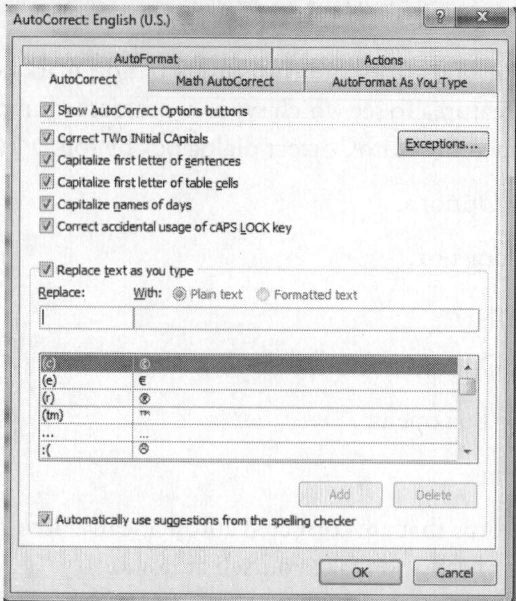

Checking for Grammatical Errors in Word

You can do your best to repair grammatical errors in Word documents by getting the assistance of the grammar checker. The grammar checker identifies grammatical errors, explains what the errors are, and gives you the opportunity to correct the errors. Sentences in which grammatical errors appear are underlined in blue in your document. Meanwhile, the grammatical errors themselves appear in bright blue in the box at the top of the Spelling and Grammar dialog box (alongwith spelling errors, which are red). When Word encounters an error, take one of these actions to correct it:

- ✓ Select a correction in the Suggestions box and click the Change button.
- ✓ Delete the grammatical error or rephrase the sentence in the top of the dialog box, enter a correction, and click the Change button.
- ✓ Click outside the Spelling and Grammar dialog box, correct the grammatical error in your document, and then click the Resume button (you find it where the Ignore Once button used to be). Click one of the Ignore buttons to let what Word thinks is a grammatical error stand.

Researching a Topic inside an Office Program

Thanks to the Research task pane, your desk needn't be as crowded as before. The Research task pane offers dictionaries, foreign language dictionaries, a thesaurus, language translators, and encyclopedias, as well as Internet searching, all available from inside the Office programs.

Finding the Right Word with the Thesaurus

To search for a good synonym, click the word in question and open the thesaurus on the Research task pane with one of these techniques:

- ✓ Press Shift+F7.
- ✓ Right-click the word and choose Synonym → Thesaurus.
- ✓ Go to the Review tab and click the Thesaurus button.

The Research task pane opens. It offers a list of synonyms and sometimes includes an antonym or two at the bottom. Now you're getting somewhere:

- ❑ **Choosing a synonym:** Move the pointer over the synonym you want, open its drop-down list, and choose Insert.
- ❑ **Finding a synonym for a synonym:** If a synonym intrigues you, click it. The task pane displays a new list of synonyms.
- ❑ **Searching for antonyms:** If you can't think of the right word, type its antonym in the Search For box and then look for an "antonym of an antonym" in the Research task pane.
- ❑ **Revisit a word list:** Click the Back button as many times as necessary. If you go back too far, you can always click its companion Forward button.

Telling Office which languages you will use

Follow these steps to inform Word, PowerPoint, Publisher, and Outlook that you will use a language or languages besides English in your files:

- ✓ On the Review tab, click the Language button and choose Language Preferences. The Options dialog box opens to the Language category.

Language

- ✓ Open the Add Additional Editing Languages drop-down list, select a language, and click the Add button to make that language a part of your presentations, documents, and messages.
- ✓ Click OK.

Marking text as foreign language text

The next step is to tell Office where in your file you're using a foreign language. After you mark the text as foreign language text, Office can spellcheck it with the proper dictionaries. Follow these steps to mark text so that Office knows in which language it was written:

✓ Select the text that you wrote in a foreign language.

✓ Go to the Review tab.

✓ Click the Language button and choose Set Proofing Language on the drop-down list.

✓ Select a language and click OK.

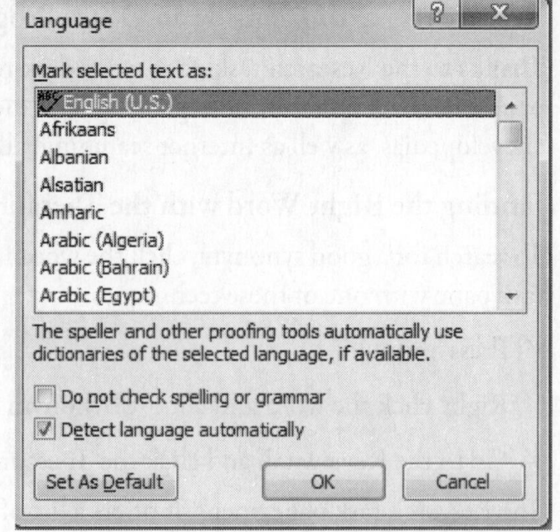

Marking text as foreign language text

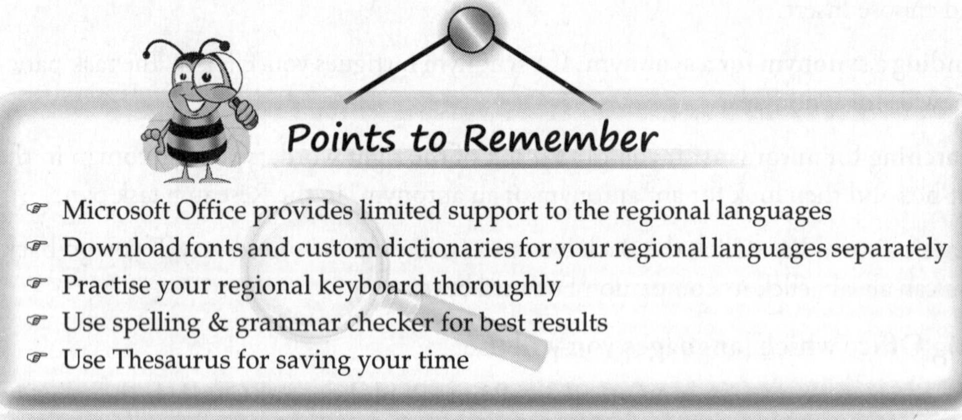

Points to Remember

- Microsoft Office provides limited support to the regional languages
- Download fonts and custom dictionaries for your regional languages separately
- Practise your regional keyboard thoroughly
- Use spelling & grammar checker for best results
- Use Thesaurus for saving your time

Tables

In this chapter you will learn

- Using table tools
- Utilising other Table Resources

Before starting the Course you need to know the following terms:

- ❑ **Cell:** The box that is formed where a row and column intersect. Each cell holds one data item.
- ❑ **Header row:** The name of the labels along the top row that explain what is in the columns below.
- ❑ **Row labels:** The labels in the first column that describe what is in each row.
- ❑ **Borders:** The lines in the table that define where the rows and columns are.
- ❑ **Gridlines:** The gray lines that show where the columns and rows are.

Unless you've drawn borders around all the cells in a table, you can't tell where rows and columns begin and end without gridlines. To display or hide the gridlines, go to the (Table Tools) Layout tab and click the View Gridlines button.

Creating a Table

- ❑ **Drag on the Table menu:** On the Insert tab, click the Table button, point in the drop-down list to the number of columns and rows you want, click, and let go of the mouse button.

Row labels Header row

	Qtr 1	Qtr 2	Qtr 3	Qtr 4
East	4	8	5	6
West	3	4	4	9
North	3	8	9	6
South	8	7	7	9

Borders Gridlines Cells

- **Use the Insert Table dialog box:** On the Insert tab, click the Table button and choose Insert Table on the drop-down list. The Insert Table dialog box appears. Enter the number of columns and rows you want and click OK. In PowerPoint, you can also open the Insert Table dialog box by clicking the Table icon in a content placeholder frame.
- **Draw a table (Word and PowerPoint):** On the Insert tab, click the Table button and then choose Draw Table on the drop-down list. The pointer changes into a pencil. Use the pencil to draw table borders, rows, and columns. If you make a mistake, click the Eraser button on the (Table Tools) Design tab and drag it over the parts of the table you regret drawing (you may have to click the Draw Borders button first). When you finish drawing the table, press Esc. You can click the Pen Colour button and choose a colour on the drop-down list to draw your table in your favourite colour.
- **Create a quick table (Word):** On the Insert tab, click the Table button and choose Quick Tables on the drop-down list. Then choose a readymade table on the submenu. You have to replace the sample data in the quick table with your own data.
- **Convert text in a list into a table (Word):** Press Tab or enter a comma in each list item where you want the columns in the table to be. Select the text you'll convert to a table, click the Table button on the Insert tab, and choose Convert Text to Table. Under Separate Text At in the Convert Text to Table dialog box, choose Tabs or Commas to tell Word how the columns are separated. Then click OK.

Entering Text and Numbers

After you create the table, you can start entering text and numbers. All you have to do is click in a cell and start typing. Select your table and take advantage of these methods to make the onerous task of entering table data a little easier:

- **Quickly changing a table's size:** Drag the bottom or side of a table to change its overall size. In Word, you can also go to the (Table Tools) Layout tab, click the AutoFit button, and choose AutoFit Window to make the table stretch from margin to margin.
- **Moving a table:** In Word, switch to Print Layout view and drag the table selector (the square in the upper-left corner of the table). In PowerPoint and Publisher, move the pointer over the table's perimeter, and when you see the four-headed arrow, click and drag.
- **Choosing your preferred font and font size:** Entering table data is easier when you're working in a font and font size you like. Select the table, visit the Home tab, and choose a font and font size there. In Word and PowerPoint, you can select a table by going to the (Table Tools) Layout tab, clicking the Select button, and choosing Select Table on the drop-down list.

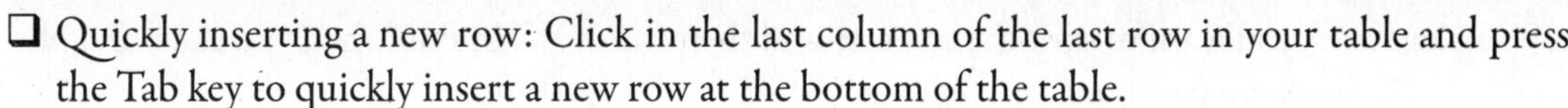

- ❑ Quickly inserting a new row: Click in the last column of the last row in your table and press the Tab key to quickly insert a new row at the bottom of the table.

Selecting different parts of a Table

- ❑ **Selecting cells:** To select a cell, click it. You can select several adjacent cells by dragging the pointer over them.
- ❑ **Selecting rows:** Move the pointer to the left of the row and click when you see the right-pointing arrow; click and drag to select several rows. You can also go to the (Table Tools) Layout tab, click inside the row you want to select, click the Select button, and choose Select Row on the drop-down list. To select more than one row at a time, select cells in the rows before choosing the Select Row command.
- ❑ **Selecting columns:** Move the pointer above the column and click when you see the down-pointing arrow; click and drag to select several columns. You can also start from the (Table Tools) Layout tab, click in the column you want to select, click the Select button, and choose Select Column in the drop-down list. To select several columns, select cells in the columns before choosing the Select Column command.
- ❑ **Selecting a table:** On the (Table Tools) Layout tab, click the Select button, and choose Select Table on the drop-down list. In PowerPoint, you can also right-click a table and choose Select Table on the shortcut menu.

Merging and Splitting Cells

Merge cells to break down the barriers between cells and join them into one cell; split cells to divide a single cell into several cells (or severalcells into several more cells).

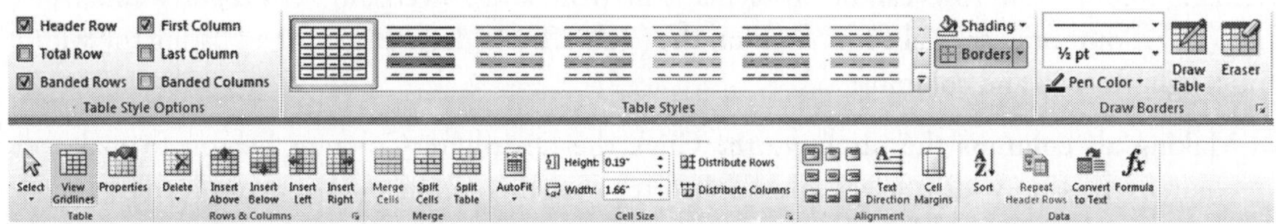

- ❑ Select the cells you want to merge or split, go to the (Table Tools) Layout tab, and follow these instructions to merge or split cells:
  - ✓ **Merging cells:** Click the Merge Cells button (in Word and PowerPoint, you can also right-click and choose Merge Cells).
  - ✓ **Splitting cells:** Click the Split Cells button (in Word and PowerPoint, you can also right-click and choose Split Cells). In the Split Cells dialog box, declare how many columns

and rows you want to split the cell into and then click OK. In Publisher, you can only split cells that were previously merged.

Laying Out your Table

- **Column or row:** Move the pointer onto a gridline or border, and when the pointer changes into a double-headed arrow, start dragging. Tug and pull, tug and pull until the column or row is the right size. In Word and PowerPoint, you can also go to the (Table Tools) Layout tab and enter measurements in the Height and Width text boxes to change the width of a column or the height of a row. The measurements affect entire columns or rows, not individual cells.
- **A table:** Select your table and use one of these techniques to change its size in Word and PowerPoint:
- **Dragging:** Drag the top, bottom, or side of the table. You can also drag the lower-right corner to change the size vertically and horizontally.
- **Height and Width text boxes:** On the (Table Tools) Layout tab, enter measurements in the Height and Width text boxes. In Publisher, these text boxes are found on the (Table Tools) Design tab. In PowerPoint, click the Lock Aspect Ratio check box if you want to keep the table's proportions when you change its height or width.
- **Table Properties dialog box (Word only):** On the (Table Tools) Layout tab, click the Cell Size group button, and on the Table tab of the Table Properties dialog box, enter a measurement in the Preferred Width text box.

Adjusting Column and Row size

Resizing columns and rows can be problematic in Word and PowerPoint. For that reason, Word and PowerPoint offer special commands on the (Table Tools) Layout tab for adjusting the width and height of rows and columns:

- **Making all columns the same width:** Click the Distribute Columns button to make all columns the same width. Select columns before giving this command to make only the columns you select the same width.
- **Making all rows the same height:** Click the Distribute Rows button to make all rows in the table the same height. Select rows before clicking the button to make only the rows you select the same height. In Word, you can also click the AutoFit button on the (Table Tools) Layout tab, and take advantage of these commands on the drop-down list for handling columns and rows.
- **AutoFit Contents:** Make each column wide enough to accommodate its widest entry.

- **AutoFit Window:** Stretch the table so that it fits across the page between the left and right margin.
- **Fixed Column Width:** Fix the column widths at their current settings.

Inserting and deleting columns and rows

- **Inserting columns:** Select a column or columns and click the Insert Left or Insert Right button. If you want to insert just one column, click in a column and then click the Insert Left or Insert Right button. You can also right-click, choose Insert, and choose an Insert Columns command.
- **Inserting rows:** Select a row or rows and click the Insert Above or Insert Below button. If you want to insert just one row, click in a row and click the Insert Above or Insert Below button. You can also right-click, choose Insert, and choose an Insert Rows command on the shortcut menu. To insert a row at the end of a table, move the pointer into the last cell in the last row and press the Tab key.
- **Deleting columns:** Click in the column you want to delete, click the Delete button, and choose Delete Columns on the drop-down list. Select more than one column to delete more than one. (Pressing the Delete key deletes the data in the column, not the column itself.)
- **Deleting rows:** Click in the row you want to delete, click the Delete button, and choose Delete Rows. Select more than one row to delete more than one. (Pressing the Delete key deletes the data in the row, not the row itself.)

Moving Columns and Rows

To move a column or row:

- Select the column or row you want to move. Earlier in this chapter, "Selecting Different Parts of a Table" explains how to select columns and rows.
- Right-click in the selection and choose Cut on the shortcut menu. The column or row is moved to the Clipboard.
- Insert a new column or row where you want the column or row to be. Earlier in this chapter, "Inserting and deleting columns and rows" explains how.

Move the whole column or row:

- **Column:** Click in the topmost cell in your new column and then click the Paste button or press Ctrl+V.
- **Row:** Click in the first column of the row you inserted and then click the Paste button or press Ctrl+V.

Designing a table with a table style

Click anywhere in your table and follow these steps to choose a table style:

- ✓ Go to the (Table Tools) Design tab.
- ✓ Open the Table Styles gallery and move the pointer over table style choices to "live-preview" the table. In Publisher, this gallery is called Table Formats.
- ✓ Select a table style. To remove a table style, open the Table Styles gallery and choose Clear (in Word) or Clear Table (in PowerPoint).

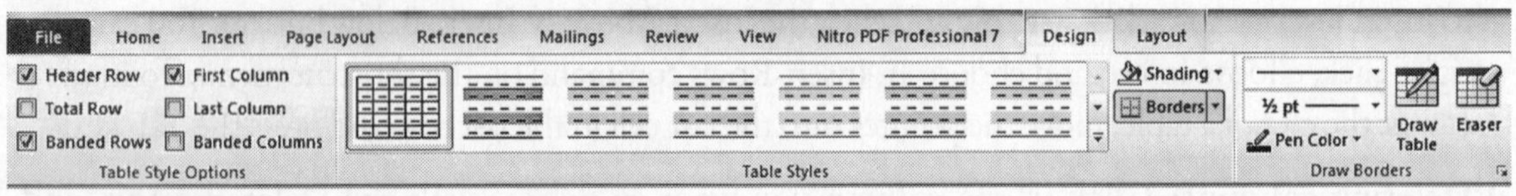

Designing borders for your table

Follow these steps to fashion a border for your table or a part of your table:

- ✓ Go to the (Table Tools) Design tab.
- ✓ Select the part of your table that needs a new border.

To select the entire table, go to the (Table Tools) Layout tab, click the Select button, and choose Select Table.

- ✓ Open the Line Style drop-down list (in Word) or the Pen Style drop down list (in PowerPoint) and choose a line style for the border (you may have to click the Draw Borders button first, depending on the size of your screen). Stay away from the dotted and dashed lines unless you have a good reason for choosing one. These lines can be distracting and keep others from focusing on the data presented in the table.
- ✓ Open the Line Weight drop-down list (in Word and Publisher) or the Pen Weight drop-down list (in PowerPoint) and choose a thickness for the border (you may have to click the Draw Borders button first).
- ✓ If you want your borders to be of another colour apart from black, click the Pen Colour button (Word and PowerPoint) or the Line Colour button (Publisher) and choose a colour on the drop-down list (you may have to click the Draw Borders button first).

✓ Open the drop-down list on the Borders button and choose where to place borders on the part of the table you selected in Step 2.

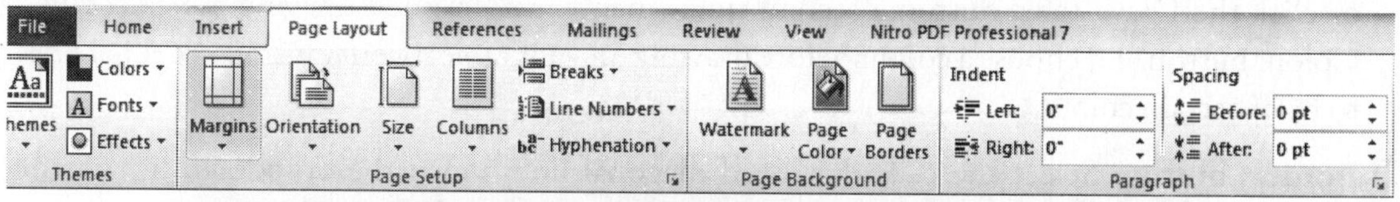

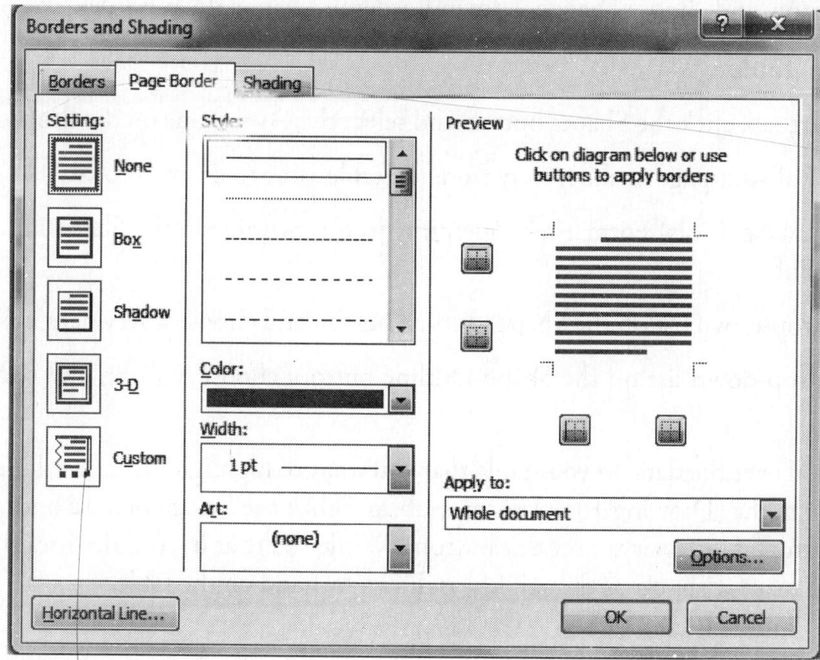

Using Math Formulas in Word Tables

You don't have to add the figures in columns and rows yourself; Word gladly does that for you. Word can perform other mathematical calculationsas well. Follow these steps to perform mathematical calculations and tell Word how to format sums and products:

✓ Put the cursor in the cell that will hold the sum or product of the cells above, below, to the right, or to the left.

✓ On the (Table Tools) Layout tab, click the Formula button.

Drawing diagonal lines on tables

Draw diagonal lines across table cells to cancel out those cells or otherwise make cells look different.

- **Draw Table button:** Click the Draw Table button (you may have to click the Draw Borders button first). The pointer changes into a pencil. Drag to draw the diagonal lines. Press Esc or click the Draw Table button a second time when you're finished drawing. Click the Pen Colour button and choose a colour before drawing on your table if you want the diagonal lines to be of certain colour.
- **Borders button:** Select the cells that need diagonal lines, open the dropdown list on the Borders button, and choose Diagonal down Border or Diagonal Up Border.

Drawing on a Table

- ✓ On the Insert tab, click the Shapes button and select the Oval shape on the drop-down list.
- ✓ On a corner of your page or slide, away from the table, drag to draw the oval.
- ✓ On the (Drawing Tools) Format tab, open the drop-down list on the Shape Fill button and choose No Fill.
- ✓ Open the drop-down list on the Shape Outline button and choose a very dark colour.
- ✓ Open the drop-down list on the Shape Outline button, choose Weight, and choose a thick line.
- ✓ Drag the oval over the data on your table that you want to highlight. If the oval is obscured by the table, go to the (Drawing Tools) Format tab, and click the Bring Forward button (click the Arrange button, if necessary,to see this button). While you're at it, consider rotating the oval a little way to make it appear as though it was drawn by hand on the table.

- Use table resources carefully
- Keep an eye on margins while drawing tables

Charts

In this chapter you will learn

- Using Charts
- Creating & designing charts
- Using other Graphical effects in your file

Anatomy of Charts

Before you start doing activities on charts, you need to know the following:

- **Plot area:** The center of the chart, apart from the legend and data labels, where the data itself is presented.
- **Values:** The numerical values with which the chart is plotted. The values you enter determine the size of the data markers — the bars, columns, pie slices, and so on — that portray values.
- **Gridlines:** Lines on the chart that indicate value measurements. Gridlines are optional in charts.
- **Worksheet:** Where you enter (or retrieve) the data used to plot the chart. The worksheet resembles a table. A worksheet is called a data table when it appears along with a chart.
- **Data series:** A group of related data points presented by category on a chart.
- **Categories:** The actual items that you want to compare or display in your chart.
- **Legend:** A text box located to the side, top, or bottom of a chart that identifies the chart's data labels.
- **Horizontal and vertical axes:** For plotting purposes, one side of the plot area.
- **Data point:** A value plotted on a chart that is represented by a column, line, bar, pie slice, dot, or other shape.

- ❑ **Data marker:** Shapes on a chart that represents data points.
- ❑ **Data label:** A label that shows the actual values used to construct the data markers.

The Basics: Creating a Chart

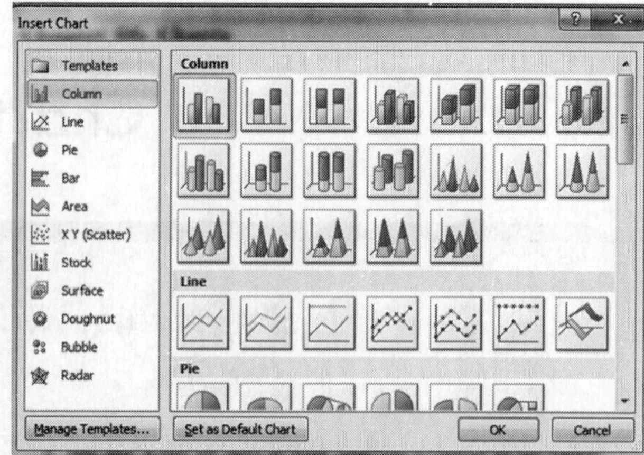

- ✓ Go to the Insert tab.
- ✓ If you're working in Excel, select the data you'll use to generate the chart.
- ✓ Select the kind of chart you want.
- ✓ To modify your chart, start by selecting it. Click a chart to select it. Selecting a chart makes the Chart Tools tabs appear in the upper-right corner of the window. Use these tabs — Design, Layout, and Format — to make your chart just-so. In Word, you must be in Print Layout view to see a chart.
- ✓ Select the (Chart Tools) Design tab when you want to change the chart's layout, alter the data with which the chart was generated, or select a different chart type.
- ✓ Select the (Chart Tools) Layout tab when you want to change the chart's title, labels, or gridlines. You can add or remove parts of a chart starting on the Layout tab.
- ✓ Select the (Chart Tools) Format tab when you want to change the appearance of your chart.

Changing chart layout

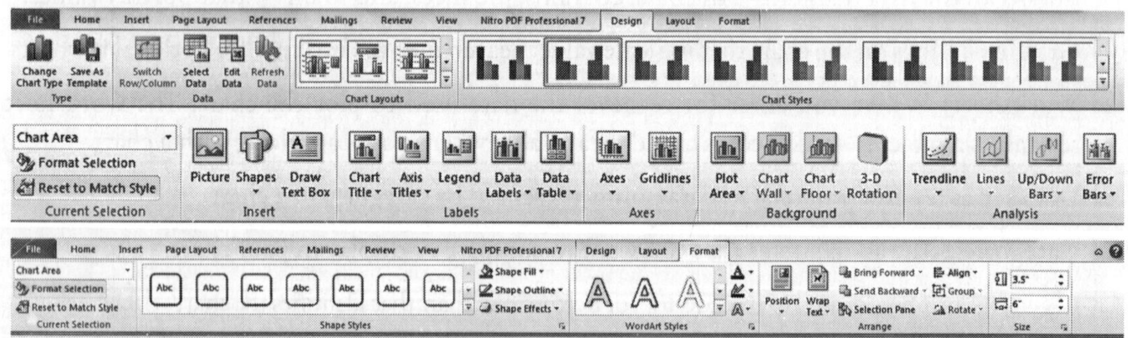

- ❑ **Design tab:** For quickly changing a chart's appearance, go to the Design tab. The ready-made gallery choices give you the opportunity to change a chart's layout and appearance in a matter of seconds. You can also choose a new chart type from the Design tab.

- ❑ **Layout tab:** For rearranging, hiding, and displaying various parts of a chart, including the legend, labels, title, gridlines, and scale, go to the Layout tab to tweak your chart and make different parts of it stand out or recede into the background.
- ❑ **Format tab:** For changing the colour, outline, font, and font size of various parts of a chart, including the labels, bars, and pie slices, you have to really know what you're doing and have a lot of time on your hands to change colours and fonts throughout a chart.

Changing Chart Type

- ✓ Click your chart to select it.
- ✓ On the (Chart Tools) Design tab, click the Change Chart Type button, or right-click your chart and choose Change Chart Type on the shortcut menu.
- ✓ Select a new chart type and click OK.

Changing Size and Shape of a Chart

To make a chart taller or wider, follow these instructions:

- ✓ Click the perimeter of the chart to select it and then drag a handle on the side to make it wider, or a handle on the top or bottom to make it taller.
- ✓ Go to the (Chart Tools) Format tab and enter measurements in the Shape Height and Shape Width boxes. You can find these boxes in the Size group (you may have to click the Size button to see them, depending on the size of your screen).

Relying on A Chart Style to change appearances

The easiest way to change the look of a chart is to choose an option in the Chart Styles gallery in the (Chart Tools) Design tab.

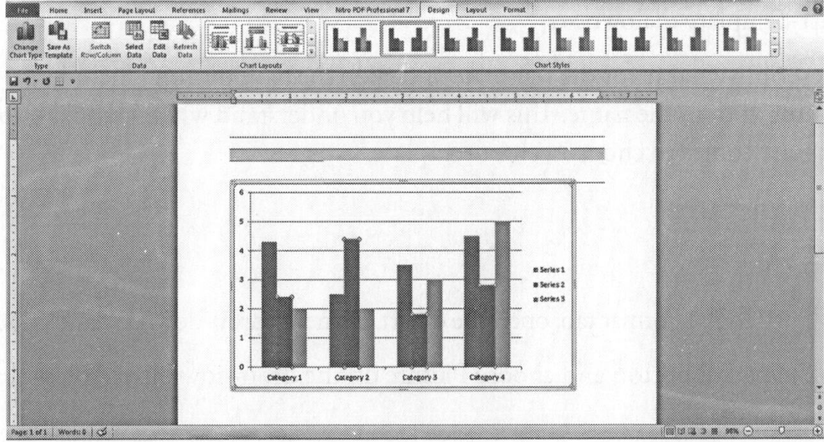

Changing a Chart elements' colour, font, or other particular

✓ Select the (Chart Tools) Format tab. The tools on the (Chart Tools) Format tab are very similar to the tools found on the (Drawing Tools) Format tab. You can find all the tools you need here to change the colour, outline, and size of a chart element.

✓ Select the chart element that needs a facelift. To select a chart element, either click it or choose its name on the Chart Elements drop-down.

✓ Format the chart element you selected.

Use one of these methods to format the chart element:

✓ Open a Format dialog box. The dialog box offers commands for formatting the element you selected.

✓ Do the work on your own. For example, to change fonts in the chart element you selected, right-click and choose a font on the shortcut menu. Or go to the Home tab to change font sizes. Or open the drop-down list on the Shape Fill button on the (Chart Tools) Format tab and select a new colour.

Saving a Chart as a Template

Follow these steps to make a template out of a chart:

✓ Save your file to make sure that the chart settings are saved on your computer.

✓ Select your chart.

✓ Go to the (Chart Tools) Design tab.

✓ Click the Save as Template button. You can find this button in the Type group. You will see the Save Chart Template dialog box.

✓ Enter a descriptive name for the template and click the Save button. Include the type of chart you're dealing with in the name. This will help you understand which template you're selecting when the time comes to choose a chart template.

Inserting a picture

✓ Select your chart.

✓ On the (Chart Tools) Format tab, open the Chart Elements drop-down list and choose Plot Area.

✓ Click the Shape Fill button and choose Picture on the drop-down list. You will see the Insert Picture dialog box.

- ✓ Locate the picture you need and select it. Try to select a light-coloured picture that will serve as a background.
- ✓ Click the Insert button. The picture lands in your chart.

Annotating a chart

- ✓ Select your chart and go to the (Chart Tools) Layout tab.
- ✓ Click the Shapes button, scroll to the Callouts section of the dropdown list, and choose a callout.
- ✓ Depending on the size of your screen, you may have to click the Insert button to get to the Shapes button.
- ✓ Drag on your slide to draw the callout shape.
- ✓ Type the annotation inside the callout shape.
- ✓ Resize the callout shape as necessary to make it fit with the chart
- ✓ Drag the yellow diamond on the callout shape to attach the callout to the chart.

Points to Remember

- ☞ Use charts judiciously & never put invalid arguments for the charts
- ☞ Practise Microsoft excel 2010 before making custom charts

SmartArt

In this chapter you will learn

- Using Diagrams & shapes in file or document
- Using hybrid layouts with diagrams & Text together

Creating a diagram

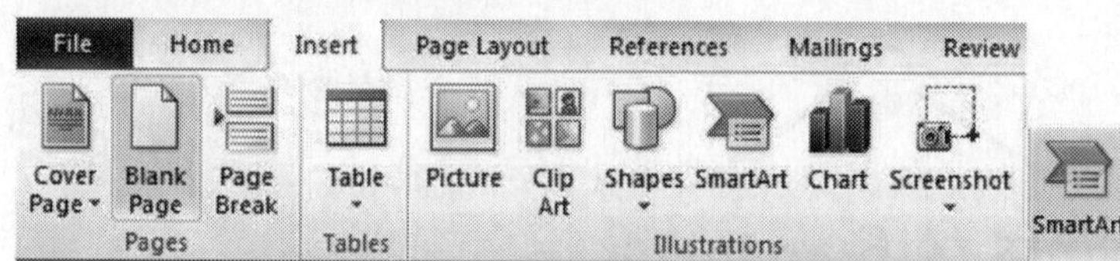

After you select a generic diagram in the Choose a SmartArt Graphic dialog box and click OK, the next step is to make the diagram your own by completing these tasks:

- ❑ **Change the diagram's size and position:** Change the size and position of a diagram to make it fit squarely on your page or slide. See "Changing the Size and Position of a Diagram," later in this chapter.
- ❑ **Add shapes to (or remove shapes from) the diagram:** Adding a shape involves declaring where to add the shape, promoting or demoting the shape with respect to other shapes, and declaring how the new shape connects to another shape. See "Laying Out the Diagram Shapes" later in this chapter.
- ❑ **Enter text:** Enter text on each shape, or component, of the diagram. See "Handling the Text on Diagram Shapes" later in this chapter. If you so desire, you can also customize your diagram by taking on some oral of these tasks:

❑ **Changing its overall appearance:** Choose a different colour scheme or 3-D variation for your diagram. See "Choosing a Look for Your Diagram" later in this chapter.

❑ **Changing shapes:** Select a new shape for part of your diagram, change the size of a shape, or assign different colours to shapes to make shapes stand out. See "Changing the Appearance of Diagram Shapes" later in this chapter.

Creating a diagram

Follow these steps to create a diagram:

✓ On the Insert tab, click the SmartArt button. You will see the Choose a SmartArt Graphic dialog box; you can also open the dialog box by clicking the SmartArt Icon in a content placeholder frame.

✓ Select a diagram in the Choose a SmartArt Graphic dialog box. Diagrams are divided into eight categories.

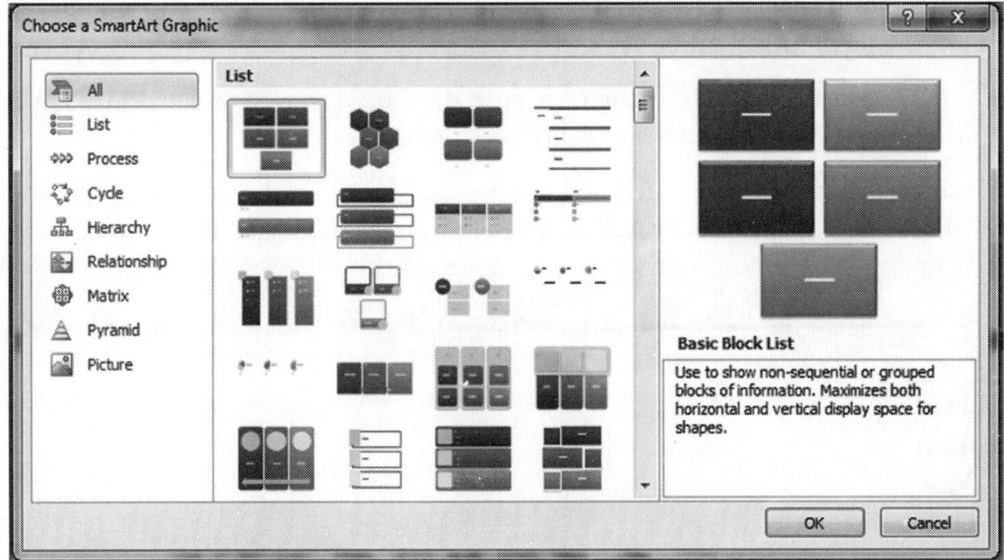

✓ Click your diagram to select it.

✓ Go to the (SmartArt Tools) Design tab.

✓ Open the Layouts gallery (you may have to click the Change Layout button first).You will see a gallery with diagrams of the same type as the diagram you're working with. Select a new diagram or choose More Layouts to open the Choose a SmartArt Graphic dialog box and select a diagram there.

Changing Size and Position of a diagram

To make a diagram fit squarely on a page or slide, you have to change its size and position.

❑ **Resizing a diagram:** Select the diagram, move the pointer over a selection handle on the corner or side, and start dragging after the pointer changes into a two-headed arrow. You can also go to the (SmartArt Tools) Format tab and enter new measurements in the Width and Height boxes. (You may have to click the Size button to see these text boxes, depending on the size of your screen.) ⟺

❑ **Repositioning a diagram:** Select the diagram, move the pointer over its perimeter, and when you see the four-headed arrow, click and start dragging.

Adding shapes to diagrams apart from hierarchy diagrams

Follow these steps to add a shape to a list, process, cycle, relationship, matrix, or pyramid diagram:

✓ In your diagram, select the shape that your new shape will appear before or after.

✓ Choose the Add Shape After or Add Shape Before command. To get to these commands, use one of these methods:

  ✓ On the (SmartArt Tools) Design tab, open the drop-down list on the Add Shape button and choose Add Shape After or Add Shape Before.

  ✓ Right-click the shape you selected, choose Add Shape on the shortcut menu, and then choose Add Shape After or Add Shape Before on the submenu.

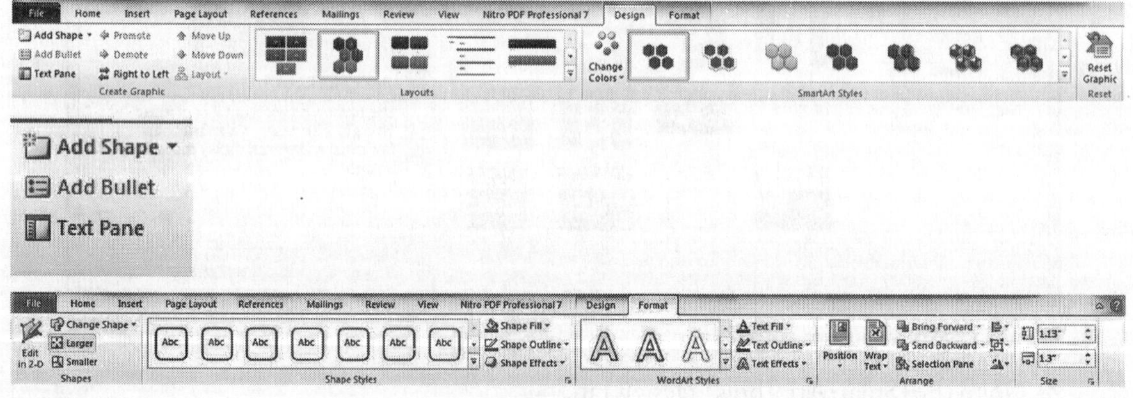

Adding an Organization Chart shape

Besides adding a shape after, before, above, or below a shape, you can add an assistant shape to an Organization Chart diagram. An assistant shape is an intermediary shape between two levels. Follow these steps to add a shape to an Organization Chart diagram:

✓ Select the shape to which you will add a new shape.

✓ Choose an Add Shape command.

You can choose Add Shape commands in two ways:

✓ On the (SmartArt Tools) Design tab, open the drop-down list on the Add Shape button and choose an Add Shape command.

✓ Right-click the shape you selected, choose Add Shape on the shortcut menu, and then choose an Add Shape command on the submenu.

Entering text on a diagram shape

Use one of these techniques to enter text on a diagram shape:

✓ Click on the shape and start typing: The words you type appear.

✓ Enter text in the Text pane: Enter the text by typing it in the Text pane

✓ On the (SmartArt Tools) Design tab, click the Text Pane button.

✓ Click the Text Pane button on the diagram. This button is not labeled, but you can find it to the left of the diagram.

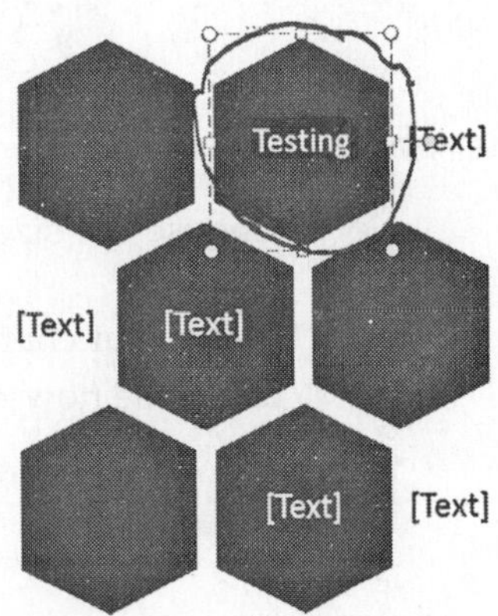

Entering bulleted lists on diagram shapes

Some diagram shapes have built-in bulleted lists, but no matter. Whether a shape is prepared to be bulleted or not, you can enter bullets in a diagram shape. Here are instructions for entering and removing bullets:

❑ **Entering a bulleted list:** Select the shape that needs bullets, and on the (SmartArt Tools) Design tab, click the Add Bullet button. Either enter the bulleted items directly into the shape (pressing Enter as you type each entry) or click the Text Pane button to open the Text pane.

❑ **Removing bulleted items:** Click before the first bulleted entry and keep pressing the Delete key until you have removed all the bulleted items.

Changing a Diagram's direction

✓ Select the diagram.

✓ On the (SmartArt Tools) Design tab, click the Right to Left button. If you don't like what you see, click the button again or click the Undo button.

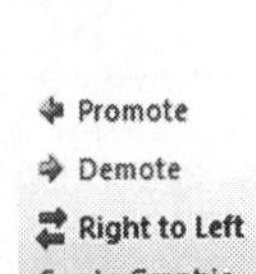

Changing the size of a diagram shape

Change Shape ▾
Larger
Smaller
Shapes

Select your shape and use one of these methods to enlarge or shrink it:

✓ On the (SmartArt Tools) Format tab, click the Larger or Smaller buttonas many times as necessary to make the shape the right size.

✓ Move the pointer over a corner selection handle, and when the pointer changes to a two-headed arrow, click and start dragging.

- Choose the size of your diagrams judiciously so that it can blend with text perfectly
- Make your chart more descriptive by adding hybrid effects
- Select the flow-charts wisely

Drawing Lines & other Shapes

In this chapter you will learn

- Ways to manipulate lines, shapes, text boxes, WordArt images, clip-art images, and graphics

The Basics: Drawing Lines, Arrows, and Shapes

Follow these basic steps to draw a line, arrow, or shape:

✓ Go to the Insert tab.

✓ Click the Shapes button to open the Insert Shapes gallery.

✓ Select a line, arrow, or shape in the Shapes gallery.

✓ Drag on your page, slide, or worksheet. As you drag, the line, arrow, or shape appears.

✓ To alter your line, arrow, or shape—that is, to change its size, colour, or outline—go to the (Drawing Tools) Format tab. This tab offers many commands for manipulating lines and shapes.

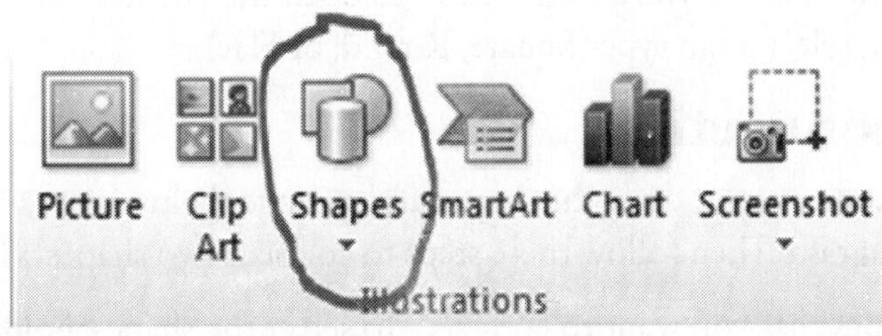

Handling Lines, Arrows, and Connectors

Changing the length and position of a line or arrow

To change anything about a line or arrow, start by clicking to select it. You can tell when a line has been selected because round selection handles appear at either end. Follow these instructions to move a line or adjust its length or angle:

- ❑ **Changing the angle of a line:** Drag a selection handle up, down, or sideways. A dotted line shows where your line will be when you release the mouse button.
- ❑ **Changing the length:** Drag a selection handle away from or toward the opposite selection handle.
- ❑ **Changing the position:** Move the pointer over the line itself and click when you see the four-headed arrow. Then drag the line to a new location.

Changing the appearance of a line, arrow, or connector

What a line looks like is a matter of its colour, its weight (how wide it is), its dash status (it can be filled out or dashed), and its cap (its ends can berounded, square, or flat). To change the appearance of a line, start by selecting it, going to the (Drawing Tools) Format tab, and opening the drop-down list on the Shape Outline button (this button is in the Shape Styles group).

- ❑ **Colour:** Select a colour on the drop-down list.
- ❑ **Width:** Choose Weight on the drop-down and then choose a line width on the submenu. You can also choose More Lines on the submenu to open the Format Shape dialog box and change the width there. Enter a setting in points to make the line heavier or thinner.
- ❑ **Dotted or dashed lines:** Choose Dashes on the drop-down list and then choose an option on the submenu. Again, you can choose More Lines to open the Format Shape dialog box and choose from many dash types and compound lines.
- ❑ **Line caps:** Click the Shape Styles group button to open the Format Shape dialog box. In the Line Style category, select a cap type (Square, Round, or Flat).

Making the connection

Before you draw the connections, draw the shapes and arrange them on the slide where you want them to be in your diagram. Then follow these steps to connect two shapes with a connector:

- ✓ Select the two shapes that you want to connect. To select the shapes, hold down the Ctrl key and click each one.

- ✓ On the (Drawing Tools) Format tab, open the Shapes gallery.
- ✓ Under Lines, select the connector that will best fit between the two shapes you want to link together.
- ✓ Move the pointer over a side selection handle on one of the shapes you want to connect. The selection handles turn red.
- ✓ Click and drag the pointer over a selection handle on the other shape, and when you see red selection handles on that shape, release the mouse button. Red, round selection handles appear on the shapes where they're connected. These red handles tell you that the two shapes are connected and will remain connected when you move them.

Handling Rectangles, Ovals, Stars, and Other Shapes

Drawing a shape

Follow these steps to draw a shape:

- ✓ On the Insert tab, click the Shapes button to open the Shapes gallery. You can also insert shapes from the Shapes gallery on the (Drawing Tools) Format tab.
- ✓ Select a shape in the gallery. If you've drawn the shape recently, you may be able to find it at the top of the gallery under Recently Used Shapes.
- ✓ Click and drag slantwise to draw the shape. Hold down the Shift key as you drag if you want the shape to retain its proportions. For example, to draw a circle, select the Oval shape and Hold down the Shift key as you draw.

Changing a shape's size and shape

Selection handles appear on the corners and sides of a shape after you select it. With the selection handles showing, you can change a shape's size and shape:

- ✓ Hold down the Shift key and drag a corner handle to change a shape's size and retain its symmetry.
- ✓ Drag a side, top, or bottom handle to stretch or scrunch a shape.

Choosing a different shape

To exchange one shape for another, select the shape and follow these steps:

- ✓ On the (Drawing Tools) Format tab, click the Edit Shape button.
- ✓ You can find this button in the Insert Shapes group.

✓ Choose Change Shape on the drop-down list.

✓ Select a new shape in the Shapes gallery.

Changing a shape's symmetry

A yellow diamond, sometimes more than one, appears on some shapes. By dragging a diamond, you can change a shape's symmetry.

Follow these instructions to handle text box shapes:

❑ **Entering the text:** Click in the shape and start typing. In Word, you can right-click and choose Add Text if you have trouble typing in the shape.

❑ **Editing the text:** Click in the text and start editing. That's all there is to it. If you have trouble getting inside the shape to edit the text, select the shape, right-click it, and choose Edit Text on the shortcut menu.

❑ **Changing the font, colour, and size of text:** Right-click in the text and choose Font. Then, in the Font dialog box, choose a font, font colour, and a font size for the text.

WordArt for Bending, Spindling, and Mutilating Text

❑ **Allowing the shape to enlarge for text:** You can allow the shape to enlarge and receive more text. Click the Shape Styles group button, and in the Text Box category of the Format Shape dialog box, select the Resize Shape to Fit Text option button.

Creating a WordArt image

Follow these steps to create a WordArt image:

✓ On the Insert tab, click the WordArt button. A drop-down list with WordArt styles appears.

✓ Select a WordArt style.

✓ Enter the text for the image in the WordArt text box.

Editing a WordArt image

On the (Drawing Tools) Format tab, click the Edit Shape button, choose Change Shape, and then select a shape in the Shapes gallery. After the conversion, you usually have to enlarge the shape to

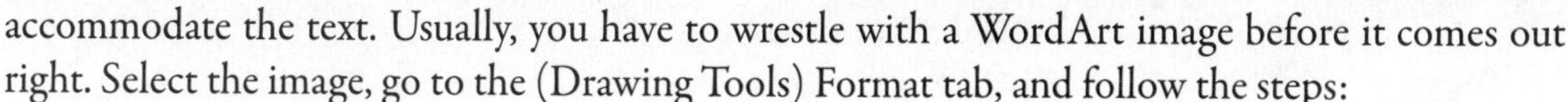

accommodate the text. Usually, you have to wrestle with a WordArt image before it comes out right. Select the image, go to the (Drawing Tools) Format tab, and follow the steps:

- **Editing the words:** Click in the WordArt text box and edit the text there.
- **Choosing a new WordArt style:** Open the WordArt Styles gallery and select a style. Depending on the size of your screen and which program you're working in, you may have to click the Quick Styles button first
- **Changing the letters' colour:** Click the Text Fill button and choose a colour on the drop-down list.
- **Changing the letters' outline:** Click the Text Outline button and make choices to change the letters' outline.

Points to Remember

- Practise the skills thoroughly
- Don't Use too much formatting.

Microsoft Word 2010

Welcome to MS Word 2010

In this chapter you will learn

- Getting started with the Word screen
- Creating a Word document
- Changing your view of a document
- Selecting text so that you can copy, move, or delete it
- Getting from place to place in long documents
- Pasting one Word document into another
- Creating data-entry forms

Introducing the Word Screen

Easy description of the screen parts:

- **Word button:** In the upper-left corner of the screen, the Word button offers a menu for restoring, moving, sizing, minimizing, maximizing, and closing the Word window.
- **Quick Access toolbar:** This toolbar offers the Save, Undo, and Repeat buttons. Wherever you go in Word, you see the Quick Access toolbar.
- **Title bar:** At the top of the screen, the title bar tells you the name of the document you're working on.
- **Minimize, Restore, Close buttons:** These three magic buttons make it very easy to shrink, enlarge, and close the window you are working in.
- **File tab:** Go to the File tab to do file-management tasks.

- **The Ribbon:** Select a tab on the Ribbon to undertake a new task
- **Scroll bars:** The scroll bars help you get from place to place in a document.
- **Status bar:** The status bar gives you basic information about where you are and what you're doing in a document. It tells you what page and what section you're in, the total number of pages and words in your document, and what language the text is written in.
- **View buttons:** Click one of these buttons — Print Layout, Full Screen Reading, Web Layout, Outline, or Draft — to change your view of a document.
- **Zoom controls:** Use these controls to zoom in and out on your work.

Creating a New Document

When you first start Word, you see a new, blank document with the generic name Document1. You can start working right away on this document, or you can create a new document by choosing a template.

A template is a special kind of file that is used as the starting point for creating documents. Each template comes with many preformatted styles. If your aim is to create an academic report, flyer, newsletter, calendar, résumé, see if you can spare yourself the formatting work by choosing the appropriate template when you create your document.

No matter what kind of document you want, start creating it by going to the File tab and choosing "New".

Click a template in this window to see, on the right side of the window, a preview of the document you will create. Double-click a template (or select it and click the Create button) to create a document.

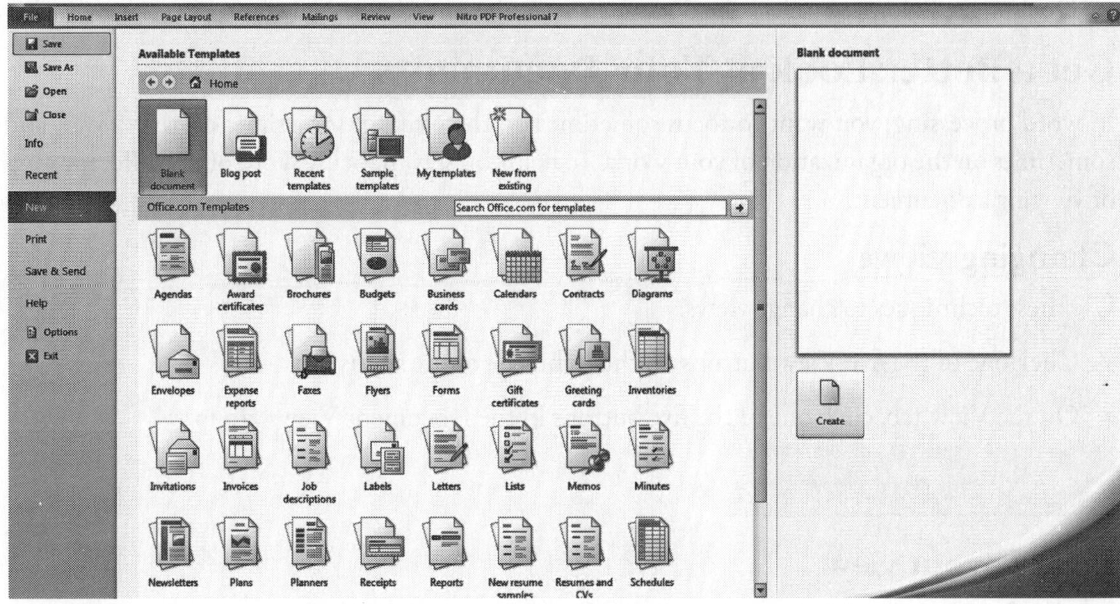

Use these methods in the Available Templates window to create a document:

- ❑ **Create a blank document:** Choose the Blank Document icon to create a bare-bones document with few styles. Blank Document is the default template for creating documents. (By pressing Ctrl+N, you can create a new, blank document without opening the Available Templates window.)
- ❑ Create a brochure, form, invoice, or other specialty document.
- ❑ **Use a template on your computer:** Choose Sample Templates. Templates that you loaded on your computer when you installed Office appear in the window.
- ❑ **Download a template from Microsoft:** Under Office.com Templates, do one of the following:
  - ✓ Choose the type of template you want, or
  - ✓ Make sure that your computer is connected to the Internet, enter a search term in the Search box, and click the Start Searching button (or press Enter). Choose a template and click the Download button to download it to your computer.
- ❑ **Use a template you created (or downloaded earlier from Microsoft or acquired from a third party):** Click the My Templates icon. The New dialog box appears so that you can choose a template.
- ❑ Create a document from a template you recently used, Templates icon and choose a template.

❑ **Create a document from another document:** If you can use another document as the starting point for creating a new document, click the New from Existing icon. In the New from Existing Document dialog box, select the document and click the Create New button.

Get a Better Look at Your Documents

In word processing, you want to focus sometimes on the writing, sometimes on the layout, and sometimes on the organization of your work. To help you stay in focus, Word offers different ways of viewing a document.

Changing views

Use these techniques to change views:

✓ Click one of the five View buttons on the right side of the status bar.

✓ On the View tab, click one of the five buttons in the Document Views group.

Print Layout view

Switch to Print Layout view to see the big picture. In this view, you can see what your document will look like when you print it. You can see graphics, headers, footers, and even page borders in Print Layout view. You can also see clearly where page breaks occur (where one page ends and the next begins). In Print Layout view, you can click the One Page, Two Pages, or Page Width button on the View tab to display more or fewer pages on your screen.

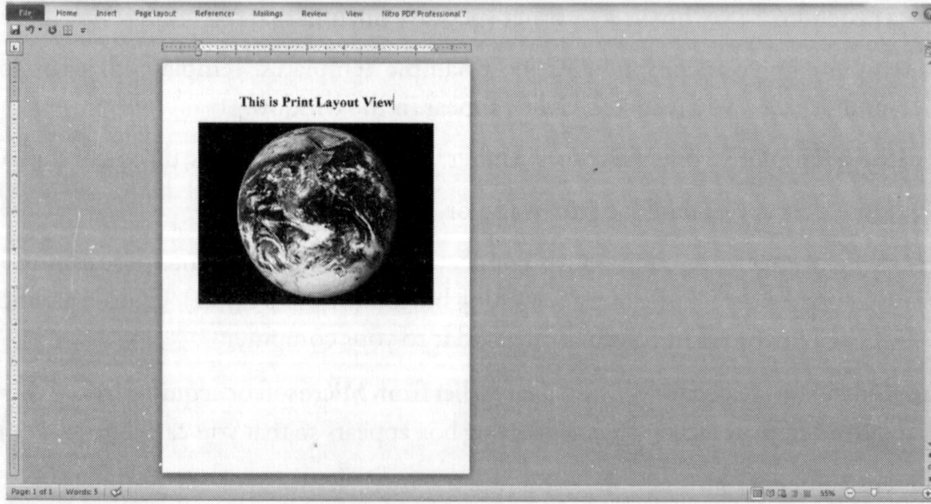

Full Screen Reading view

Switch to Full Screen Reading view to focus on the text itself and proofread your documents. In this view, everything gets stripped away — the Ribbon, scroll bars, status bar, and all. All you see is the text and artwork in your documents. You can't enter or edit text.

Web Layout view

Switch to Web Layout view to see what your document would look like as a web page. Background colours appear (if you chose a theme or background colour for your document). Text is wrapped to the window rather than around the artwork in the document.

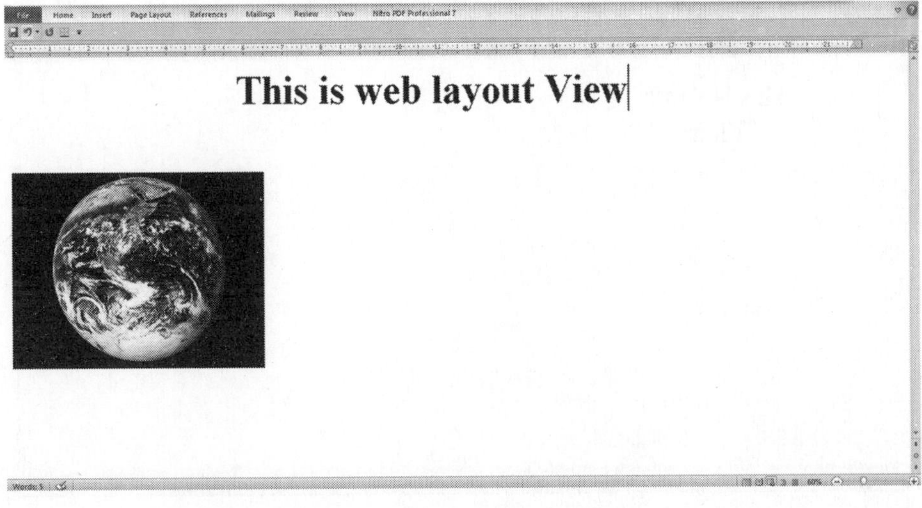

Outline view

Switch to Outline view to see how your work is organized. In this view, you can see only the headings in a document. You can get a sense of how your document unfolds and easily move sections of text backward and forward in a document. In other words, you can reorganize a document in Outline view.

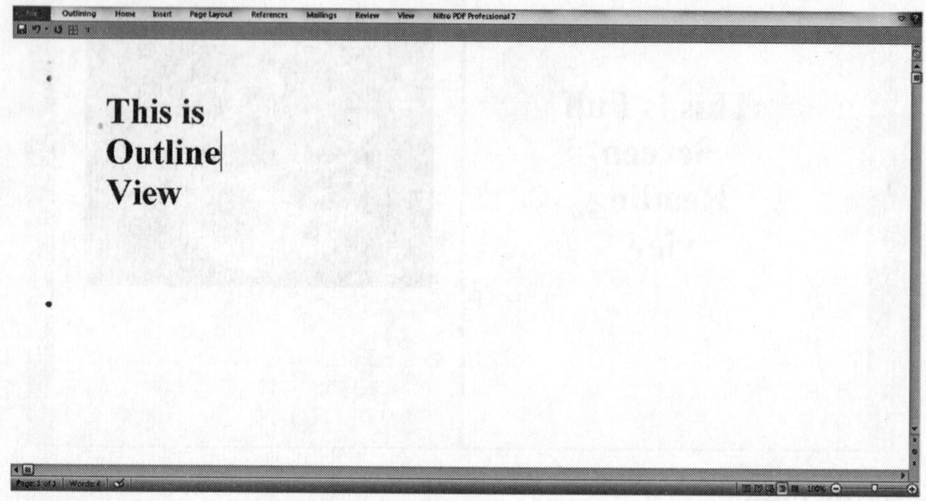

Draft view

Switch to Draft view when you're writing a document and you want to focus on the words. Clip-art images, shapes, and other objects don't appear in this view, nor do page breaks (although you can clearly see section breaks). Draft view is best for writing first drafts.

Splitting the screen

Besides opening a second window on a document you can be two places at one time in a Word document by splitting the screen. Word offers two ways to split the screen:

✓ Move the mouse pointer to the split box at the top of the scroll bar on the right. Move it just above the View Ruler button. When the pointer turns into double arrows, click and drag the gray line down the screen. When you release the mouse button, you have a split screen.

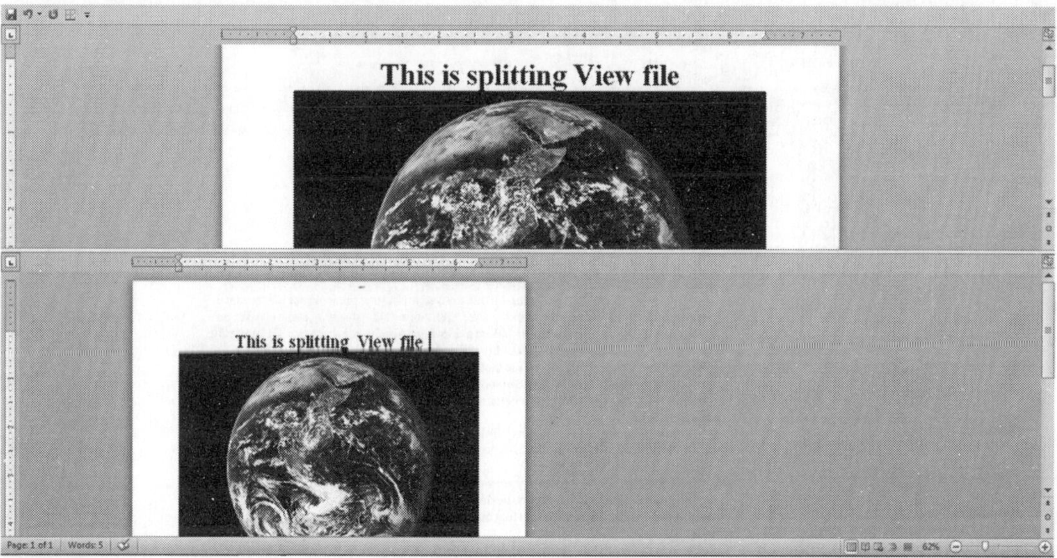

✓ On the View tab, click the Split button. A gray line appears on-screen. Roll the mouse down until the gray line is where you want the split to be, and click. You get two screens split down the middle.

Moving in Documents

Besides sliding the scroll bar, Word offers a handful of methods for navigation of documents

Keys for Navigation

Checkout this table:

Key to Press	Where it Takes You
PgUp	Up the length of one screen
PgDn	Down the length of one screen
Ctrl+PgUp	To the previous page in the document
Ctrl+PgDn	To the next page in the document

Ctrl+Home	To the top of the document
Ctrl+End	To the bottom of the document

Navigating from page to page or heading to heading

In lengthy documents such as the one in the best way to get from place to place is to make use of the Navigation pane.

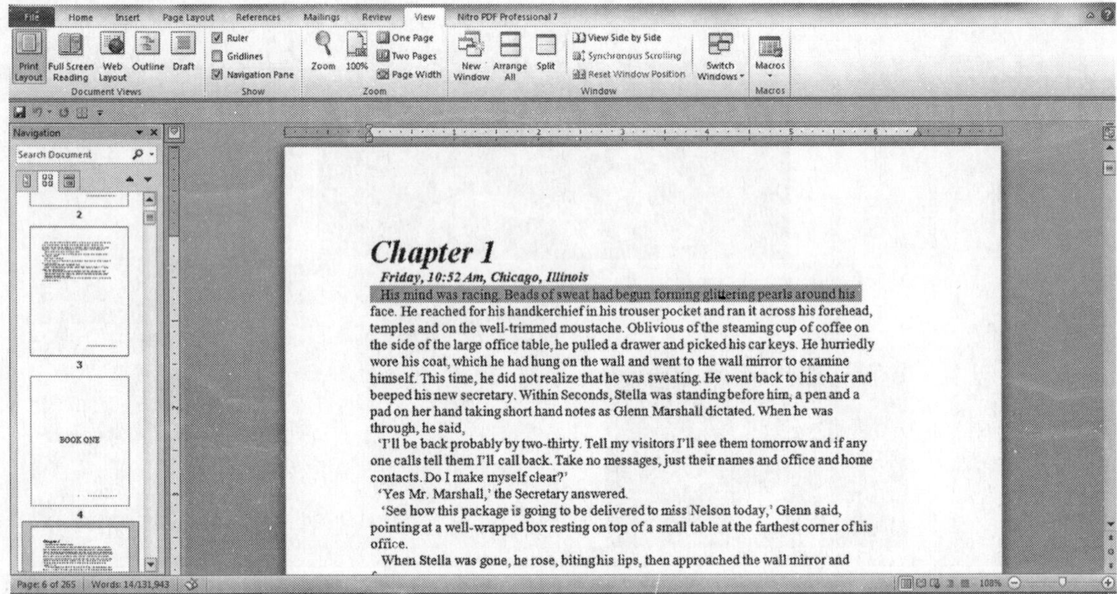

To display the Navigation pane, go to the View tab and click the Navigation Pane check box (you may have to click the Show button first). Then select a tab in the Navigation pane and go to it:

- ❑ **Going from heading to heading:** Select the Browse the Headings tab. Headings in your document appear (provided you assigned heading styles to headings). You can use the Navigation pane like a table of contents and click headings to get from place to place. Right-click a heading and choose a heading-level option on the shortcut menu to tell Word which headings to display. You can also right-click a heading and choose Expand All or Collapse All to see or hide lower-level headings.
- ❑ **Going from page to page:** Select the Browse the Pages tab. A thumbnail image of each page in the document appears. To quickly move from page to page, use the scroll bar in the Navigation pane or click a page thumbnail. Each thumbnail is numbered so that you always know which page you are viewing.

Using 'Go To' command

- Another fast way to go from place to place in a document is to use the Go To command. On the Home tab, open the drop-down list on the Find button and choose Go To (you may have to click the Editing button first). You will see a box as shown below –

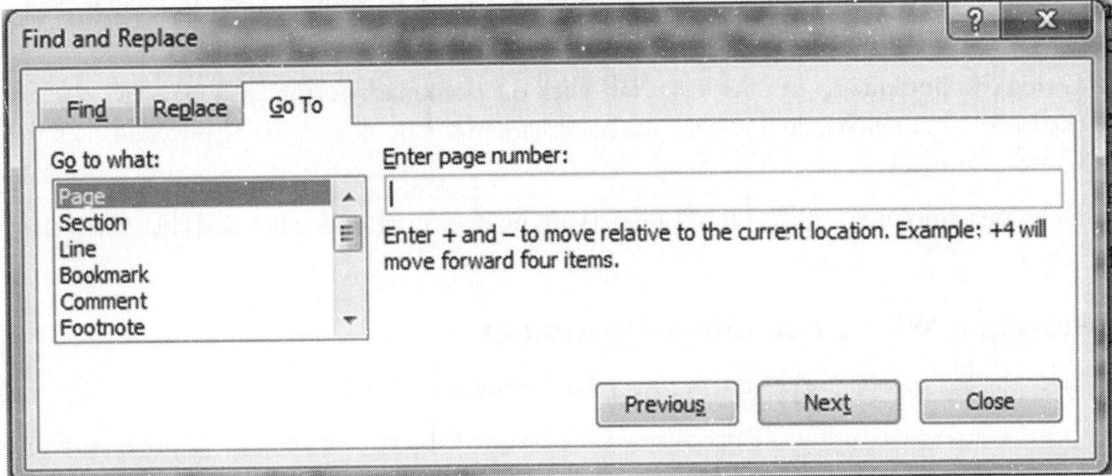

Bookmarks

Rather than press PgUp or PgDn or click the scroll bar to thrash around in a long document, you can use bookmarks. All you do is put a bookmark in an important spot in your document that you'll return to many times. To return to that spot, open the Bookmark dialog box and select a bookmark name.

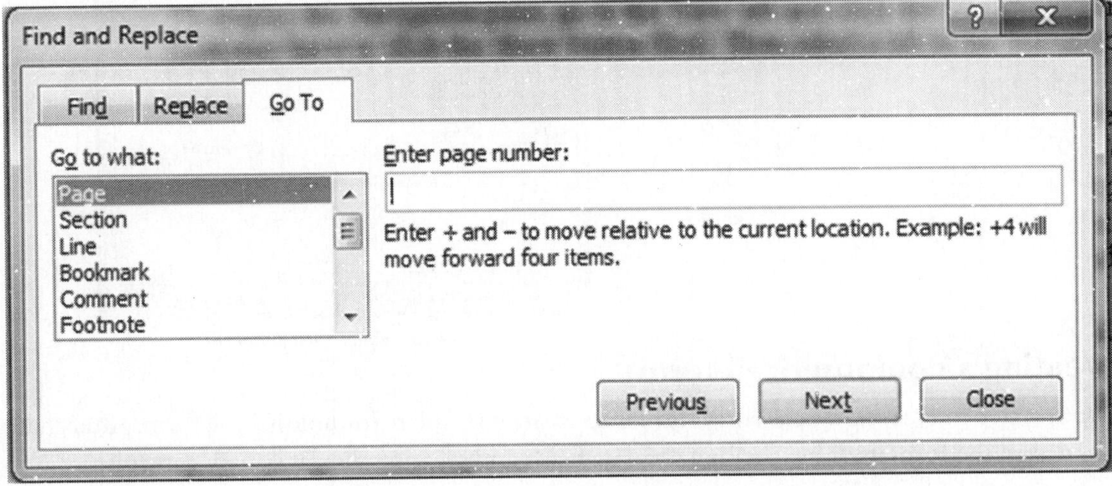

Follow these instructions to handle bookmarks:

- ❑ **Adding a bookmark:** Click where you want the bookmark to go, visit the Insert tab, and click the Bookmark button (you may have to click the Links button first, depending on the size of your screen). Then, in the Bookmark dialog box, type a descriptive name in the Bookmark Name box, and click the Add button. Bookmarks can't start with numbers or include blank spaces. You can also open the Bookmark dialog box by pressing Ctrl+Shift+F5.
- ❑ **Going to a bookmark:** On the Insert tab, click the Bookmark button (you may have to click the Links button first), double-click the bookmark in the Bookmark dialog box, and click the Close button.
- ❑ **Deleting a bookmark:** Select the bookmark in the Bookmark dialog box and click the Delete button.

Inserting a Whole File into a Document

- ✓ Place the cursor where you want to insert the document.
- ✓ On the Insert tab, open the drop-down list on the Object button and choose Text from File.
- ✓ You see the Insert File dialog box.
- ✓ Find and select the file you want to insert.
- ✓ Click the Insert button.

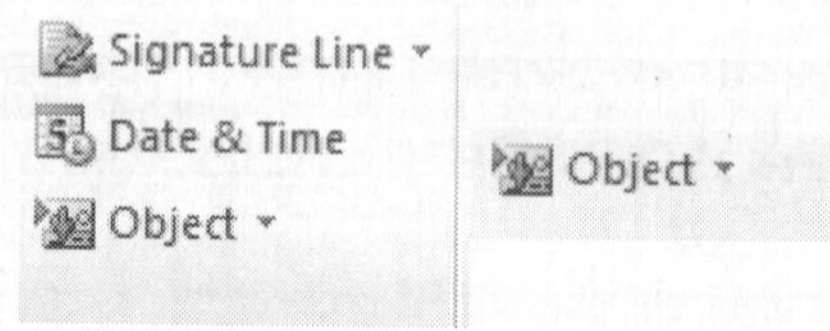

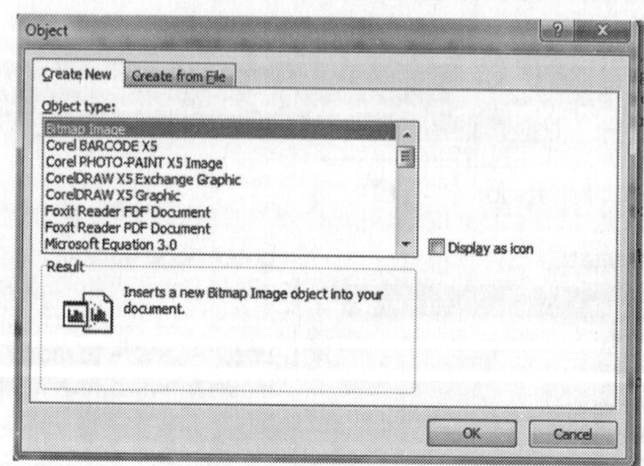

Inserting a file into a document

Creating a computerized form

The first step in creating a data-entry form is to create a template for holding the form. After that, you design the form itself by labelling the data fields and creating the data-entry controls.

Creating a template to hold the form

Follow these steps to create a new template:

- ✓ On the File tab, choose New. You see the Available Templates window.
- ✓ Click the My Templates icon. The New dialog box appears. It lists Word templates that are on your computer.
- ✓ Click the Template option button. You can find this button under Create New in the lower-right corner of the dialog box.
- ✓ Click OK.
- ✓ Click the Save button (or press Ctrl+S) to open the Save As dialog box.
- ✓ Enter a descriptive name for your template and click the Save button.

Creating the form and data-entry controls

Your next task is to create the form and data-entry controls for your template.

- ✓ Display the Developer tab, if necessary. If this tab isn't showing, go to the File tab, choose Options, and on the Customize Ribbon tab of the Word Options dialog box, select the Developer check box and click OK.
- ✓ Click where you want to place a control, and then create the control by clicking the Controls button followed by the Properties button on the Developer tab.

Entering Information Quickly in a Computerized Form

- ❑ **Combo box:** Like a drop-down list, a combo box "drops" to reveal choices. However, as well as choosing an option on the drop-down list, data-entry clerks can enter information in the box Click the Combo Box Content Control button and then the Properties button. In the Content Control Properties dialog box, enter option names the same way you enter them in a drop-down list.
- ❑ **Date picker:** A date picker is a mini-calendar from which data-entry clerks can enter a date. Click the Date Picker Content Control button and then the Properties button. In the Content Control Properties dialog box, choose a display format for dates and click OK. Click the Save button to save your template. Now you're ready to use your newly made form to enter data.

Entering data in the form

Now that you have the template, you or someone else can enter data cleanly in easy-to-read forms:

- ✓ On the File tab, choose New. You see the Available Templates window.
- ✓ Click the My Templates icon.
- ✓ The New dialog box opens and shows you Word templates on your computer.

Entering Information Quickly in a Computerized Form

✓ Double-click the name of the template you created for entering data in your form. The form appears.

✓ Enter information in the input fields.

✓ Press the up or down arrow, or press Tab and Shift+Tab to move from field to field. You can also click input fields to move the cursor there. When you're done, print the document or save it.

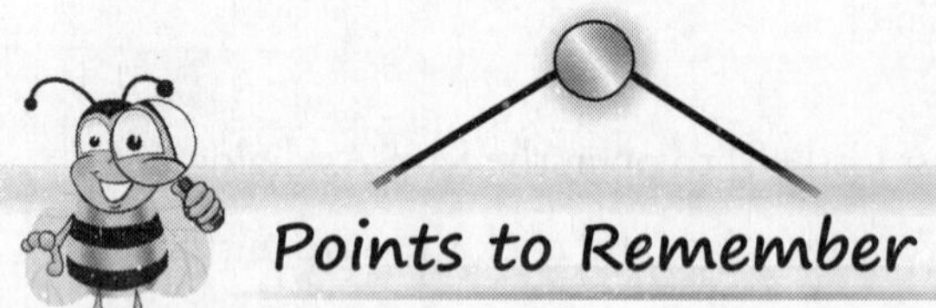

Points to Remember

- Practise the skills thoroughly
- Always save your templates in secured environment

Composing Text & Pages

In this chapter you will learn

- entering a section break
- Starting a new line and page
- changing the margins
- Indenting text
- Numbering pages and handling headers and footers
- adjusting the space between lines and paragraphs
- handling numbered and bulleted lists
- hyphenating the text

Format text and pages

Paragraphs and Formatting

Inserting a Section Break for Formatting Purposes

When you want to change page numbering schemes, headers and footers, margin sizes, and page orientations in a document, you have to create a section break to start a new section. Word creates a new section for you when you create newspaper-style columns or change the size of margins.

Follow these steps to create a new section:

✓ Click where you want to insert a section break.

✓ On the Page Layout tab, click the Breaks button. You open a drop-down list.

✓ Under Section breaks on the drop-down list, select a section break.

All four section break options create a new section, but they do so in different ways:

- **Next Page:** Inserts a page break as well as a section break so that the new section can start at the top of a new page (the next one). Select this option to start a new chapter, for example.
- **Continuous:** Inserts a section break in the middle of a page. Select this option if, for example, you want to introduce newspaper-style columns in the middle of a page.
- **Even Page:** Starts the new section on the next even page. This option is good for two-sided documents in which the headers on the left- and right-side pages are different.
- **Odd Page:** Starts the new section on the next odd page. You might choose this option if you have a book in which chapters start on odd pages. (By convention, that's where they start.) To delete a section break, make sure that you are in Draft view so that you can see section breaks, click the dotted line, and press the Delete key.

Breaking a Line

To break a line of text before it reaches the right margin without startinga new paragraph, press Shift+Enter.

Starting a New Page

Word gives you another page so that you can keep going when you fill up one page. But what if you're impatient and want to start a new page right away? Whatever you do, don't press Enter again and again until you fill up the page. Instead, create a hard page break by doing the following on the Insert tab:

- ✓ Click the Page Break button (or press Ctrl+Enter). Word starts a new page at the cursor position. (You can also go to the Page Layout tab, click the Breaks button, choose Page on the drop-down list.)
- ✓ Click the Blank Page button. Word enters two hard page breaks to create an empty, blank page at the cursor position.

Setting Up and Changing the Margins

To set up or change the margins, go to the Page Layout tab and click the Margins button. You will see a drop-down list with margin settings. Either choose a setting or select Custom Margins to open the Margins tab of the Page Setup dialog box and choose among these commands for handling margins:

- **Changing the size of the margins:** Enter measurements in the Top, Bottom, Left, and Right boxes to tell Word how much blank space to put along the sides of the page.

- **Making room for the gutter:** The gutter is the part of the paper that the binding eats into when you bind a document. Enter a measurement in the Gutter box to increase the left or inside margin and make room for the binding. Notice on the pages of this book, for example, that the margin closest to the binding is wider than the outside margin. Choose Top on the Gutter Position menu if you intend to bind your document from the top, not the left, or inside, of the page. Some legal documents are bound this way.

Using mirror margins (inside and outside margins) in two-sided documents:

- In a bound document in which text is printed on both sides of the pages, the terms left margin and right margin are meaningless. What matters instead is in the inside margin, the margin in the middle of the page spread next to the bindings, and the outside of the page spread that isn't affected by the Choose Mirror Margins on the Multiple Pages drop-down list and adjust the margins accordingly if you intend to print on both sides of the paper.

- **Applying margin changes:** On the Apply To drop-down list, choose Whole Document to apply your margin settings to the entire document. This Section to apply them to a section; or This Point Forward to change margins in the rest of a document. When you choose This Point Forward, Word creates a new section.

© Bittu Kumar, December 2011

This Book is dedicated To-

Nirankari Baba Hardev Singh Ji Maharaj

Who, Inspired Me to Do something new something innovative.

Acknowledgements

I would like to express the deepest appreciation to my Parents. They constantly and convincingly conveyed a spirit of adventure in regard to writing. Without Their guidance and persistent help this publication would not have been possible.

In addition, a thank you to V&S Publishers. Who gave me the opportunity to develop this Book.

I must acknowledge as well the many friends, colleagues, teachers, other artists who assisted, advised, and supported my work and writing efforts over the years. Especially, I need to express my gratitude and deep appreciation to my maternal Uncle Narendra Kumar. Nirankari Mission's hospitality, knowledge, and wisdom have supported, enlightened, and entertained me; they have consistently helped me keep perspective on what is important in life and shown me how to deal with reality.

I am grateful too for the support of my Dear Friend Mukesh Kumar. I need to thank Makis Starfield (Kyoto, Japan) and Texas Writers Foundation (USA) to advise me in this Project.

Thank You Once again...

Bittu Kumar

Author, Become Millionaire Online

Indenting Paragraphs and First Lines

Clicking an Indent button (for left-indents)

On the Home tab, click the Increase Indent or Decrease Indent button (or press Ctrl+M or Ctrl+Shift+M) to move a paragraph a half inch farther away from or closer to the left margin. If you created tab stops, text is indented to the next or previous tab stop as well as to the next or previous half inch. This is the fastest way to indent text, although you can't indent first lines or Indent from the right margin this way.

- ❑ **Indenting an entire paragraph from the left margin:** Drag the left-indent marker on the ruler to the right. Dragging the left-indent marker moves the first-line indent marker as well.
- ❑ **Indenting an entire paragraph from the right margin:** Drag the right indent marker to the left.
- ❑ **Indenting the first line of a paragraph:** Drag the first-line indent marker to the right. This marker determines how far the first line of the paragraph is indented.
- ❑ **Making a hanging indent:** Drag the hanging indent marker to the right. This marker determines how far the first line of the paragraph is indented.

Numbering the Pages

In which the first line of a paragraph appears to "hang" into the margin because the second and subsequent lines are indented to the right of the start of the first line. Bulleted and numbered lists employ hanging indents.

Indenting in Paragraph dialog box

Yet another way to indent a paragraph or first line is to visit the Paragraph dialog box. Click in or select the paragraph or paragraphs in question, go to the Home tab, and click the Paragraph group button. You see the Indents and Spacing tab of the Paragraph dialog box. Change the indentation settings.

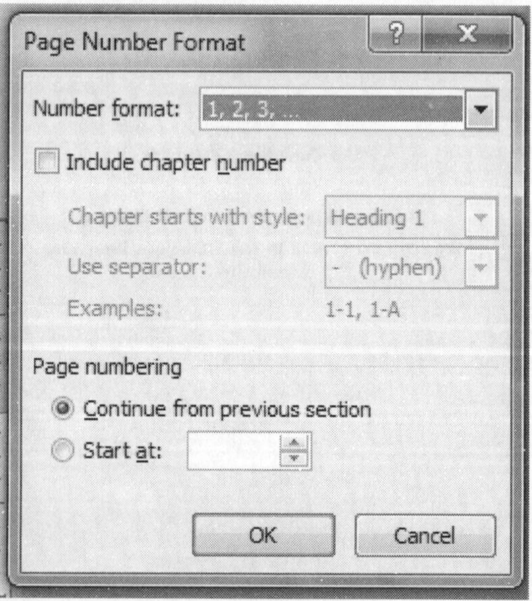

Numbering pages

If you want to indent the first line or create a hanging indent, choose FirstLine or Hanging on the Special drop-down list and enter a measurement in the By box.

Numbering with page numbers only

Follow these steps to insert page numbers by itself in the header, footer, or margin of the pages:

- ✓ On the Insert tab, click the Page Number button.
- ✓ On the drop-down list, choose where on the page you want to put the page number (Top of Page, Bottom of Page, or Page Margins).
- ✓ On the submenu that appears, choose a page number option. The farther you scroll on the submenu, the fancier the page number formats are.

Including a page number in header or footer

To put the page number part in a header or footer, click in the header or footer where you want the page number to appear (later in this chapter, "Putting Headers and Footers on Pages" explains headers and footers). Then follow these steps to insert page numbers:

- ✓ On the (Header & Footer Tools) Design tab, click the Page Numbers button.
- ✓ Choose Current Position. You see a submenu with page number choices.
- ✓ Scroll through the submenu and choose a page number format.

Header Footer Page Number
Header & Footer

Changing page number formats

Change page number formats in the Page Number Format dialog box. To display this dialog box, make sure that you're in Print Layout view and double-click your header or footer. Then use one of the following methods to change page number formats:

- ✓ On the Insert tab, click the Page Number button and choose Format Page Numbers.
- ✓ On the (Header & Footer Tools) Design tab, click the Page Number button and choose Format Page Numbers.

In the Page Number Format dialog box, make your page numbers just so:

- ❑ **Choosing a different number format:** Open the Number Format drop down list and choose a page-numbering format. You can use numbers, letters, or roman numerals.
- ❑ **Including chapter numbers in page numbers:** If your document generates chapter numbers automatically from headings, you can include the chapter number in the page number. Click

the Include Chapter Number check box, choose a style, and choose a separator to go between the chapter number and page number.

- ❑ **Numbering each section separately:** Click the Start At option button (not Continue from Previous Section button) to begin counting pages anew at each section in your document. Earlier in this chapter, "Inserting a Section Break for Formatting Purposes" explains the same.
- ❑ **Start numbering pages at a number other than 1:** Click the Start At option button and enter a number other than 1.

Putting Headers and Footers on Pages

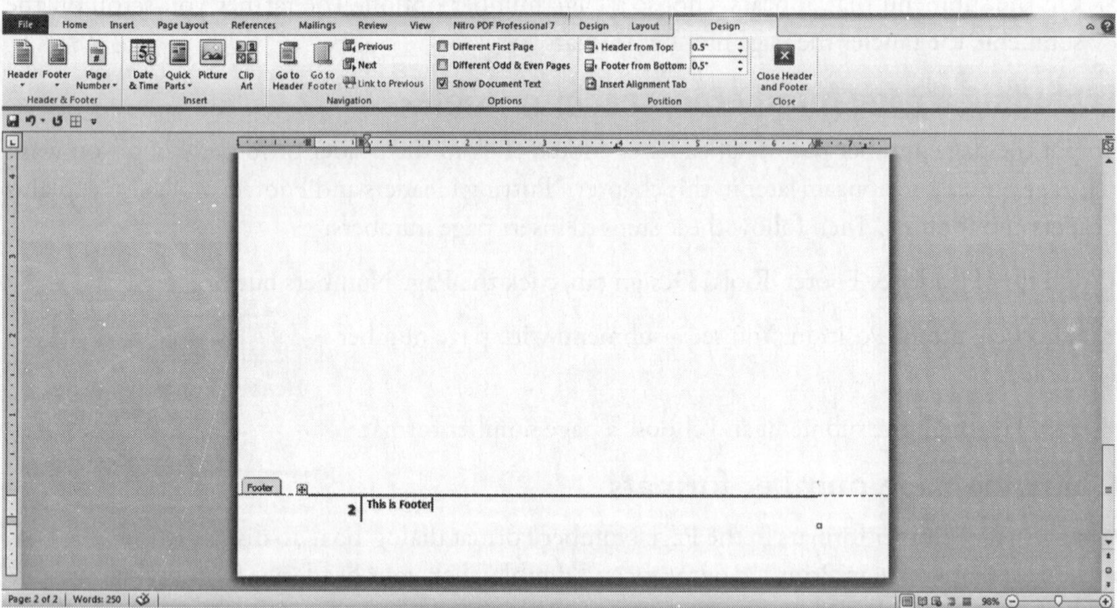

A header is a little description that appears along the top of a page so that the reader knows what's what. Usually, headers include the page number and a title, and often the author's name appears in the header as well. A footer is the same thing as a header except that it appears along the bottom of the page, as befits its name.

Here are rules how you can do it:

- ❑ **Switching to Print Layout view:** To enter, read, edit, or delete headers and footers, you must be in Print Layout view. You can't see headers and footers in the other views.
- ❑ **Displaying the (Header & Footer Tools) Design tab:** To display this tab after you create a header or footer, switch to Print Layout view and double-click a header or footer.

- **Closing the (Header & Footer Tools) Design tab:** Click the Close Header & Footer button or double-click outside the header or footer.
- **Placing different headers and footers in the same document:** To change headers or footers in the middle of a document, you have to create a new section.

Creating, editing, and removing headers and footers

Follow these instructions to create, edit, and delete headers and footers:

- **Creating a header or footer:** On the Insert tab, click the Header or Footer button, and choose a header or footer on the gallery. The gallery presents headers or footers with preformatted page numbers, dates, and places to enter a document title and author's name. Click More Headers (or Footers) from Office.com to download headers or footers from Microsoft.
- **Choosing a different header or footer:** If necessary, double-click your header or footer to display the (Header & Footer Tools) Design tab. Then click the Header or Footer button and choose a new header or footer from the gallery.
- **Editing a header or footer:** Click the Header or Footer button and choose Edit Header or Edit Footer on the drop-down list. The cursor moves into the header or footer so that you can enter or format text.
- **Changing the appearance of a header or footer:** Click a shape or text box in a header or footer and visit the (Drawing Tools) Format tab to change the shape or text box's colour, background, or size.
- **Removing a header or footer:** Click the Header or Footer button and choose Remove Header or Remove Footer on the drop-down list.

Fine-tuning a header or footer

Follow these steps for making a perfect header on the (Header & Footer Tools)Design tab:

- Inserting a page number: See "Including a page number in a header or footer" and "Changing page number formats" earlier in this chapter.
- Inserting the date and time: Click the Date & Time button, choose a date format in the Date and Time dialog box, and click OK. Click the Update Automatically check box if you want the date to record when you print the document, not when you created your header or footer.

Adjusting Space between Lines

To change the spacing between lines, select the lines whose spacing you want to change, or simply put the cursor in a paragraph if you're changing the line spacing throughout a paragraph. Then, on the Home tab, click the Line and Paragraph Spacing button and choose an option on the drop-down list. To take advantage of more line-spacing options, click the Paragraph group button on the Home tab or choose Line Spacing Options on the Line and Paragraph Spacing button drop-down list. You will see the Paragraph dialog box.

Select an option on the Line Spacing drop-down list:

- ❑ **At Least:** Choose this one if you want Word to adjust for tall symbols or other unusual text. Word adjusts the lines but makes sure that there is, at minimum, the number of points you enter in the At box between each line.
- ❑ **Exactly:** Choose this one and enter a number in the At box if you want a specific amount of space between lines.
- ❑ **Multiple:** Choose this one and put a number in the At box to get triple spaced, quadruple-, quintuple-, or any other number of spaced lines.

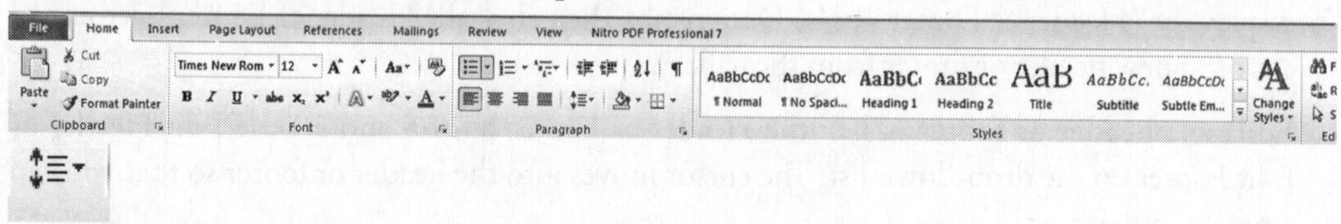

Creating Numbered and Bulleted Lists

Simple numbered and bulleted lists

Just press Enter at the end of each step or bulleted entry. When you're done, select the list, go to the Home tab, and click the Numbering or Bullets button. You can also click the Numbering or Bullets button and start typing the list. Each time you press Enter, Word enters the next number or another bullet.

Meanwhile, here are some tricks for handling lists:

- ❑ **Ending a list:** Press the Enter key twice after typing the last entry in the list. You can also right-click the list, choose Bullets or Numbering, and choose None on the submenu.
- ❑ **Removing the numbers or bullets:** Select the list and click the Numbering or Bullets button.
- ❑ **Adjusting how far a list is indented:** Right-click anywhere in the list, choose Adjust List Indents, and enter a new measurement in the Text Indent box.
- ❑ **Resuming a numbered list:** Suppose that you want a numbered list to resume where a list you entered earlier ended. In other words, suppose that you left off writing a four-step list, put in a

graphic or some paragraphs, click the Numbering a button to start numbering again. The Auto Correct Options button appears. Click it and choose Continue Numbering, or right-click and choose Continue Numbering on the shortcut menu.

Points to Remember

- Use all the tools for formatting for saving your time
- Pay attention to the spacing options
- Use custom designs for different purposes
- Adjust page Margins before printing to make sure that file is compatible for printing
- Use header & footer, numbering, Page layout tools for making page attractive
- Before finalizing the document review it in every formats & do necessary corrections if required

Desktop Publishing on Word

In this chapter you will learn

- Considering ways to desktop-publish in Word
- Fine-tuning tables
- Wrapping text around graphics and other objects
- Running text in newspaper-style columns
- Putting text boxes in documents
- Putting borders on pages
- Decorating pages with drop caps and watermarks
- Printing landscape documents and on varying sizes of paper

Making Use of Charts, Diagrams, Shapes, Clip Art, and Photos

- **Charts:** A chart is an excellent way to present data for comparison purposes. Chart
- **Diagrams:** A diagram allows readers to quickly grasp an idea, relationship, or concept. Shapes SmartArt
- **Shapes and lines:** Shapes and lines can also illustrate ideas and concepts. Shapes
- **Clip-art images:** Clip-art images make a document livelier. They add a little colour to documents. Clip Art
- **Photos:** A well-placed photo or two can make a newsletter or brochure that much more attractive. Picture

Positioning/Wrapping Objects Relative to the Page & Text

Note....

"Object" is just Office's generic term for a shape, line, text box, clip-art image, photo, diagram, WordArt image, or chart that you insert in a document.

Wrapping text around an object

Select the object you want to wrap text around, go to the Format tab, and use one of these methods to wrap text around the object:

✓ Click the Wrap Text button and choose an option on the drop-down list.

✓ Click the Wrap Text button and choose More Layout Options on the drop-down list, or click the Size group button and select the Text Wrapping tab in the Layout dialog box. Then choose a wrapping style and side around which to wrap text.

Positioning an object on a page

To position an object in a Word page, you can drag it to a new location.

Use one of these methods to move your object precisely into place:

✓ Click the Position button and select a With Text Wrapping option on the drop-down list. These options position an object squarely in a corner, a side, or the middle of the page.

✓ Click the Position button and choose More Layout Options on the dropdown list, or click the Size group button and select the Position tab in the Layout dialog box. Then choose position options. Go to the Layout dialog box when you want to place objects in the very same position on different pages.

Working with Text Boxes

Put text in a text box when you want a notice or announcement to stand out on the page. Like other objects, text boxes can be shaded, filled with colour, and given borders. You can also lay them over graphics to make for interesting effects.

Inserting a text box

To create a text box, go to the Insert tab, click the Text Box button, and use one of these methods:

✓ **Choose a ready-made text box:** Scroll in the drop-down list and choose a preformatted text box.

✓ **Draw a conventional text box:** Choose Draw Text Box on the drop-down list, and then click and drag to draw the text box. Lines show you how big it will be when you release the mouse button.

Making text flow from text box to text box

Text Box

You can link text boxes so that the text in the first box is pushed into the next one when it fills up. To link text boxes, start by creating all the text boxes that you need. You cannot link one text box to another if the second text box already has text in it. follow these directions to link text boxes:

✓ **Creating a forward link:** Click a text box and then click the Create Link button to create a forward link.

✓ **Breaking a link:** To break a link, click the text box that is to be the last in the chain, and then click the Break Link button.

Decorating a page with a border

Page Borders

Word offers a means of decorating title pages, certificates, menus, and similar documents with a page border. Besides lines, you can decorate the sides of a page with stars, pieces of cake, and other artwork. If you want to place a border around a page in the middle of a document, you must create a sectionbreak where the page is. Before you create your border, place the cursor on the page where the border is to appear. Place the cursor on the first page of a document if you want to put a border around only the first page. If your document is divided into sections and you want to put borders around certain pages in a section, place the cursor in the section — either in the first page if you want the bordersto go around it, or in a subsequent page. With the cursor in the right place, follow these steps to decorate your page or pages with a border:

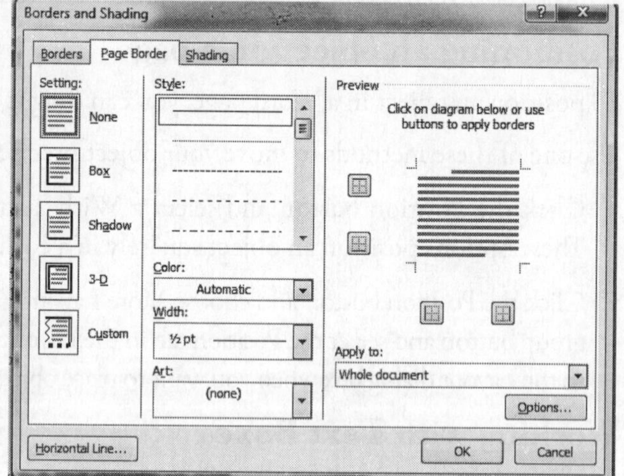

✓ Go to the Page Layout tab and click the Page Borders button.

✓ Under Setting, choose which kind of border you want. The Custom setting is for putting borders on one, two, or three sides of the page, not four. Use the none setting to remove borders.

✓ On the Apply To drop-down list, tell Word which page or pages in the document get borders.

✓ Select options to construct the border you want and then click OK.

Putting a background colour on pages

If you intend to save your Word document as a web page, you will be glad to know that putting a background colour on pages is easy. You can't, however, pick and choose which pages get a background colour. Putting background colours on the pages of a document is an all-or-nothing proposition.

To give a page with a background colour or gradient colour mixture, go to the Page Layout tab, click the Page Colour button, and choose a colour on the drop-down list. Choose Fill Effects to open the Fill Effects dialog box and apply gradient colour mixtures or patterns to the pages.

Dropping in a Drop Cap

To create a drop cap, start by clicking anywhere in the paragraph whose first letter you want to "drop." If you want to "drop" more than one character at the start of the paragraph, select the characters. Then go to the Insert tab, click the Drop Cap button, and choose Dropped or Drop Cap Options. You can configure the following:

- ❑ **Position:** Choose which kind of drop cap you want. In Margin, place the drop cap to the left of the paragraph, not in the paragraph itself.
- ❑ **Font:** Choose a font from the Font drop-down list. Choose a different font from the text in the paragraph.
- ❑ **Lines to Drop:** Enter the number of text lines to drop the letter.
- ❑ **Distance from Text:** Keep the 0 setting unless you're dropping and I, 1, or other skinny letter or number.

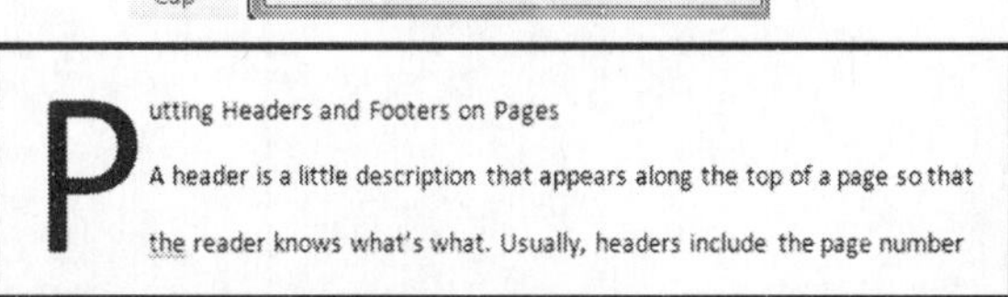
Putting Headers and Footers on Pages
A header is a little description that appears along the top of a page so that the reader knows what's what. Usually, headers include the page number

- ❑ Click the Drop Cap button and choose none to remove a drop cap.

Watermark

To create a watermark for every page of a document, go to the Page Layout tab and click the Watermark button. From the drop-down list, create yourwatermark:

- ❑ **Prefabricated text watermark:** Scroll down the list and choose an option. You will find "Confidential," "Urgent," and other text watermarks.

- **Picture watermark:** Choose Custom Watermark, and in the Printed Watermark dialog box, click the Picture Watermark option button. Then click the Select Picture button. In the Insert Picture dialog box, select a graphic file to use for the watermark and click the Insert button. Back in the Printed Watermark dialog box, choose or enter a size for the graphic on the Scale drop-down list. I don't recommend deselecting the Washout check box — do so and your image may be so dark that it obscures the text.
- **Text watermark:** Choose Custom Watermark and, in the Printed Watermark dialog box, click the Text Watermark option button. Type a word or two in the Text box (or choose an entry from the drop-down list). Choose a font, size, colour, and layout for the words. If you deselect the semi-transparent check box, you do so at your peril because the watermark words may be too dark on the page.

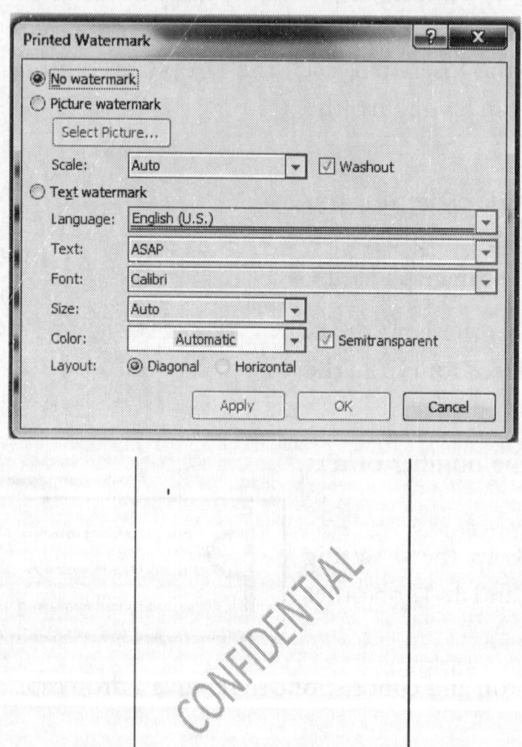

Landscape Documents

A landscape document is one in which width is more than the length. Most documents, are printed in portrait style, with the short sides of the page on the top and bottom. However, creating a landscape document is sometimes a good idea because a landscape document stands out from the usual crowd of portrait documents and sometimes printing in landscape mode is necessary to fit text, tables, and graphics on a single page.

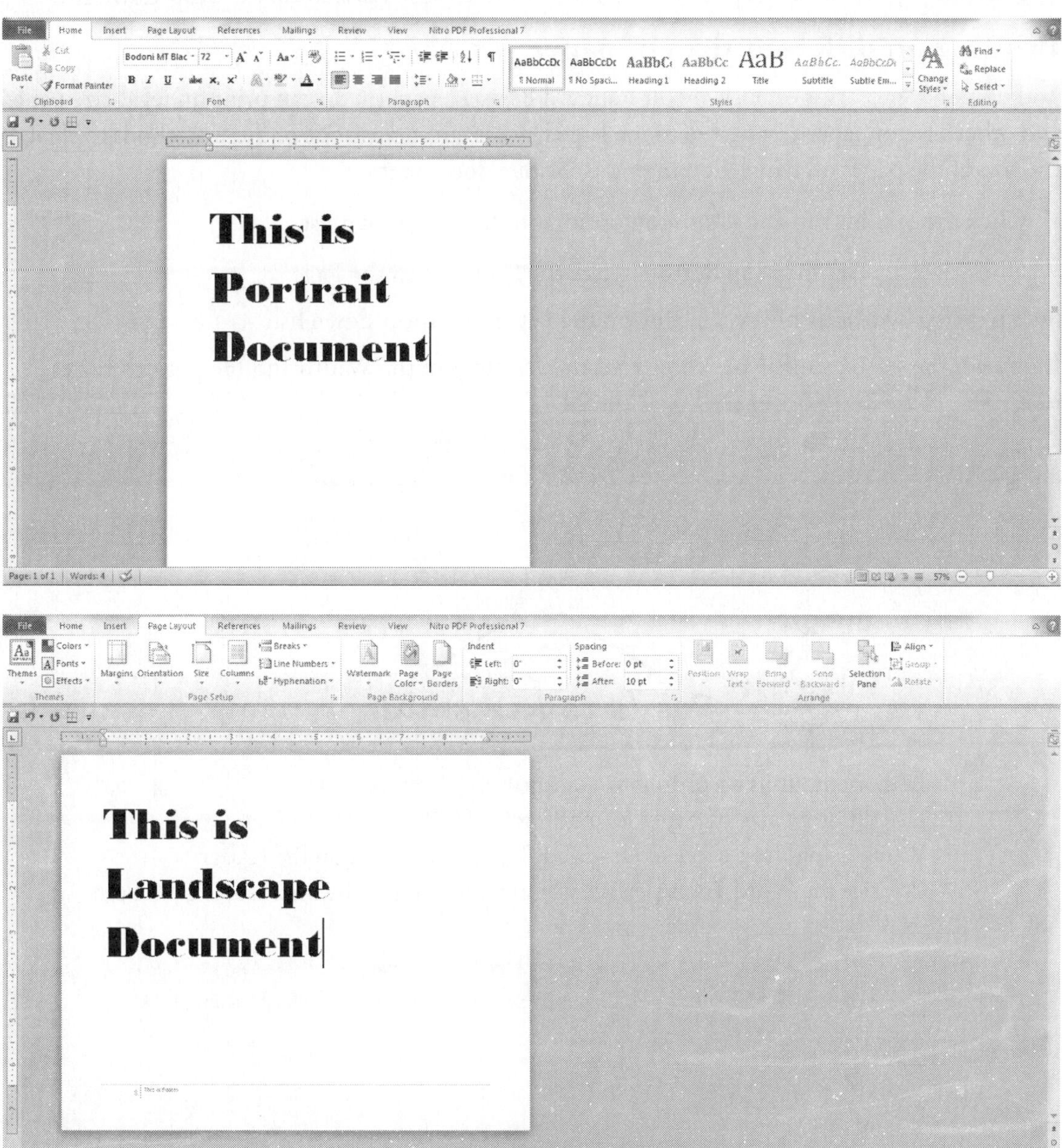

Starting on the Page Layout tab, follow these steps to change the page orientation:

- ✓ **Landscape pages:** Click the Orientation button and choose Landscape on the drop-down list.
- ✓ **Portrait pages:** Click the Orientation button and choose Portrait on the drop-down list.

Printing on different sizes of paper

You don't have to print exclusively on standard 8.5-x-11 paper; you can print on legal-size paper and other sizes of paper as well. Go to the Page Layout tab and use one of these methods to change the size of the paper on which you intend to print a document:

- ✓ Click the Size button and choose an option on the drop-down list.
- ✓ Click the Page Setup group button, select the Paper tab in the Page

Set up dialog box, and choose a setting on the Paper Size drop-down list.

If none of the settings suits you, enter your own settings in the Width and Height text boxes.

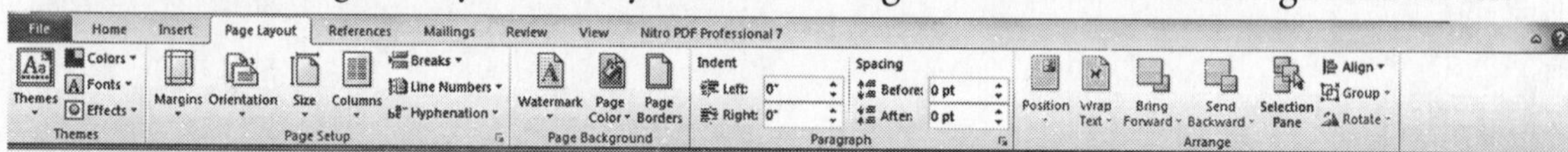

- Use orientations according to your use
- Use different size of paper formatting for DTP
- While using drop cap keep in mind that it has impact on the reader.
- Practice the Word Tools perfectly before jumping to the Microsoft PowerPoint 2010.

Microsoft Power Point 2010

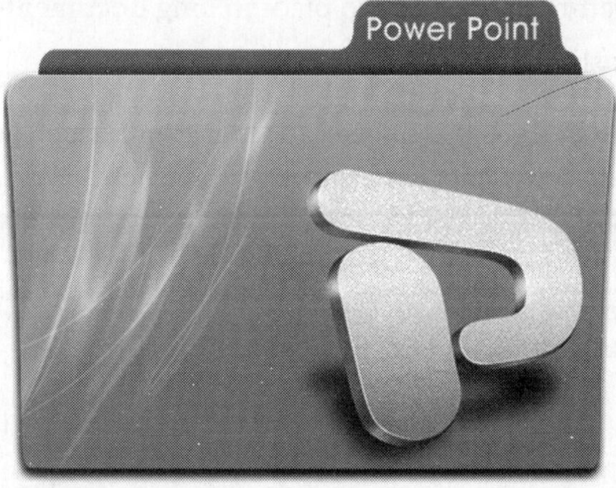

Welcome to MS PowerPoint 2010

In this chapter you will learn

- Getting started with the PowerPoint screen
- Creating a Slide show
- Changing your view of a document
- Selecting text so that you can copy, move, or delete it
- Getting from place to place in long documents
- Pasting one slide document into another

It is practically impossible to sit through a conference, seminar, or trade show without seeing at least one PowerPoint presentation. PowerPoint has found its way into nearly every office and boardroom.

Note...

- Presentation: All the slides, from start to finish, that you show your audience. Sometimes presentations are called "slide shows." Presentations are saved in presentation files (.pptx files).
- Slides: The images you create with PowerPoint. During a presentation, slides appear on-screen one after the other. Don't be put off by the word slide and dreary memories of sitting through your uncle's slide show vacation memories. You don't need a slide projector to show these slides. You can now plug a laptop or other computer into special monitors that display PowerPoint slides.

Creating PowerPoint Presentation

Creating a PowerPoint presentation entails completing these basic tasks:

- **Creating the slides:** Once you open the PPT Window, your next task is to create the slides. PowerPoint offers many preformatted slide layouts, each designed for presenting information a certain way.
- **Notes:** As you create slides, you can jot down notes in the Notes pane. You can use these notes later to formulate your presentation and decide what you're going to say to your audience while each slide is on-screen.
- **Designing your presentation:** After you create a presentation, the next step is to think about its appearance. You can change slides' colours and backgrounds, as well as choose a theme for your presentation, an all-encompassing design that applies to all (or most of) the slides.
- **Inserting tables, charts, diagrams, and shapes:** A PowerPoint presentation should be more than a loose collection of bulleted lists. Starting on the Insert tab, you can place tables, charts, and diagrams on slides, as well as adorn your slides with text boxes, WordArt images, and shapes.
- **"Animating" your slides:** PowerPoint slides can play video and sound, as well as be "animated". You can make the items on a slide move on the screen. As a slide arrives, you can make it spin or flash.
- Delivering your presentation: During a presentation, you can draw on the slides. You can also blank the screen and show slides out of order. In case you can't be there in person, PowerPoint

gives you the opportunity to create self-running presentations and presentations that others can run on their own. You can also distribute presentations on CDs and videos.

Creating a New Presentation

No matter what kind of presentation you want to create, start creating it by going to the File tab and choosing New. You will see the Available Templates and Themes window. This window offers templates for creating many types of presentations. Click a template to preview it on the right side of the window. Double-click a template (or select it and click the Create button) to create a presentation. Apply following methods to create apresentation:

- **Blank presentation:** Double-click the Blank Presentation icon. A new presentation appears. Try visiting the Design tab and choosing a theme or background style to get a taste of all the things you can do to decorate a presentation. (By pressing Ctrl+N, you can create a new, blank Presentation without opening the Available Templates and Themes window.)
- **Recently used template:** Click the Recent Templates icon to use a template listed there.
- **Template on your computer:** Click the Sample Templates icon. Templates that you loaded on your computer when you installed PowerPoint appear.
- **Template you created (or downloaded earlier from Microsoft):** Click the My Templates icon. The New Presentation dialog box appears. Select a template and click OK.

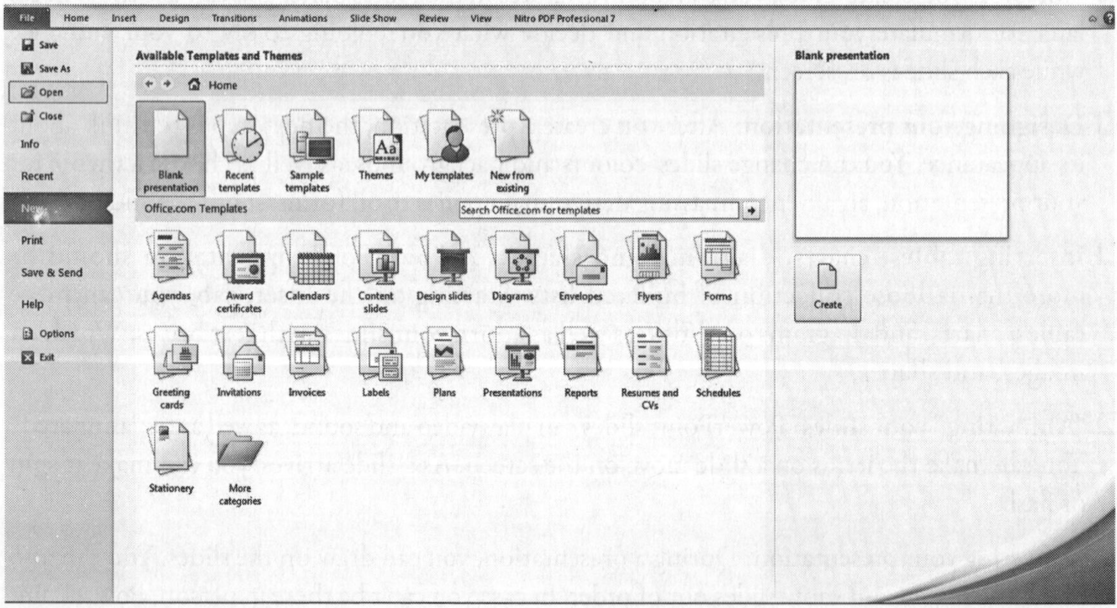

- ❑ **Template available online at Office.com:** Enter a search term in the Search box, make sure that your computer is connected to the Internet, and click the Start Searching button. Templates appear in the window. Double-click a template to download and use it to create a presentation.
- ❑ **Recycle another presentation:** If you can use another presentation as the starting point for creating a new presentation, nab slides from the other presentation. Click the New from Existing icon. In the New from ExistingPresentation dialog box, select the presentation and click the Open button.

Creating New Slides for Your Presentation

Inserting a new slide

Follow these steps to insert a new slide in your presentation:

- ✓ Select the slide that you want to insert. In Normal view, select the slide on the Slides pane. In Slide Sorter view, select the slide in the main window.
- ✓ On the Home tab, click the bottom half of the New Slide button. You see a drop-down list of slide layouts. (If you click the top half of the New Slide button, you insert a slide with the same layout as the one you selected in Step 1.)
- ✓ Select the slide layout that best approximates the slide you want to create.

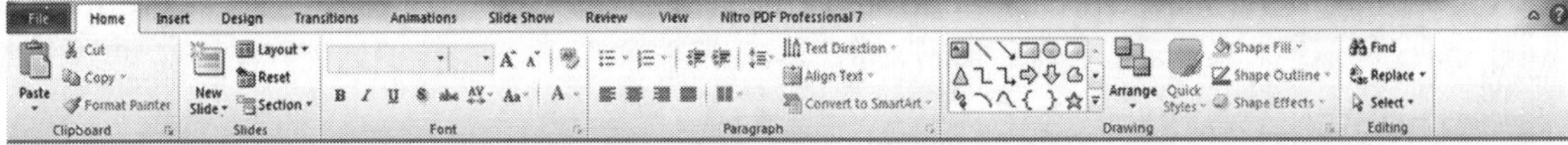

- ❑ **Creating a duplicate slide:** Select the slide or slides you want to duplicate, and on the Home tab, open the drop-down list on the New Slide button and choose Duplicate Selected Slides. You can also open the drop-down list on the Copy button and choose Duplicate.
- ❑ **Copying and pasting slides:** Click the slide you want to copy (or Ctrl+click to select more than one slide) and then click the Copy button on the Home tab (or press Ctrl+C). Next, click to select the slide that you want the copied slide (or slides) to appear after and click the Paste button (or press Ctrl+V).
- ❑ **Recycling slides from other presentations:** Select the slide that you want the recycled slides to follow in your presentation, and on the Home tab, open the drop-down list on

the New Slide button and choose Reuse Slides. The Reuse Slides task pane opens. Open the drop-down list on the Browse button, choose Browse File, and select a presentation in the Browse dialog box. The Reuse Slides task pane shows thumbnail versions of slides in the presentation you selected. One at a time, click slides to add them to your presentation. You can right-click a slide and choose Insert All Slides to grab all the slides in the presentation.

Selecting a different layout for a slide

If you mistakenly choose the wrong layout for a slide, you can start all over. You can graft a new layout onto your slide with one of these techniques:

- ✓ On the Home tab, click the Layout button and choose a layout on the drop-down list.
- ✓ Right-click the slide (being careful not to right-click a frame or object), choose Layout, and choose a layout on the submenu.

You can use Reset command also.

Changing views

PowerPoint offers two places to change views:

- ❑ **View buttons on the status bar:** Click the View button — Normal, Slide Sorter, Slide Show, or Reading View — on the status bar to change views.
- ❑ **View tab:** On the View tab, click a button on the Presentation Views or Master Views group.

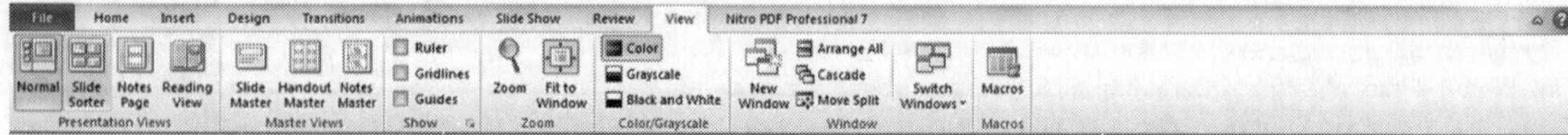

- ❑ **Normal/Slides view for examining slides:** Switch to Normal view, move the pointer to the Slides pane, and select the Slides tab when you want to examine a slide. In this view, thumbnail slides appear in the Slides pane, and you can see your slide in all its glory in the middle of the screen.
- ❑ **Slide Sorter view for moving and deleting slides:** In Slide Sorter view, you will see thumbnails of all the slides in the presentation (use the Zoom Slider to change the size of thumbnails). From here, moving slides around is easy, and seeing many slides simultaneously gives you a sense of whether the different slides are consistent with one another and how the whole presentation is shaping up. The slides are numbered so thatyou can see where they appear in a presentation.

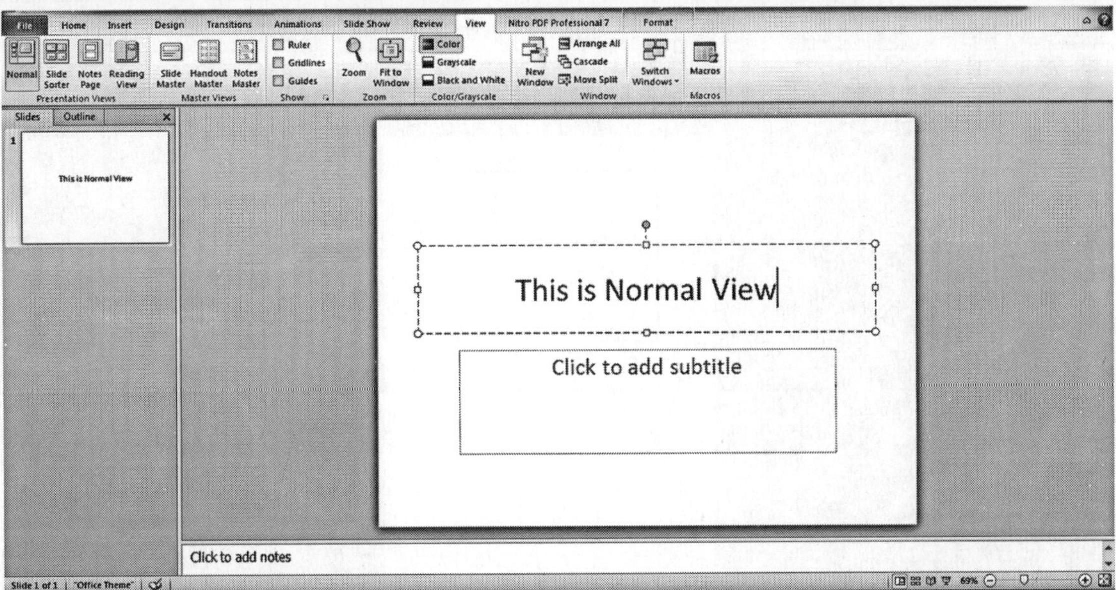

- **Notes Page view for reading your speaker notes:** In Notes Page view, you see notes you've written to aid you in your presentation, if you've written any. You can write notes in this view as well as in the Notes pane in Normal view.

- Reading View **Reading View for focusing on slides' appearance:** In Reading View, you also see a single slide, but it appears on-screen with the View buttons and with buttons for moving quickly from slide to slide. Switch to Reading View to proofread slides and put the final touches on presentation.

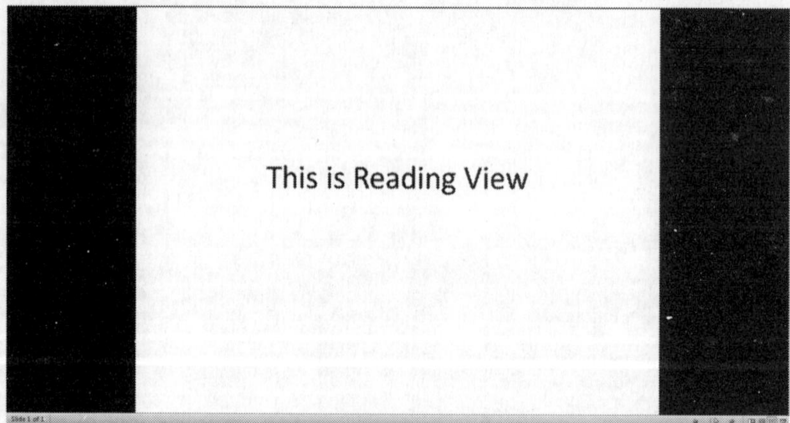

- **Slide Show view for giving a presentation:** In Slide Show view, you see a single slide. Not only that, but the slide fills the entire screen. This is what your presentation looks like when you show it to an audience.

- **The Master views for a consistent presentation:** The master views — Slide Master, Handout Master, and Notes Master — are for handling master styles, the formatting commands that pertain to all the slides in a presentation, handouts, and notes. To switch to these views, go to the View tab and click the appropriate button.

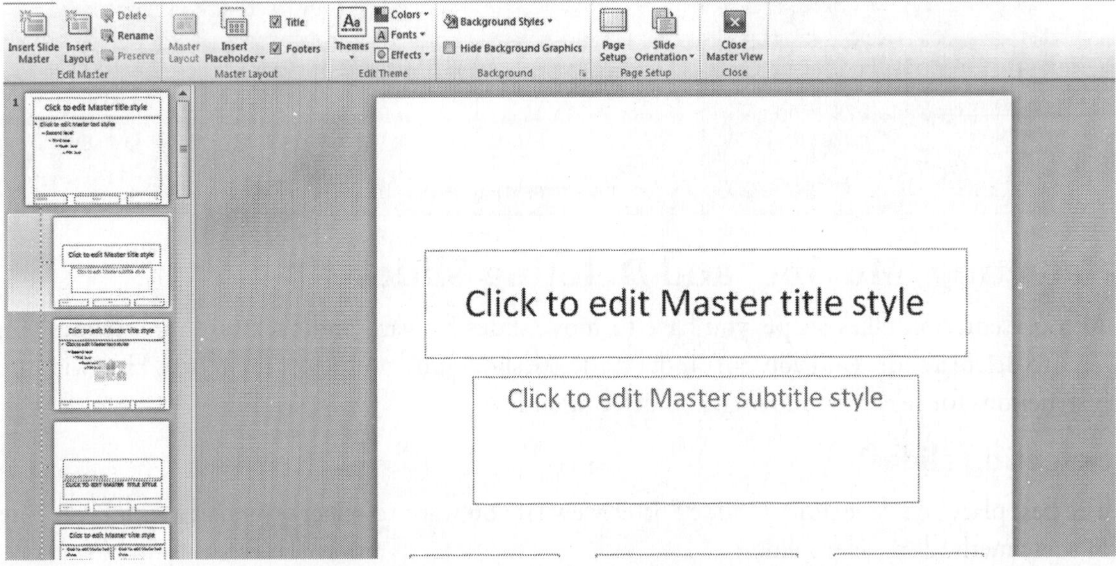

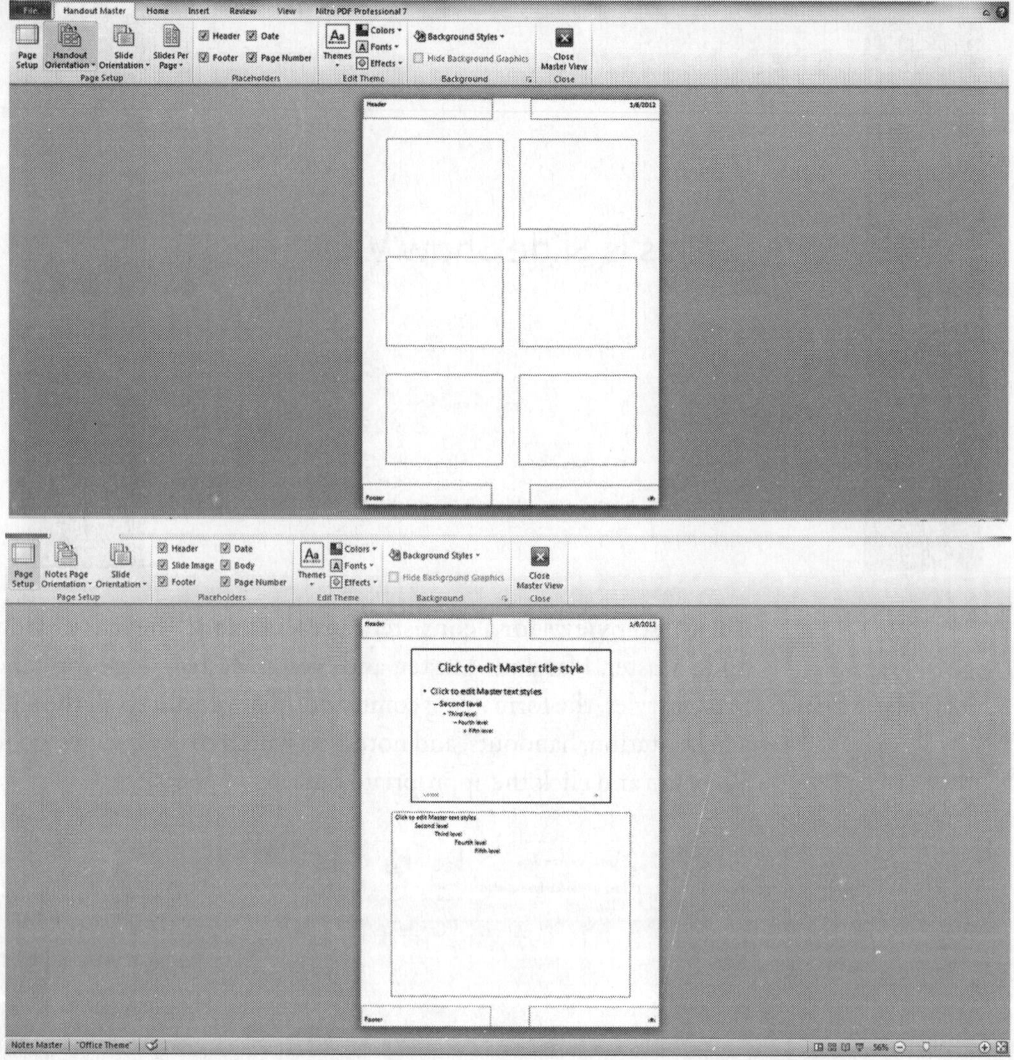

Selecting, Moving, and Deleting Slides

As a presentation takes shape, you have to move slides forward and backward. Sometimes you have to delete a slide. And you can't move or delete slides until you select them first. Herewith are instructions for selecting, moving, and deleting slides.

Selecting slides

The best place to select slides is Slide Sorter view (if you want to select several at a time). Use one of these methods to select slides:

- ❑ **Select one slide:** Click the slide.
- ❑ **Select several different slides:** Hold down the Ctrl key and click each slide in the Slides pane or in Slide Sorter view.
- ❑ **Select several slides in succession:** Hold down the Shift key and click the first slide and then the last one.

Moving slides

To move or rearrange slides, you're advised to go to Slide Sorter view. Select the slide or slides that you want to move and use one of these methods to move slides:

- ❑ **Dragging and dropping:** Click the slides you selected and drag them to a new location. You will see the drag pointer, and in Slide Sorter view, a vertical line shows you where the slide or slides will land when you release the mouse button. On the Slides pane, a horizontal line appears between slides to show you where the slide or slides will land when you release the mouse button.
- ❑ **Cutting and pasting:** On the Home tab, cut the slide or slides to the Windows Clipboard (click the Cut button, press Ctrl+X, or right-click and choose Cut). Then select the slide that you want the slide or slides to appear after and give the Paste command (click the Paste button, press Ctrl+V, or right-click and choose Paste). You can right-click between slides to paste with precision.

Deleting slides

Select the slide or slides you want to delete and use one of these methods to delete slides:

- ✓ Press the Delete key.
- ✓ Right-click and choose Delete Slide on the shortcut menu.

Points to Remember

- ☞ Before finalizing your slideshow, review it on your system
- ☞ Select slides setup according to your need
- ☞ Save a presentation style as template you like

Let's Start PowerPoint

In this chapter you will learn

- Selecting theme for your presentation
- Creating background & designs for your presentation
- Customising the slide appearance
- Editing the Slide styles

Choosing a Theme for Your Presentation

After you initially select a theme, you can do one or two things to customize it. These pages explain how to find and select a theme for your presentation and diddle with a theme after you select it. By the way, the name of the theme that is currently in use is listed on the left side of the status bar, in case you're curious about a theme you want to replace.

Selecting a theme

Use one of these methods to select a new theme for your presentation:

- **Selecting a theme in the Themes gallery:** On the Design tab, open the Themes gallery and move the pointer over different themes to "live preview" them. Click a theme to select it.
- **Borrowing a theme from another presentation:** On the Design tab, open the Themes gallery, and click Browse for Themes. Select and click the Apply button.

Tweaking a theme

Starting on the Design tab, you can customize a theme with these techniques and in so doing alter all the slides in your presentation:

- **Choosing a new set of colours:** The easiest and best way to experiment with customizing a theme is to select a different colour set. Click the Colours button, slide the pointer over the different colour sets on the dropdown list, and see what effect they have on your slides.
- **Change the fonts:** Click the Fonts button and choose a font combination on the drop-down list. The first font in each pair applies to slide titles and the second to slide text. You can also choose Create New Theme Fonts on the list and select theme fonts of your own.
- **Change theme effects:** Click the Effects button and choose a theme effect on the drop-down list. A theme effect is a slight refinement to a theme.
- **Choosing background style variation:** Most themes offer background style variations. Click the Background Styles button to open the Background Styles gallery and select a style.

Creating Slide Backgrounds on Your Own

Besides a theme or background style, your other option for creating slide backgrounds is to do it on your own. For a background, you can have a solid colour, a transparent colour, a gradient blend of colours, a picture, or a clip-artimage.

- **Solid colour:** A single, uniform colour. You can adjust a colour's transparency and in effect "bleach out" the colour to push it farther into the background.
- **Gradient:** A mixture of different colours with the colours blending into one another.
- **Clip art:** A clip-art image from the Microsoft Clip Organizer.
- **Picture:** A photograph or graphic.
- **Texture:** A uniform pattern that gives the impression that the slide is displayed on a material such as cloth or stone.

Using a solid (or transparent) colour for the slide background

Follow these steps to use a solid or transparent colour as the background for slides:

✓ On the Design tab, click the Background Styles button and choose Format Background on the drop-down list. You see the Fill category of the Format Background dialog box.

✓ Select the Solid Fill option button.

✓ Click the Colour button and choose a colour on the drop-down list. The muted theme colours are recommended because they look better in the background, but you can select a standard colour or click the More Colours button and select a colour in the Colours dialog box.

✓ Drag the Transparency slider if you want a "bleached out" colour rather than a slide colour. At 0% transparency, you get a solid colour; at 100%, you get no colour at all.

✓ Click the Apply to All button and then the Close button.

Follow these steps to create a gradient background for slides:

✓ On the Design tab, click the Background Styles button, and choose Format Background on the drop-down list. You see the Fill category of the Format Background dialog box. Drag this dialog box to the left side of the screen so that you can get a better view of your slide.

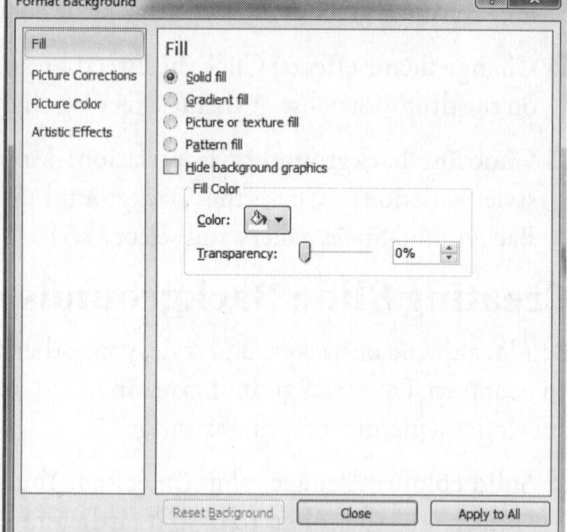

Creating gradient background

✓ Click the Gradient Fill option button.

✓ On the Type drop-down list, choose what type of gradient you want — Linear, Radial, Rectangular, Path, or Shade from Title. If you choose Linear, you can enter a degree measurement in the Angle box to change the angle at which the colours blend. At 90 degrees, for example, colours blend horizontally across the slide; at 180 degrees, they blend vertically.

✓ Create a gradient stop for each colour transition you want on yourslides. Gradient stops determine where colours are, how colours transition fromone to the next, and which colours are used. You can create as many gradient stops as you want. Here are methods for handling gradient stops:

- ❑ **Adding a gradient stop:** Click the Add Gradient Stop button. A new gradient stop appears on the slider. Drag it to where you want the colour blend to occur.
- ❑ **Removing a gradient stop:** Select a gradient stop on the slider and click the Remove Gradient Stop button.

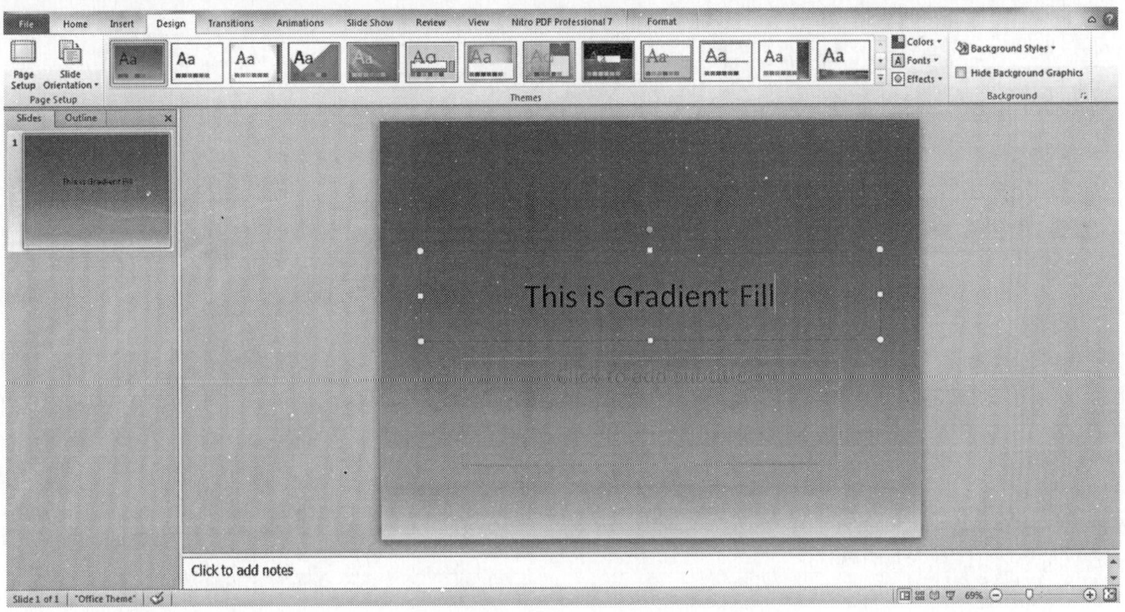

- ❑ **Choosing a colour for a gradient stop:** Select a gradient stop on the slider, click the Colour button, and choose a colour on the drop-down list.
- ❑ **Positioning a gradient stop:** Drag a gradient stop on the slider or use the Position box to move it to a different location.
- ❑ Drag the Brightness slider to make the colours dimmer or brighter.

Creating Slide Backgrounds on Your Own

Drag the Transparency slider to make the colours on the slides more or less transparent. At 0% transparency, you get solid colours; at 100%, you get no colour at all. Click the Apply to All button.

Placing a clip-art image in the slide background

- ✓ On the Design tab, click the Background Styles button and choose Format Background on the drop-down list. The Fill category of the Format Background dialog box appears
- ✓ Click the Picture or Texture Fill option button.
- ✓ Click the Clip Art button. You see the Select Picture dialog box.
- ✓ Find and select a clip-art image that you can use in the background of your slides. You can scroll through the clip-art images until you find a good one, enter a search term in the Search Text

box and click the Go button (click the Include Content from Office Online check box to search online at Microsoft for a clip-art image), or click the Import button to get an image from your computer.

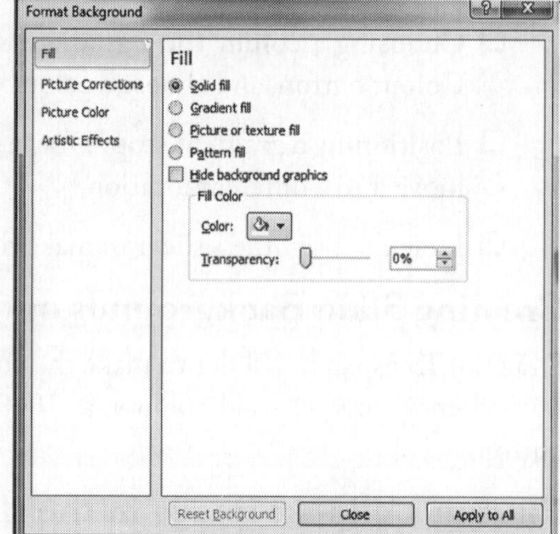

Formatting background

- ✓ In the Format Background dialog box, enter a Transparency measurement. Drag the Transparency slider or enter a measurement in the box. The higher the measurement, the more transparent the image is.
- ✓ Enter measurements in the Offsets boxes to make your clip-art image fill the slide.
- ✓ Click the Apply to All button and then click Close.

Follow these steps to use a picture as a slide background:

- ✓ On the Design tab, click the Background Styles button and choose Format Background on the drop-down list. You see the Fill category of the Format Background dialog box.
- ✓ Click the Picture or Texture Fill option button.

- ✓ Click the File tab. The Insert Picture dialog box appears.
- ✓ Locate the picture you want, select it, and click the Insert button. The picture lands on your slide.
- ✓ Enter a Transparency measurement to make the picture fade a bit in to the background. Using the Offsets text boxes, enter measurements to make your picturefit on the slides.
- ✓ Click the Apply to All button.

Using a texture for a slide background

- ✓ On the Design tab, click the Background Styles button and choose Format Background on the drop-down list.
- ✓ Click the Picture or Texture Fill option button.
- ✓ Click the Texture button and choose a texture on the drop-down list.
- ✓ Enter a Transparency measurement to make the texture less imposing.
- ✓ Drag the slider or enter a measurement in the Transparency box.

✓ Click the Apply to All button and then click Close.

Points to Remember

- Create all formatting on the frame only, since any formatting done outside the frame will be unavailable during slide show
- Choose colours and other formatting elements wisely

Text &Text Boxes

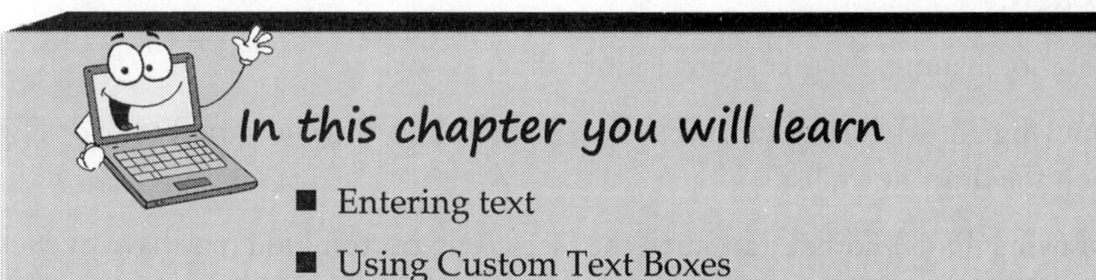

- Entering text
- Using Custom Text Boxes

Entering Text

Here we will discuss how to enter text in a slide in a Powerpoint presentation.

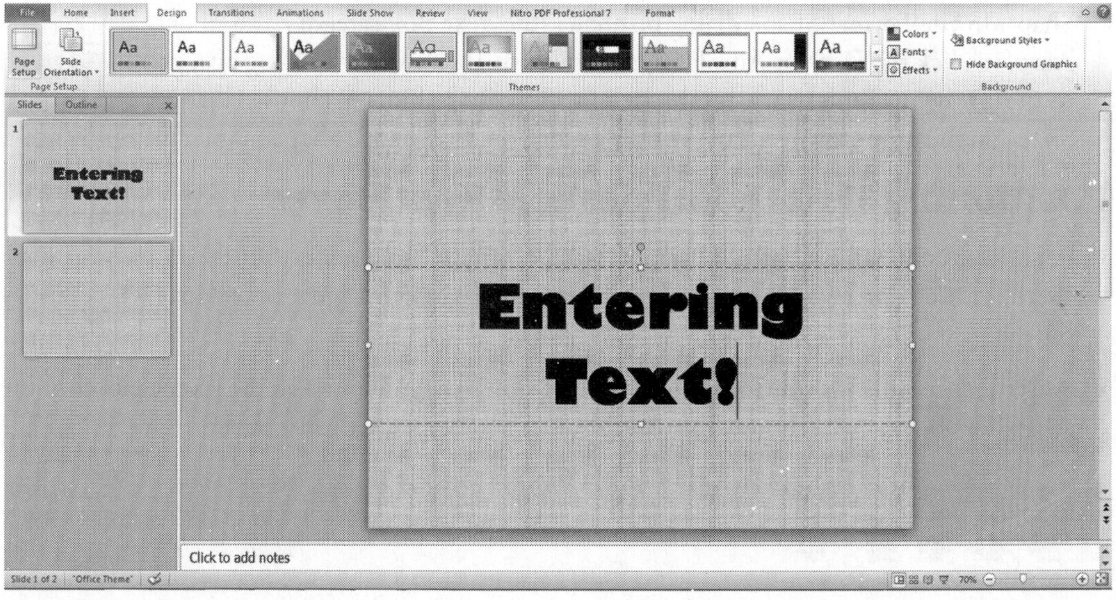

Text Boxes and Text Box Shapes

- ❑ **Creating a text box:** On the Insert tab, click the Text Box button and move the pointer to a part of the slide where you can see the text box pointer, a downward-pointing arrow. Then click and start dragging to create your text box, and enter the text.
- ❑ **Filling a text box with a colour style:** On the (Drawing Tools) Format tab, choose a style on the Shape Styles gallery.
- ❑ **Rotating a text box (text included):** Use one of these techniques to rotate a text box along with the text inside it:
  - ✓ Drag the rotation handle, the green circle above the text box.
  - ✓ On the (Drawing Tools) Format tab, click the Rotate button and choose a Rotate or Flip command on the drop-down list.
  - ✓ On the (Drawing Tools) Format tab, click the Size group button (you may have to click the Size button first) and, in the Size category of the Format Shape dialog box, enter a measurement in the Rotation box.
- ❑ **Turning a shape into a text box:** Create the shape, and then click in the shape and start typing.
- ❑ **Turning a text box into a shape:** Right-click the text box and choose Format Shape. In the Format Shape dialog box, click the Text Box category and under AutoFit, click the Do Not AutoFit option button. Then close the dialog box, go to the (Drawing Tools) Format tab, click the Edit Shape button, choose Change Shape on the drop-down list, and choose a shape on the Change Shape submenu.

Positioning Text in Frames and Text Boxes

- ✓ Align text commands control horizontal (left-to-right) alignments. On the Home tab, click the Align Left (press Ctrl+L), Center (press Ctrl+E), Align Right (press Ctrl+R), or Justify button.
- ✓ Align Text commands control vertical (up-and-down) alignments. On the Home tab, click the Align Text button and choose Top, Middle, or Bottom on the drop-down list.

Format Text Effects

Text Fill
Text Outline
Outline Style
Shadow
Reflection
Glow and Soft Edges
3-D Format
3-D Rotation
Text Box

Text Box
Text layout
Vertical alignment: Top
Text direction: Horizontal
Autofit
Do not Autofit
Shrink text on overflow
Resize shape to fit text
Internal margin
Left: 0.1" Top: 0.05"
Right: 0.1" Bottom: 0.05"
Wrap text in shape
Columns...
Close

Format text effects

☞ Place the text box in the frame only, it will not appear out of the frame during slide show

Transitions & Animations

In this chapter you will learn

- Using Animations in Slide show
- Using Transitions to slides
- Inserting Sound & Video clips in presentation
- Converting presentation into Video

In PowerPoint, a transition is a little bit of excitement that occurs as one slide leaves the screen and the next slide climbs aboard. An animation is movement on the slide.

Tools for tweaking a transition:

- ❑ **Effect Options:** Click the Effect Options button and choose an effect on the drop-down list. For example, choose From Top or From Bottom to make a transition arrive from the top or bottom of the screen. Not all transitions offer effect options.
- ❑ **Sound:** Open the Sound drop-down list and choose a sound to accompany the transition. The Loop Until Next Sound option at the bottom of the drop-down list plays a sound continuously until the next slide in the presentation appears.
- ❑ **Duration:** Enter a time period in the Duration box to declare how quickly or slowly you want the transition to occur. As mentioned earlier, you can click the Apply To All button to assign the same.

Altering and removing slide transitions

In the Slides pane and Slide Sorter view, the transition symbol, a flying star, appears next to slides that have been assigned a transition. Select the slides that need a transition change, go to the Transitions tab, and follow these instructions to alter or remove transitions:

- ❑ **Altering a transition:** Choose a different transition in the Transition to This Slide gallery. You can also choose different effect options and sounds, and change the duration of the transition.
- ❑ **Removing a transition:** Choose None in the Transition to This Slide gallery.

Animating parts of a slide

Follow these steps to preview and choose an animation scheme for slides:

- ✓ Go to the Animations tab.
- ✓ Click to select the element on the slide that you want to animate. For example, select a text frame with a bulleted list. You can tell when you've selected an element because a selection box appears around it.
- ✓ In the Animation Styles gallery, choose an animation effect.

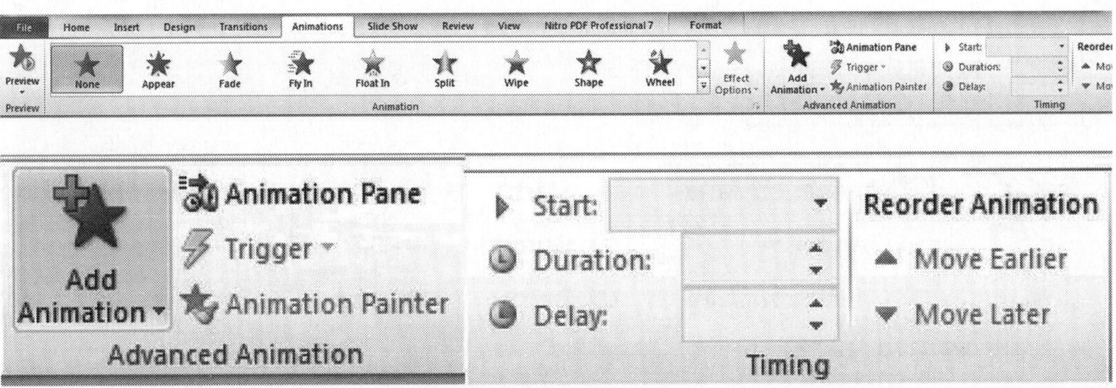

You can choose Entrance, Emphasis, and Exit animation effects. As soon as you make your choice, the animation springs to life, and you can click the Preview button at any time to see your animation in all its glory.

- ✓ Click the Effect Options button and experiment with choices on the drop-down list to tweak your animation. Which options are available depends on the animation you chose.

- ✓ **All at Once:** All the text is animated at the same time.
- ✓ **By Paragraph:** Each paragraph is treated separately and is animated on its own.

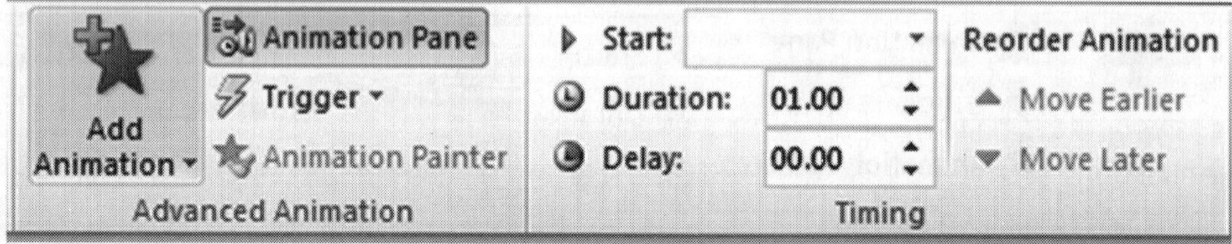

To remove an animation, return to the Animation Styles gallery and choose None.

Audio Part of Your Presentation

PowerPoint offers two ways to make audio part of a presentation:

- ❑ **As part of slide transitions:** A sound is heard as a new slide arrives on-screen. On the Transitions tab, open the Sound drop-down list and choose a sound.

- [ ] **On the slide itself:** The means of playing audio appears on the slide in the form of an Audio icon. By moving the mouse over this icon, you can display audio controls, and you can use these controls to play audio. You can also make audio play as soon as the slide arrives on-screen.

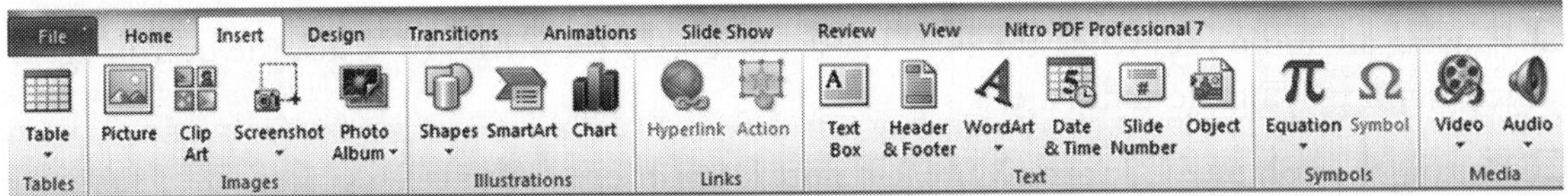

Inserting an audio file on a slide

Follow these steps to insert an audio file in a slide:

✓ Go to the Insert tab.

✓ Click the Audio button. You will see the Insert Audio dialog box.

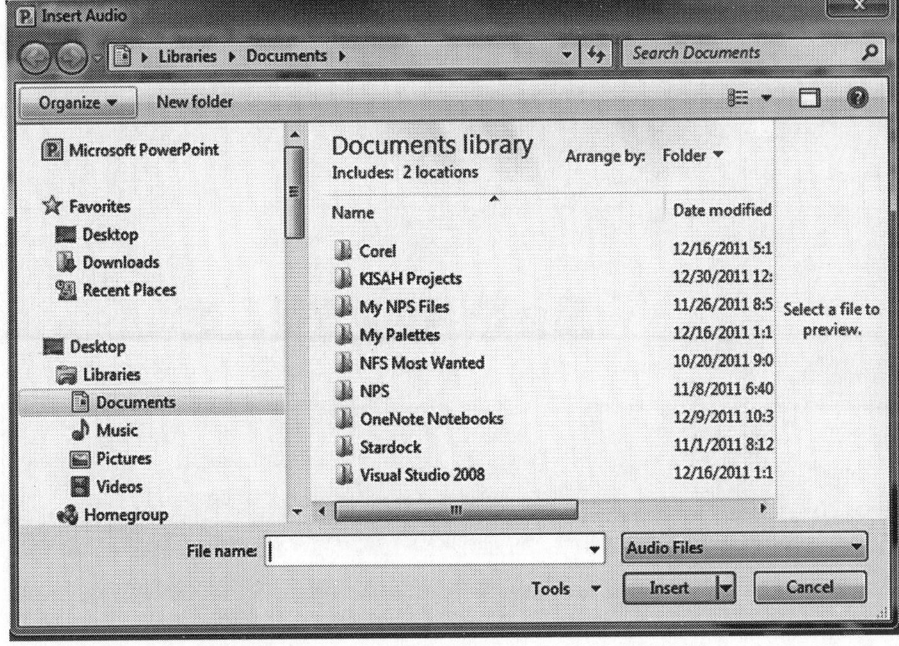

✓ Locate and select a sound file and then click Insert.

Playing audio during a presentation

While an audio file is playing during a presentation, controls for starting, pausing, and controlling the volume appear on-screen.

Follow these instructions to start, pause, and control the volume of an audio recording during a presentation:

- ❑ **Starting an audio file:** Move the pointer over the Audio icon, and when you see the Audio controls, click the Play/Pause button (or press Alt+P).
- ❑ **Pausing an audio file:** Click the Play/Pause button (or press Alt+P). Click the button again to resume playing the audio file.
- ❑ **Muting the volume:** Click the Mute/Unmute icon (or press Alt+U).
- ❑ **Controlling the volume:** Move the pointer over the Mute/Unmute icon to display the volume slider and then drag the volume control on the slider.

Inserting a video on a slide

Follow these steps to insert a video on a slide:

- ❑ Open the Insert Video dialog box. You can open the dialog box with one of these methods:
  - ✓ Click the Media icon in a content place holder frame.
  - ✓ On the Insert tab, click the Video button.

❑ Select a video file in the Insert Video dialog box and click Insert.

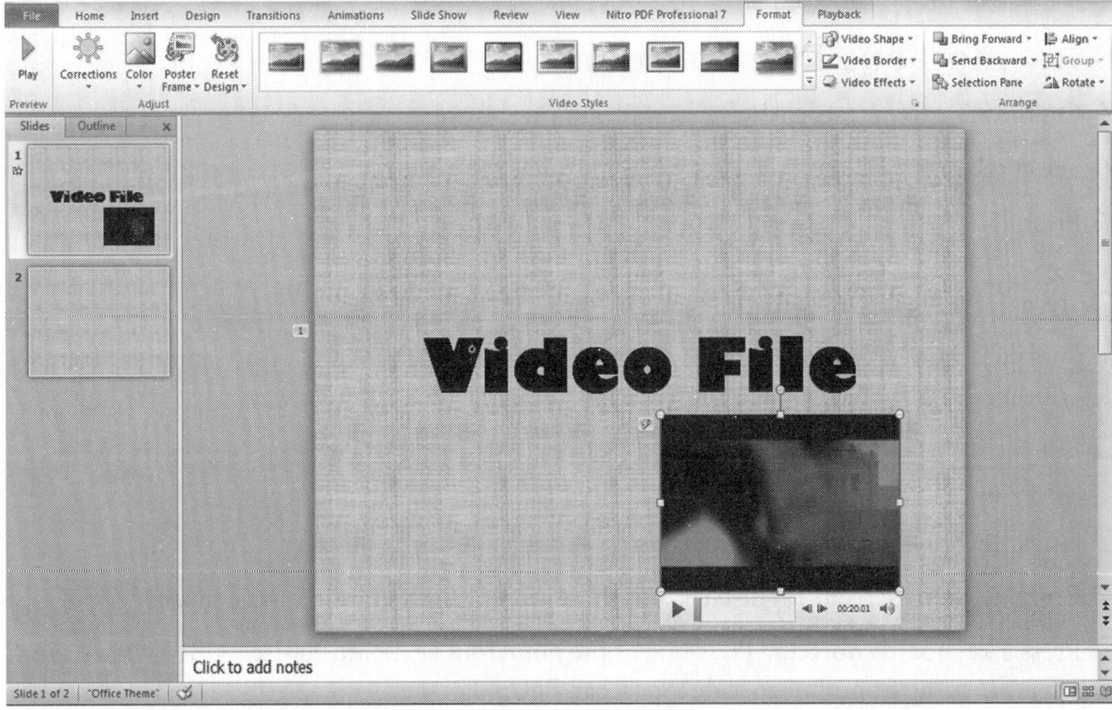

❑ **Controlling the volume:** Click the Volume button and choose Low, Medium, High, or Mute to control how loud the video sound is.

❑ **Playing the video automatically or when you click the Play/Pause button:** Open the Start drop-down list and choose Automatically or On Click to tell PowerPoint when to start playing the video.

❑ **Playing the video at full screen:** Make a video fill the entire screen by selecting the Play Full Screen check box. Be careful of this one. Videos can look terribly grainy when they appear on the big screen.

❑ **Hiding the video when it isn't playing:** You can hide the video until you start playing it by selecting the Hide While Not Playing check box. Be sure to choose Automatically on the Start drop-down list if you select this check box.

❑ **Continuously playing, or looping the video:** Play a video continuously or until you go to the next slide by selecting the Loop Until Stopped check box.

- ❑ **Rewinding the video when it's finished playing:** Rewind a video if you want to see the first frame, not the last, when the video finishes playing.

Showing Your Presentation

- ✓ On the Slide Show tab, click the From Beginning button.
- ✓ Select the first slide and then click the Slide Show view button
- ✓ Press F5

Going from slide to slide

In a nutshell, PowerPoint offers four ways to move from slide to slide in a presentation. Here we describe methods for navigating a presentation, using the four different ways:

- ❑ **Use the slide control buttons:** Click a slide control button — Previous, Next — in the lower-left corner of the screen.
- ❑ **Click the Slide button:** Click this button and make a choice on the pop-up menu.
- ❑ **Right-click on-screen:** Right-click and choose a navigation option on the shortcut menu.
- ❑ **Press a keyboard shortcut:** Press one of the numerous keyboard shortcuts. That PowerPoint offers for going from slide to slide (Spacebar, PgUp, PgDn...)

Wielding a pen or highlighter in a presentation

Follow these instructions so that you can draw on a slide:

- ❑ **Selecting a pen or highlighter:** PowerPoint offers Pen for writing on slides and Highlighter for highlighting text on slides. To select the Pen or Highlighter, click the Pen button and choose Pen or Highlighter. You can also right-click, choose Pointer Options, and make a selection on the submenu.
- ❑ **Choosing a colour for drawing:** After you select the Pen or Highlighter, click the Pen button, choose Ink Colour, and select a colour on the submenu

Follow these steps to make yours a kiosk-style, self-running presentation:

- ✓ Go to the Slide Show tab.
- ✓ Click the Set Up Slide Show button.

You will see the Set Up Slide Show dialog box.

- ✓ Under Show Type, select the Browsed at a Kiosk (Full Screen) option. When you select this option, PowerPoint automatically selects the Loop Continuously Until 'Esc' check box.
- ✓ Make sure that the Using Timings, If Present option button is selected.
- ✓ Click OK.

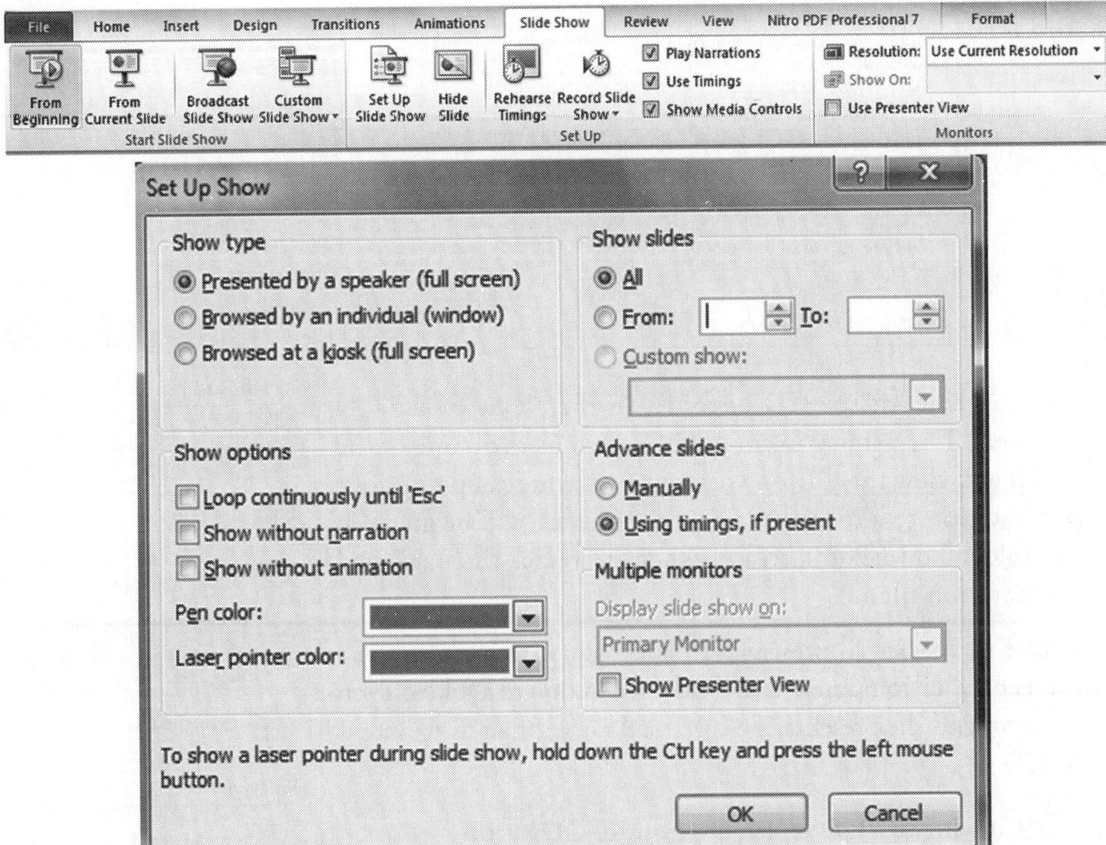

Packaging a presentation on a CD

Follow these steps to copy your presentation and the PowerPoint Viewer to a CD or a folder:

- ✓ Open the presentation you want to package.
- ✓ On the File tab, choose Save & Send.
- ✓ Choose Package Presentation for CD, and click the Package for CD button.

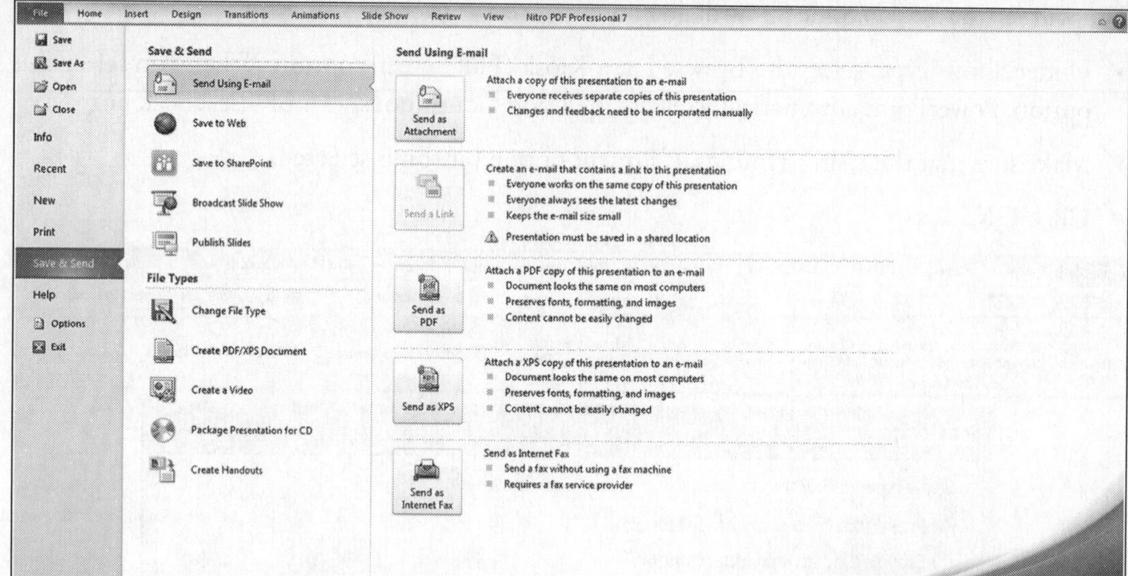

✓ Enter a name for the CD or folder in the Name of the CD text box. The name you enter will appear as the name of the CD if you view the CD on Computer; if you're copying your presentation to a folder, the name you enter will be given to the folder PowerPoint creates when it creates the packaged presentation file.

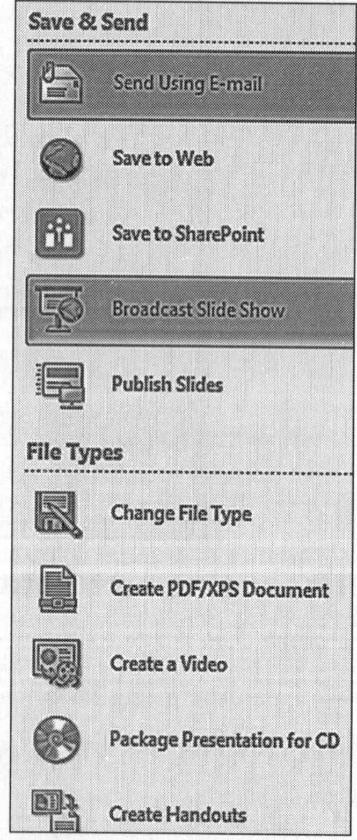

✓ Create the packaged presentation and copy it to a CD or to a folder on your computer. Copy the presentation to a folder if you want to send the presentation by e-mail rather than distribute it by CD.

- ❑ **Copying to a CD:** Click the Copy to CD button.
- ❑ **Copying to a folder:** Click the Copy to Folder button. In the Copy to Folder dialog box, click the Browse button, and in the ChooseLocation dialog box, select a folder for storing the folder where you will keep your packaged presentation. Then click the Select button and click OK in the Copy to Folder dialog box.

- ✓ Click Yes in the message box that asks if you want to include linked content in the presentation. It can take PowerPoint several minutes to assemble the files and copy them to the CD or folder.

Creating a presentation video

Follow these steps to create a WMV-file version of a PowerPoint presentation:

- ✓ On the File tab, choose Save & Send.
- ✓ Choose Create a Video. You see the Create a Video window.
- ✓ Open the first drop-down list and choose a display resolution for your video.

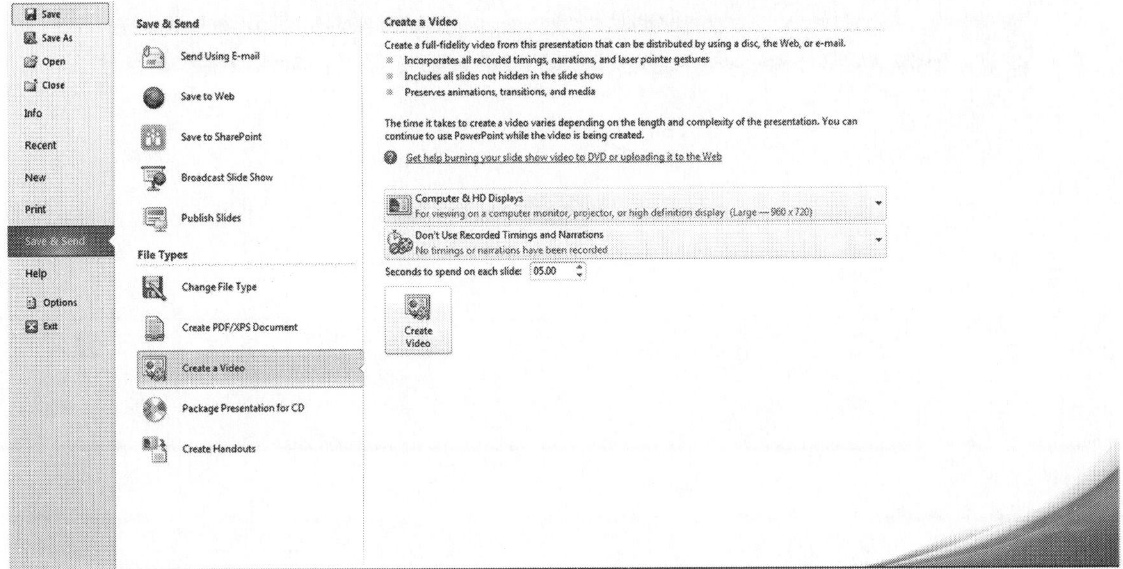

- ✓ Open the second drop-down list and choose whether to use recorded timings and narrations.
- ✓ Open the second drop-down list and choose Preview Timings and Narrations. Your presentation video plays. How do you like it? This is what your video will look and sound like after you save it in a WMV file.
- ✓ Click the Create Video button. The Save As dialog box opens.
- ✓ Choose a folder for storing the WMV file, enter a name for the file, and click the Save button.

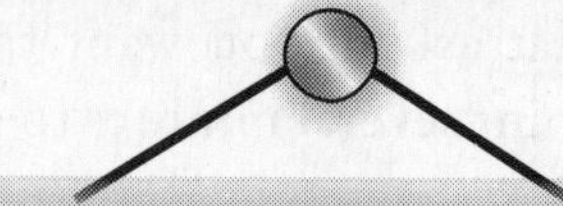

Points to Remember

- Use Animation & transition with tools to ensure that which object will appear on click & which will appear automatically
- Use suitable frame for videos
- Your Sound clip button should appear on frame during slide show
- While converting the file into Video, please set the sound clips & Video playback in auto-mode by setting time limits.

Microsoft Excel 2010

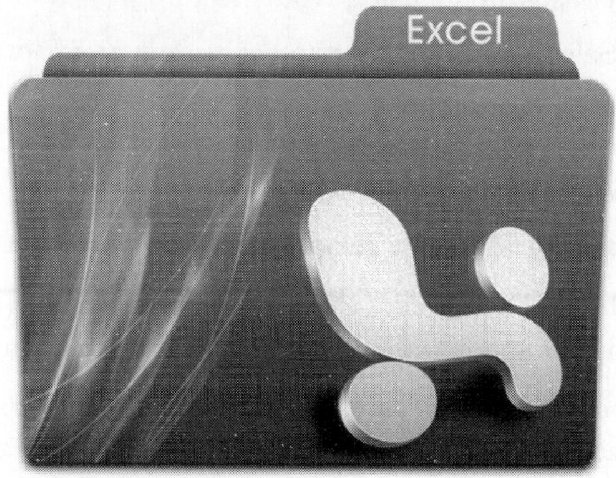

Welcome to MS Excel

In this chapter you will learn

- Getting started with the Excel screen
- Creating an Excel worksheet
- Formatting & using worksheet
- Selecting text so that you can copy, move, or delete it
- Making custom rules

Creating a New Excel Workbook

Use one of these methods in the Available Templates window to create a workbook:

- **Create a blank workbook:** Double-click the Blank Workbook icon. (By pressing Ctrl+N, you can create a new, blank workbook without opening the Available Templates window.)
- **Create a workbook from a template:** Use a template on your computer: Click Sample Templates. Templates that you loaded on your computer when you installed Office appear in the window.
- **Download a template from Office.com:** Under Office.com Templates, either choose the type of template you want or make sure that your computer is connected to the Internet, enter a search term in the Search box, and click the Start Searching button (or press Enter). Choose a template and click the Download button to download it to your computer.
- **Use a template you created (or downloaded earlier from Microsoft):** Click the My Templates icon. The New dialog box appears. Select a template and click OK.
- **Select a recently used template:** Click the Recent Templates icon and double-click on a template name.

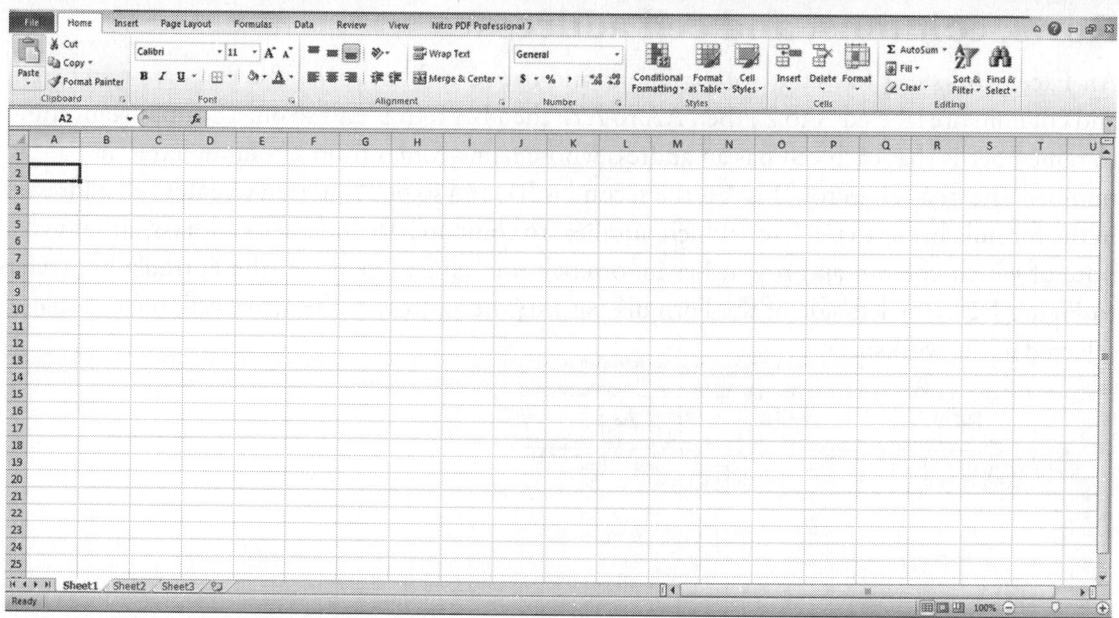

- **Recycle another workbook:** If you can use another workbook as the starting point for creating a new one, click the New from Existing icon. In the New from Existing Workbook dialog box, select the workbook and click the Create New button.

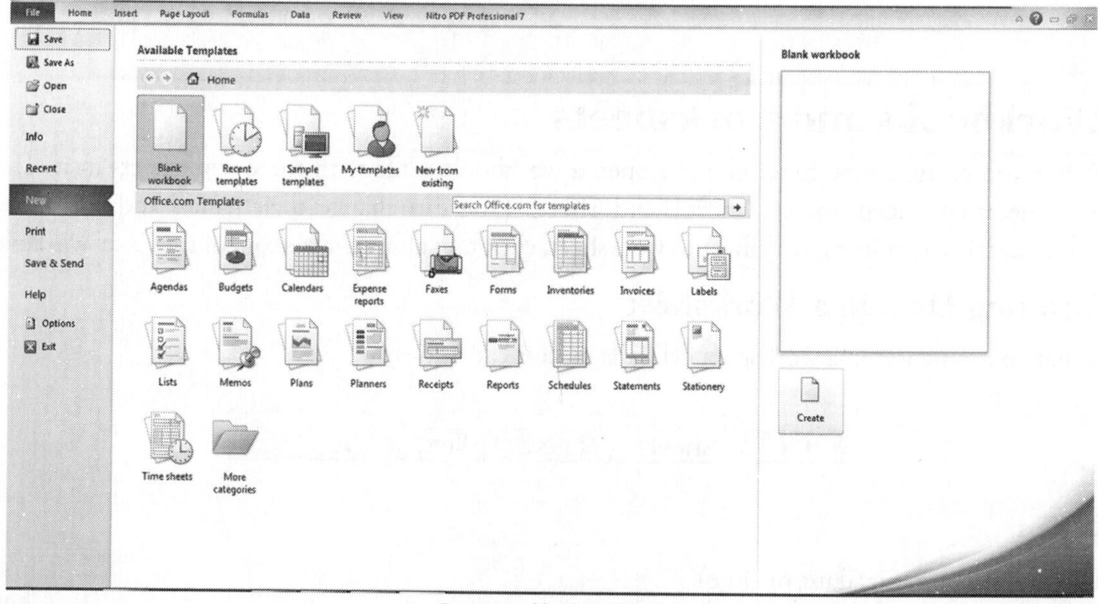

Creating a blank workbook

Rows, columns, and cell addresses

An Excel worksheet has numerous columns and over 1 million rows. The rows are numbered, and columns are labeled A to Z; then AA to AZ; then BA to BZ, and so on. The important thing to remember is that each cell has an address whose name comes from a column letter and a row number. The first cell in row 1 is A1, the second is B1, and so on. You need to enter cell addresses in the formula bar as to tell Excel which numbers to compute. To find a cell's address, either make note of which column and row it lies in, or click the cell and glance at the Formula bar (refer to Figure 1-2). The left side of the Formula bar lists the address of the active cell, the cell that is selected in the worksheet.

Workbooks and worksheets

When you create a new Excel file, you open a workbook, a file with three worksheets in it. The worksheets are called Sheet1, Sheet2, and Sheet3 (you can change their names and add more worksheets). To get from worksheet to worksheet, click tabs along the bottom of the Excel window.

Entering Data in a Worksheet

What you can enter in a worksheet cell falls in four categories:

- Text
- A value (numeric, date, or time)

- ❑ A logical value (True or False)
- ❑ A formula that returns a value, logical value, or text

Procedure

Click the cell where you want to enter the data or text label. The cell you clicked is now the active cell. Glance at the left side of the Formula bar if you're not sure of the address of the cell you're about to enter data in. The Formula bar lists the cell address.

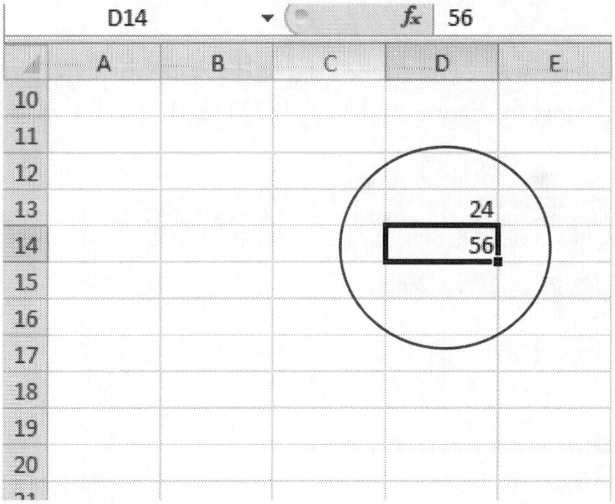

Entering date values

You can enter a date value in a cell in just any format you choose, and Excel understands that you're entering a date. For example, enter a date in any of the following formats and you'll be all right:

m/d/yy 8/31/11

m-d-yyyy 8-31-2011

d-mmm-yy 31-Aug-11

Here are some basic things to remember about entering dates:

- ❑ **Date formats:** You can quickly apply a format to dates by selecting cells and using one of these methods:
    - ✓ On the Home tab, open the Number Format drop-down list and choose Short Date (m/d/yyyy; 8/31/2011) or Long Date (day-of-the-week, month, day, year; Saturday, Aug 31, 2011).

✓ On the Home tab, click the Number group button to open the Number tab of the Format Cells dialog box.

❑ **Current date:** Press Ctrl+; (semicolon) and press Enter to enter the current date.

❑ **Current year's date:** If you don't enter the year as part of the date, Excel assumes that the date you entered is in the current year. For example, if you enter a date in the m/d (8/31) format during the year 2011, Excel enters the date as 8/31/11. As long as the date you want to enter is the current year, you can save a little time when entering dates by not entering the year, as Excel enters it for you.

❑ **Dates on the Formula bar:** No matter which format you use for dates, dates are displayed in the Formula bar in the format that Excel prefers for dates: m/d/yyyy (8/31/2010). How dates are displayed in the worksheet is up to you.

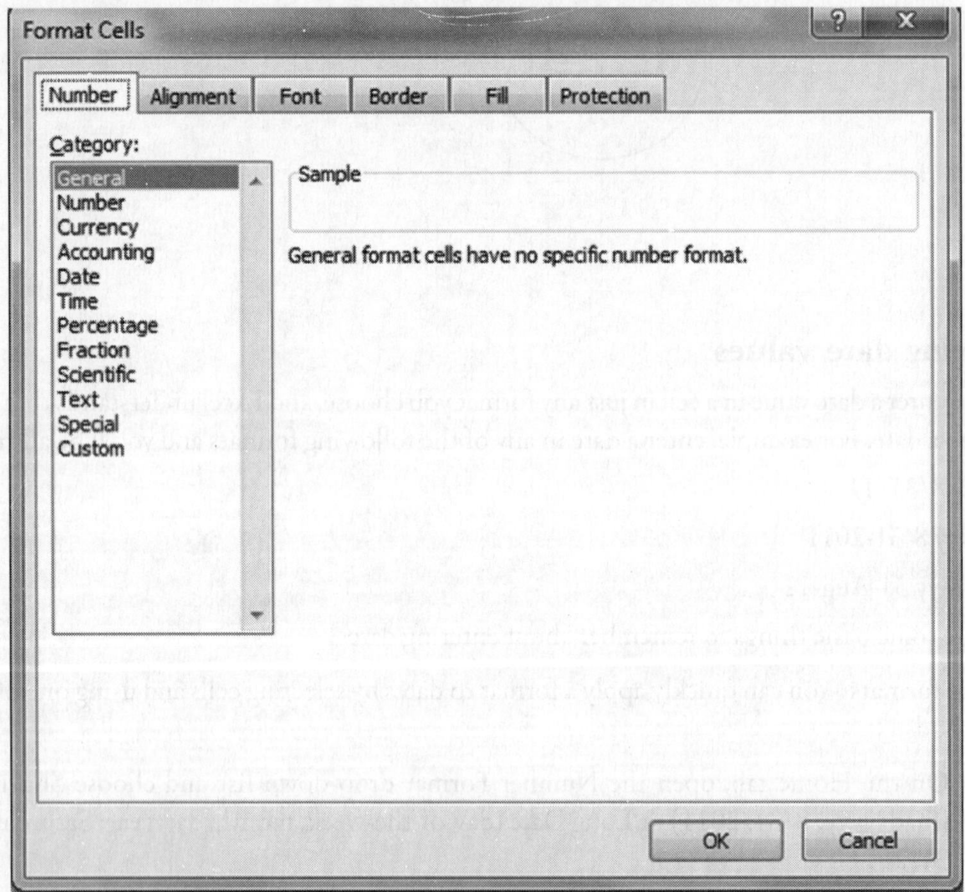

Format cells

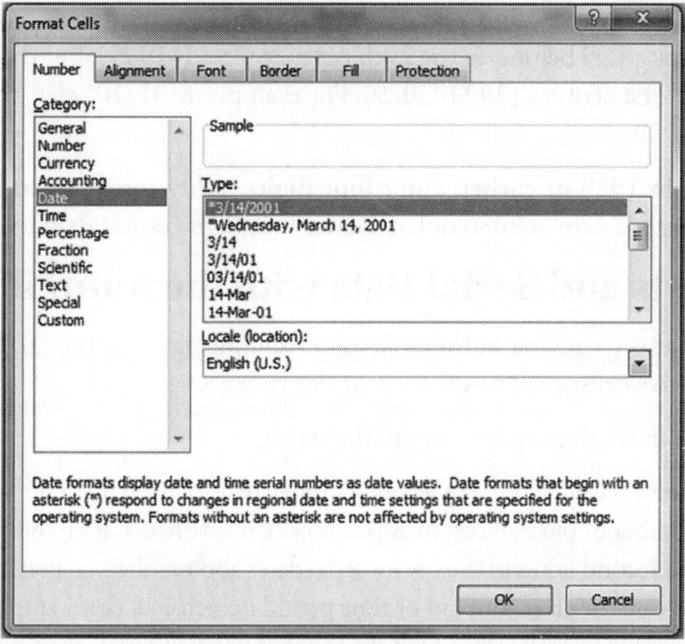

Entering date

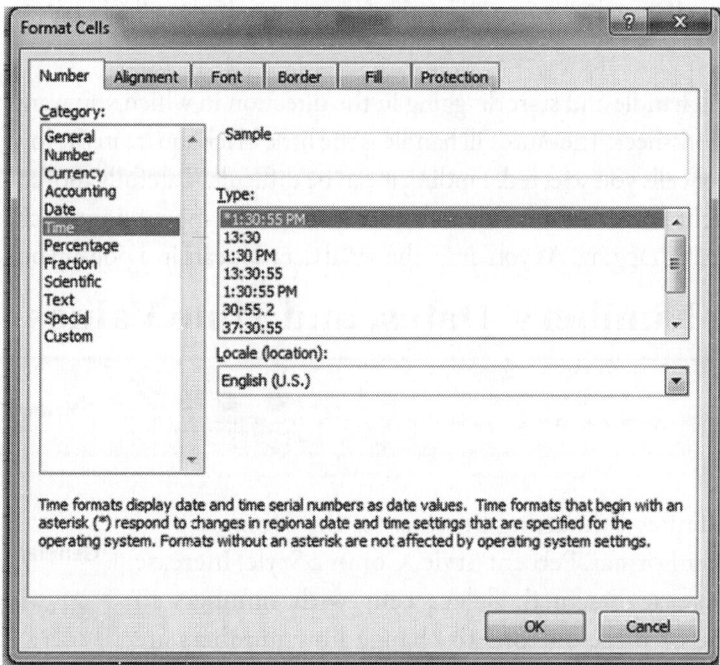

Entering time

- ❑ **20th and 21st century two-digit years:** When it comes to entering two digit years in dates, the digits 30 through 99 belong to the 20th century (1930–1999), but the digits 00 through 29 belong to the 21st century (2000–2029). For example, 8/31/10 refers to August 31, 2010, not August 31,1910.
- ❑ **To enter a date in 1929 or earlier, enter four digits rather than two to describe the year:** 8-31-1929. To enter a date in 2030 or later, enter four digits rather than two: 8-31-2030.

Entering Lists and Serial Data with the AutoFill Command

- ✓ Click the cell that is to be first in the series. For example, if you intend to list the days of the week in consecutive cells, click where the first day is to go.
- ✓ Enter the first number, date, or list item in the series.
- ✓ Move to the adjacent cell and enter the second number, date, or list item in the series. If you want to enter the same number or piece of text in adjacent cells, it isn't necessary to take this step, but Excel needs the first and second items in the case of serial dates and numbers so that it can tell how much to increase or decrease the given amount or time period in each cell. For example, entering 5 and 10 tells Excel to increase the number by 5 each time so that the next serial entry is 15.
- ✓ Select the cell or cells you just entered data in. To select a single cell, click it; to select two, drag over the cells.
- ✓ Click the AutoFill handle and start dragging in the direction in which you want the data series to appear on your worksheet. The AutoFill handle is the little black square in the lower-right corner of the cell or block of cells you selected. Finding it can be difficult. Carefully move the mouse pointer over the lower-right corner of the cell, and when you see the mouse pointer change into a black cross, click and start dragging. As you drag, the serial data appears in a pop-up box, 1.

Formatting Numbers, Dates, and Time Values

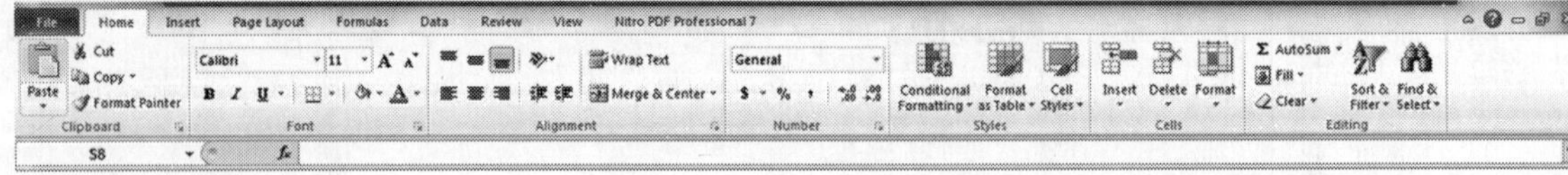

Excel offers five number-formatting buttons on the Home tab — Accounting Number Format, Percent Style, Comma Style, Increase Decimal, and Decrease Decimal. Select cells with numbers in them and click one of these buttons to change how numbers are formatted:

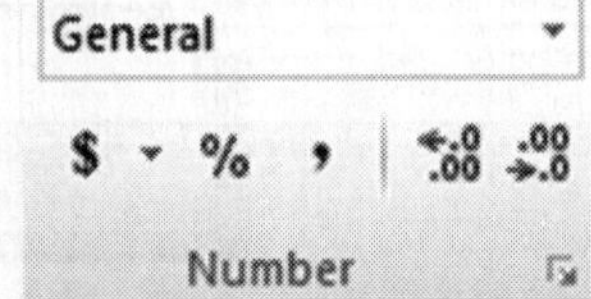

- **Accounting Number Format:** Places a dollar sign before the number and gives it two decimal places. You can open the drop-down list on this button and choose a currency symbol apart from the dollar sign. $ ▾
- **Percent Style:** Places a percent sign after the number and converts the number to a percentage.
- **Comma Style:** Places commas in the number. ,
- **Increase Decimal:** Increases the number of decimal places by one.
- **Decrease Decimal:** Decreases the number of decimal places by one.
- To strip formats from the data in cells, select the cells, go to the Home tab,click the Clear button, and choose Clear Formats. Clear ▾

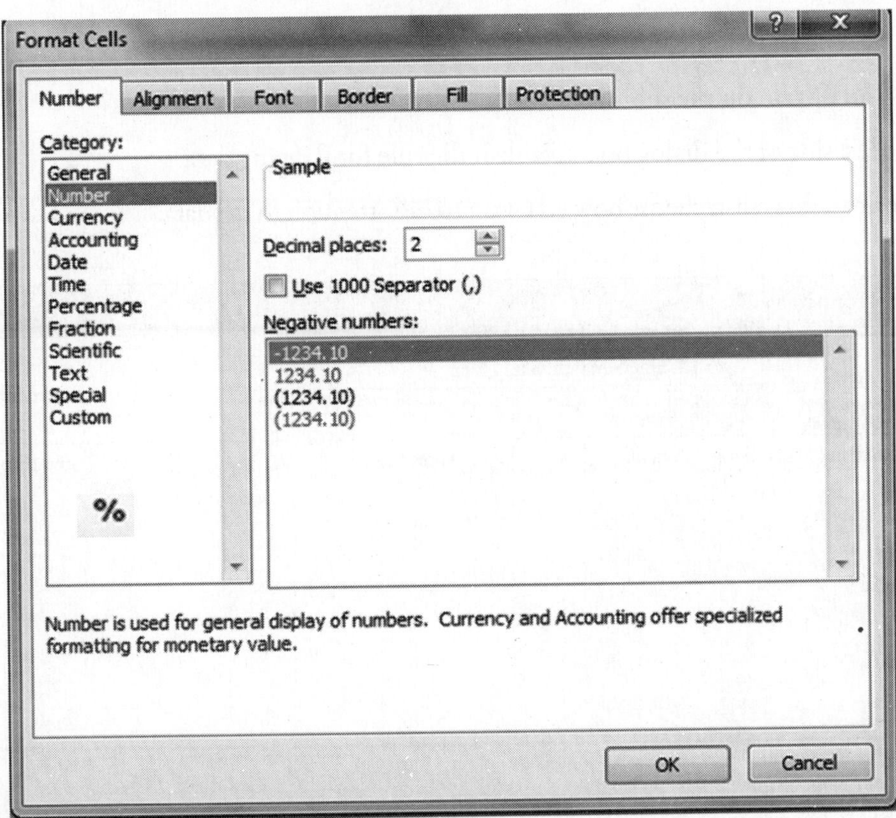

Formatting numbers

Conditional Formats

Select the cells that are candidates for conditional formatting and follow these steps to tell Excel when and how to format the cells:

✓ On the Home tab, click the Conditional Formatting button (you may have to click the Styles button first, depending on the size of your screen).

✓ Choose Highlight Cells Rules or Top/Bottom Rules on the drop-downlist.

You will see a submenu with choices about establishing the rule for whether values in the cells are highlighted or otherwise made more prominent:

❑ **Highlight Cells Rules:** These rules are for calling attention to data if it falls in a numerical or date range, or it's greater or lesser than a specific value. For example, you can highlight cells that are greater.

❑ **Top/Bottom Rules:** These rules are for calling attention to data if it falls within a percentage range relative to all the cells you selected.

For example, you can highlight cells with data that falls in the bottom 50 percent range.

✓ Choose an option on the submenu.

✓ On the left side of the dialog box, establish the rule for flagging data.

✓ On the drop-down list, choose how you want to call attention to the data.

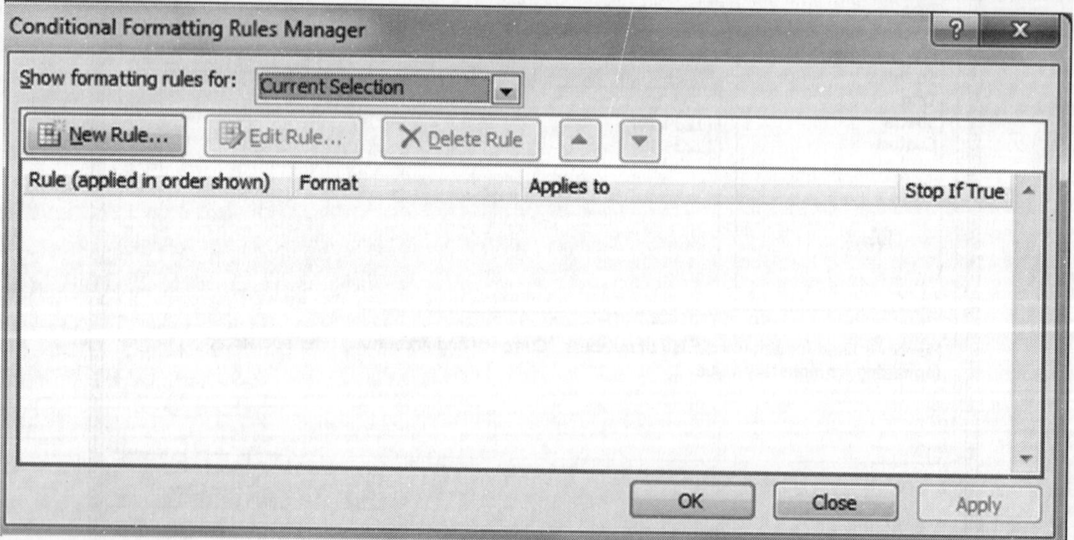

Conditional formatting rules manager

Follow these steps to establish a data-validation rule:

- ✓ Select the cell or cells that need a rule.
- ✓ On the Data tab, click the Data Validation button.
- ✓ On the Allow drop-down list, choose the category of rule you want.
- ✓ Enter the criteria for the rule.

What the criteria is depends on what rule category you're working in. You can refer to cells in the worksheet by selecting them. To do that, either select them directly or click the Range Selector button and then select them.

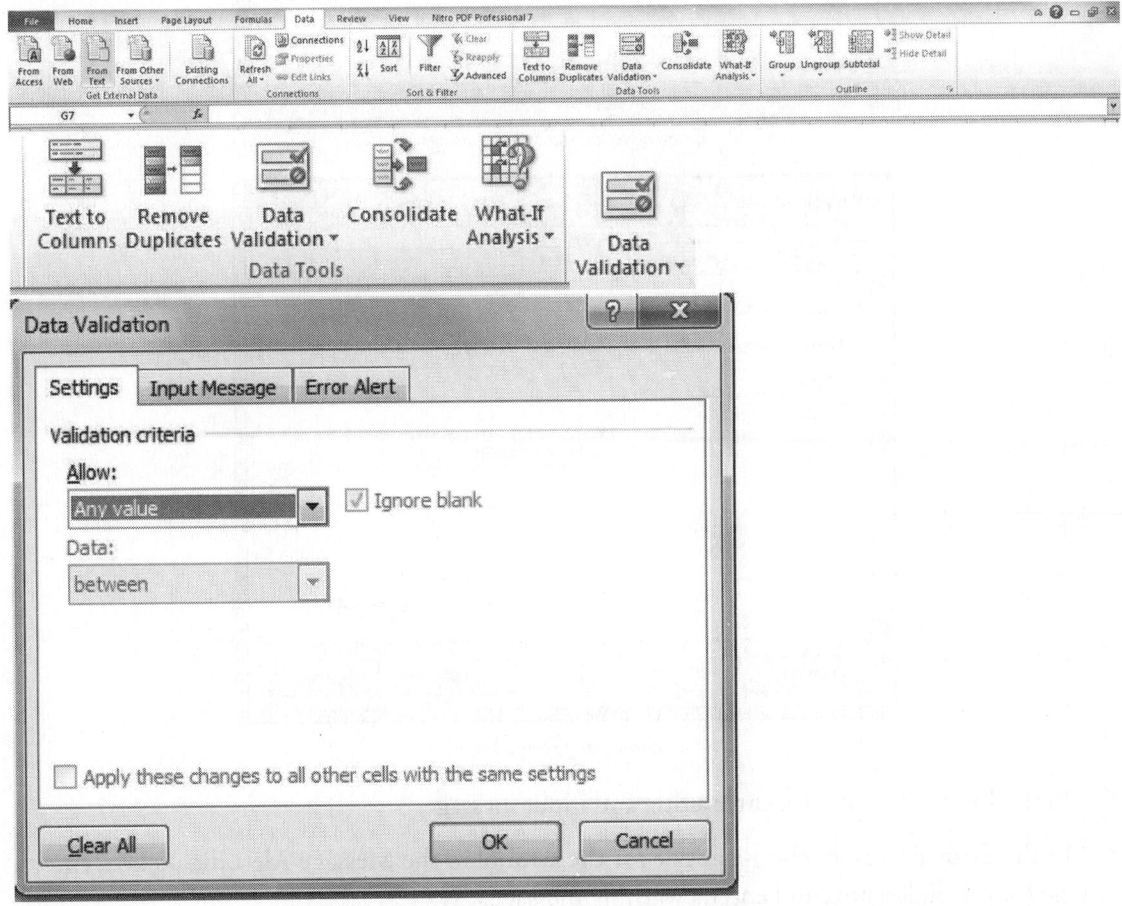

. Establishing date validation

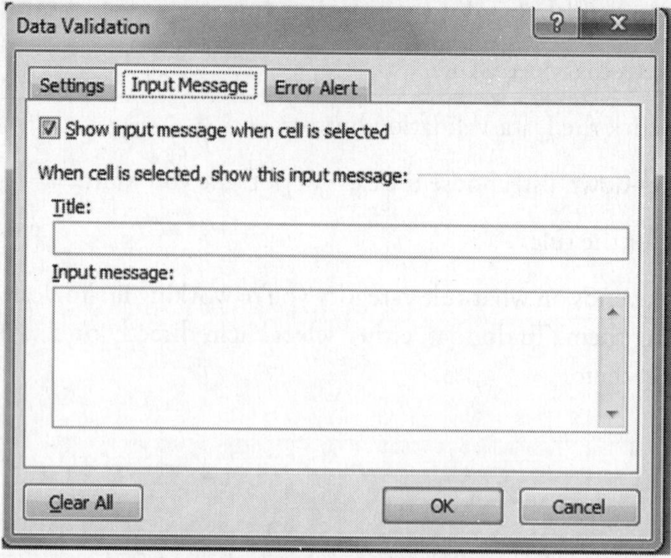

Entering letter and input massage

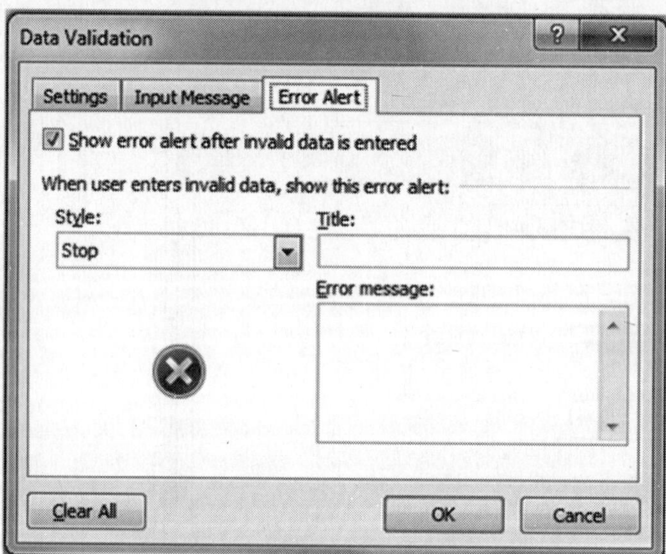

Formatting error alert

- ✓ On the Input Message tab, enter a title and input message.
- ✓ On the Error Alert tab, choose a style for the symbol in the Message Alert dialog box, enter a title for the dialog box, and enter a warning message.
- ✓ Click OK.

To remove data-validation rules from cells, select the cells, go to the Data tab, click the Data Validation button, and on the Settings tab of the Data Validation dialog box, click the Clear All button, and click OK.

Points to Remember

- Use correct arguments while using Validating data
- Using wrong arguments will produce problems for operators
- While formatting worksheet, keep an eye that invalid function does not exist in any cell.

Working on Your Worksheet

In this chapter you will learn

- Editing the worksheet
- Encrypting the document

Editing Worksheet Data

Not everyone enters data correctly the first time. To edit data you entered in a cell, do one of the following:

✓ Double-click the cell. Doing so places the cursor squarely in the cell, where you can start deleting or entering numbers and text.

✓ Click the cell and press F2. This method also lands the cursor in the cell.

✓ Click the cell you want to edit. With this technique, you edit the data on the Formula bar.

Moving in a Worksheet

Keyboard Shortcuts for Worksheets

Press	To Move the Selection
Home	To column A
Ctrl+Home	To cell A1, the first cell in the worksheet
Ctrl+End	To the last cell in the last row with data in it
←, →, ↑, ↓	To the next cell
Ctrl+←, →, ↑, ↓	In one direction toward the nearest cell with data in it or to the first or last cell in the column or row
PgUp or PgDn	Up or down one screen's worth of rows
Ctrl+PgUp or Ctrl+PgDn	Backward or forward through the workbook, from worksheet to worksheet

- ❑ **Scroll bars:** Use the vertical and horizontal scroll bars to move to different areas. Drag the scroll box to cover long distances. To cover long distances very quickly, hold down the Shift key as you drag the scroll box on the vertical scroll bar.
- ❑ **Scroll wheel on the mouse:** Turn the wheel to quickly scroll up and down.
- ❑ **Name box:** Enter a cell address in the Name box and press Enter to go to the cell. The Name box is found to the left of the Formula bar.
- ❑ **Go To command:** On the Home tab, click the Find & Select button, and choose Go To on the drop-down list (or press Ctrl+G or F5). You will see the Go To dialog box. Enter a cell address in the Reference box and click OK. Cell addresses you've already visited with the Go To command are already listed in the dialog box. Click the Special button to open the Go To Special dialog box and visit a formula, comment, or other esoteric item.
- ❑ **Find command:** On the Home tab, click the Find & Select button, and choose Find on the drop-down list (or press Ctrl+F). Enter the data you seek in the Find What box and click the Find Next button.

Find & Select

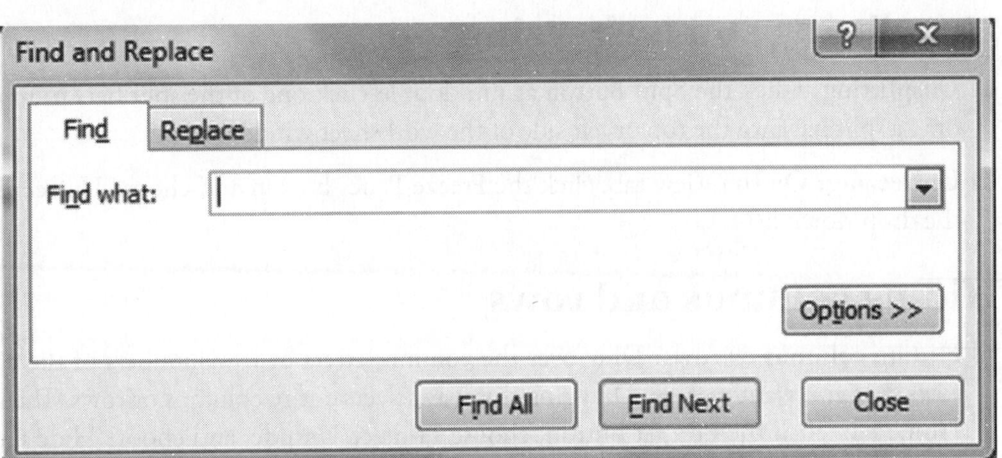

Giving the Split or Freeze Panes command

Follow these steps to split or freeze columns and rows on-screen:

✓ Click the cell directly below the row you want to freeze or split, and click in the column to the right of the column that you want to freeze or split. In other words, click where you want the split to occur.

- ✓ On the View tab, split or freeze the columns and rows. Go to the View tab and use one of these techniques:
  - ❑ **Splitting:** Click the Split button and then click and drag the split bars to split the screen horizontally or vertically. The other way to split a worksheet is to grab hold of a split bar, the little division markers directly above the vertical scroll bar and directly to the right of the horizontal scroll bar (in the lower-right corner of your screen). You can tell where split bars are because the pointer turns into a double arrow when it's over a split bar.
  - ❑ **Freezing:** Click the Freeze Panes button and choose one of three Freeze options on the drop-down list.

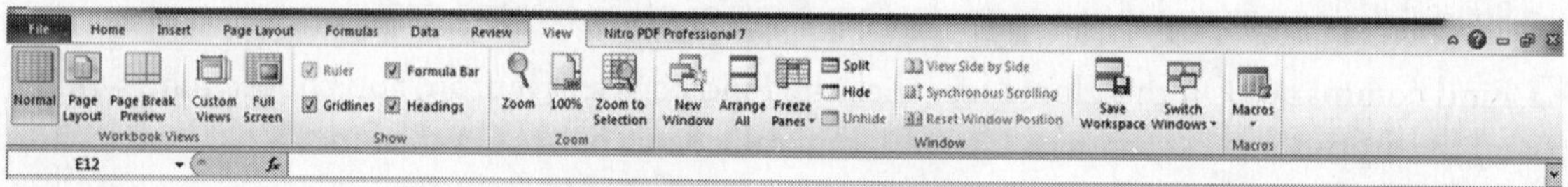

Unsplitting and unfreezing

- ❑ **Unsplitting:** Click the Split button again; double-click one of the split bars to remove it; or drag a split bar into the top or left side of the worksheet window.
- ❑ **Unfreezing:** On the View tab, click the Freeze Panes button and choose Unfreeze Panes on the drop-down list.

Hiding columns and rows

- ❑ **Hiding columns or rows:** Drag over the column letters or row numbers of the columns or rows that you want to hide. Dragging this way selects entire columns or rows. Then go to the Home tab, click the Format button, choose Hide & Unhide, and choose Hide Columns or Hide Rows.
- ❑ **Unhiding columns and rows:** Select columns to the right and left of the hidden columns, or select rows above and below the hidden rows. To select columns or rows, drag over their letters or numbers. Then go to the Home tab, click the Format button, choose Hide & Unhide, and choose Unhide Columns or Unhide Rows.

Comments for Your Worksheet

- **Entering a comment:** Click the cell that deserves the comment, go to the Review tab, and click the New Comment button. Enter your comment in the pop-up box. Click in a different cell when you finish entering your comment.
- **Reading a comment:** Move the pointer over the small red triangle and read the comment in the pop-up box.
- **Finding comments:** On the Review tab, click the Previous or Next button to go from comment to comment.
- **Editing a comment:** On the Review tab, select the cell with the comment, click the Edit Comment button, and edit the comment in the pop-upbox. You can also right-click the cell and choose Edit Comment.
- **Deleting comments:** On the Review tab, click a cell with a comment, and then click the Delete button, or right-click the cell and choose Delete Comment. To delete several comments, select them by Ctrl+clicking and then click the Delete button.
- **Deleting all comments in a worksheet:** Select all comments and then, on the Review tab, click the Delete button. You can select all comments by clicking the Find & Select button on the Home tab, choosing Go To, and in the Go To dialog box, clicking the Special button and choosingComments in the Go To Special dialog box.

Hiding a worksheet

Follow these instructions to hide and unhide worksheets:

- **Hiding a worksheet:** Select the worksheet you want to hide, go to the View tab, and click the Hide button. You can also right-click the worksheet's tab and choose Hide on the shortcut menu. And you can also display the worksheet, go to the Home tab, click the Format button, and choose Hide &Unhide→Hide Sheet.

❑ **Unhiding a worksheet:** On the View tab, click the Unhide button, select the name of the worksheet you want to unhide in the Unhide dialog box, and click OK. To open the Unhide dialog box, you can also right-click any worksheet tab and choose Unhide; or go to the Home tab.

Protecting a worksheet

- ✓ Select the worksheet that needs protection.
- ✓ On the Review tab, click the Protect Sheet button.
- ✓ Enter a password in the Password to Unprotect Sheet box if you want only people with the password to be able to open the worksheet after you protect it.
- ✓ On the Allow All Users of This Worksheet To list, select the check box next to the name of each task that you want to permit others to do. For example, click the Format Cells check box if you want others to be able to format cells. Deselect the Select Locked Cells check box to prevent any changes from being made to the worksheet. By default, all worksheet cells are locked, and by preventing others from selecting locked cells, you effectively prevent them from editing any cells.
- ✓ Click OK.

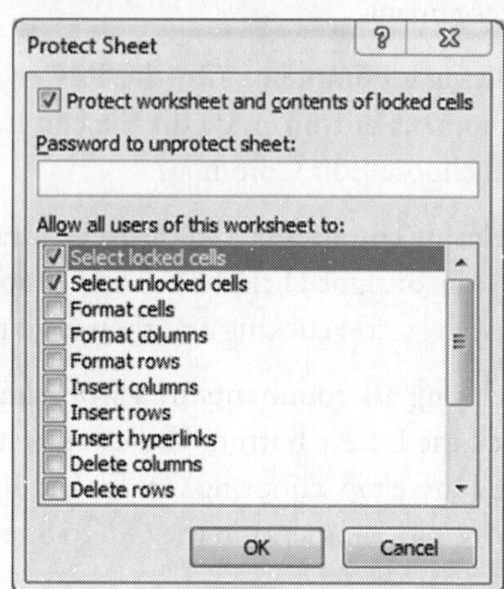

Protection a worksheet

Points to Remember

- ☞ While encrypting document with a password, please make sure that you remember the password, it is impossible to open the document with wrong password once encrypted

Formulas & Functions

In this chapter you will learn

- Using mathematical Formula in the worksheet
- Using Operators in the Worksheet
- Common error messages
- Inserting functions

Referring to cells in formulas

As well as numbers, Excel formulas can refer to the contents of different cells. When a formula refers to a cell, the number in the cell is used to compute the formula. For example, cell A1 contains the number 2; cell A2 contains the number 3; and cell A3 contains the formula =A1+A2. As shown in cell A3, the result of the formula is 5. If I change the number in cell A1 from 2 to 3, the result of the formula in cell A3 (=A1+A2) becomes 6, not 5. When a formula refers to a cell and the number in the cell changes, the result of the formula changes as well.

A3 | =A1+A2

	A	B	C	D
1	2			
2	3			
3	5			

Similarly for Subtraction,

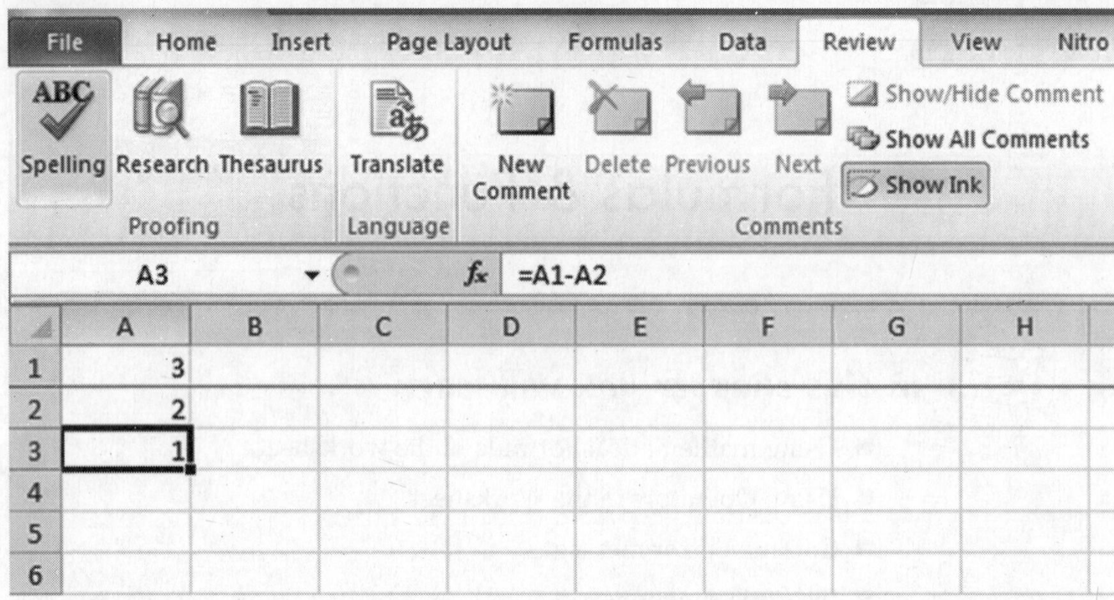

Similarly for Multiplication,

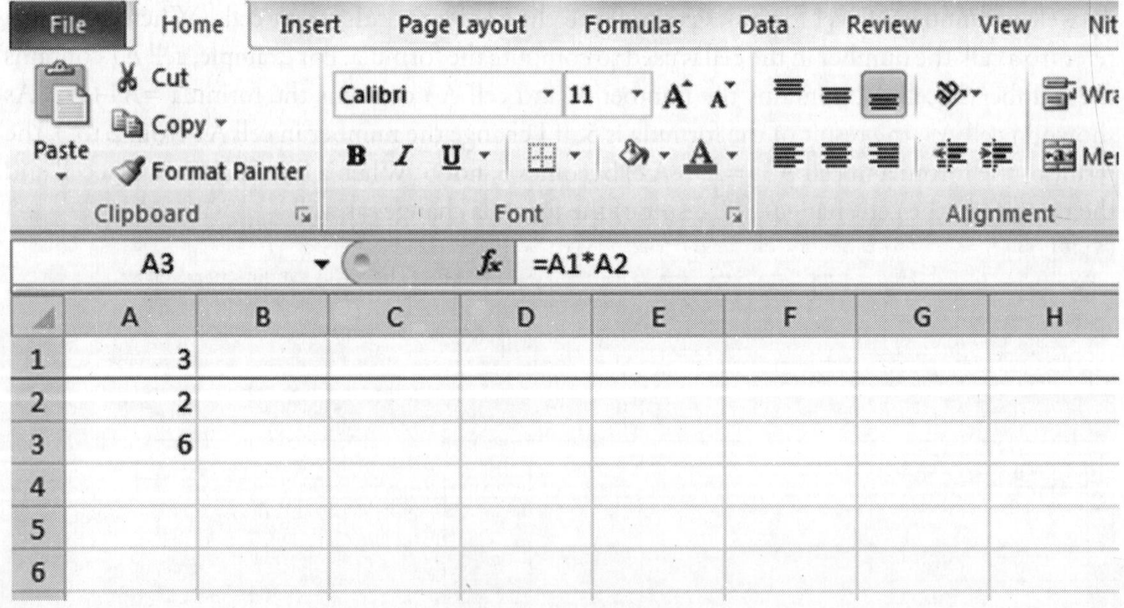

Operators Table

(Most Important! You will need to use these in formulas)

Operator	Example Formula
% (Percent)	=50%
^ (Exponentiation)	=50^2
* (Multiplication)	=E2*4
/ (Division)	=E2/3
+ (Addition)	=F1+F2+F3
– (Subtraction)	=G5–8
= (Equal to)	="Part No."&D4 =C5=4
<> (Not equal to)	=F3<>9
< (Less than)	=B9<E11
<= (Less than or equal to)	=A4<=9
> (Greater than)	=E8>14
>= (Greater than or equal to)	=C3>=D3

Creating a cell range name

Follow these steps to create a cell range name:

✓ Select the cells that you want to name.

✓ On the Formulas tab, click the Define Name button. You see the New Name dialog box.

✓ Enter a descriptive name in the Name box. Names can't begin with a number or include blank spaces.

✓ On the Scope drop-down list, choose Workbook or a worksheet name.

✓ Enter a comment to describe the range name, if you want.

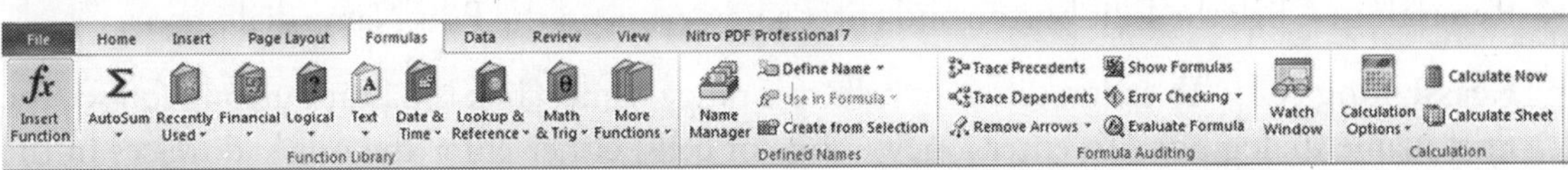

✓ Click OK.

Entering a range name as part of a formula

To include a cell range name in a formula, click in the Formula bar where you want to enter the range name and then use one of these techniques to enter the name:

- ✓ On the Formulas tab, click the Use in Formula button and choose a cell range name on the drop-down list
- ✓ Press F3 or click the Use in Formula button and choose Paste Names on the drop-down list.

Managing cell range names

To rename, edit, or delete cell range names, go to the Formulas tab and click the Name Manager button.

- ✓ **Renaming:** Click the Edit button and enter a new name in the Edit Name dialog box.
- ✓ **Reassigning cells:** To assign different cells to a range name, click the Edit button. You see the Edit Name dialog box. To enter a new range of cells, either enter the cells' addresses in the Refers To text box or click the Range Selector button (it's to the right of the text box), drag across the cells on your worksheet that you want for the cell range, and click the Cell Selector button again to return to the Edit Name dialog box.

✓ Deleting: Click the Delete button and click OK in the confirmation box.

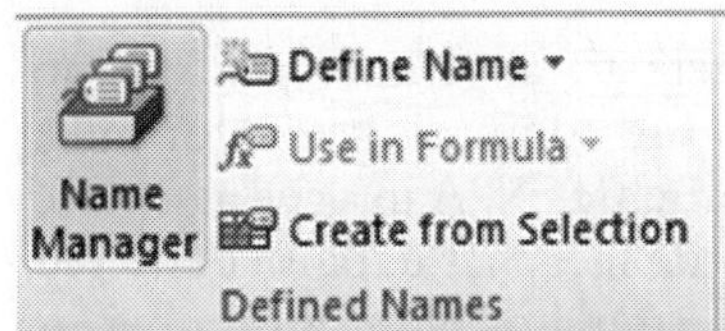

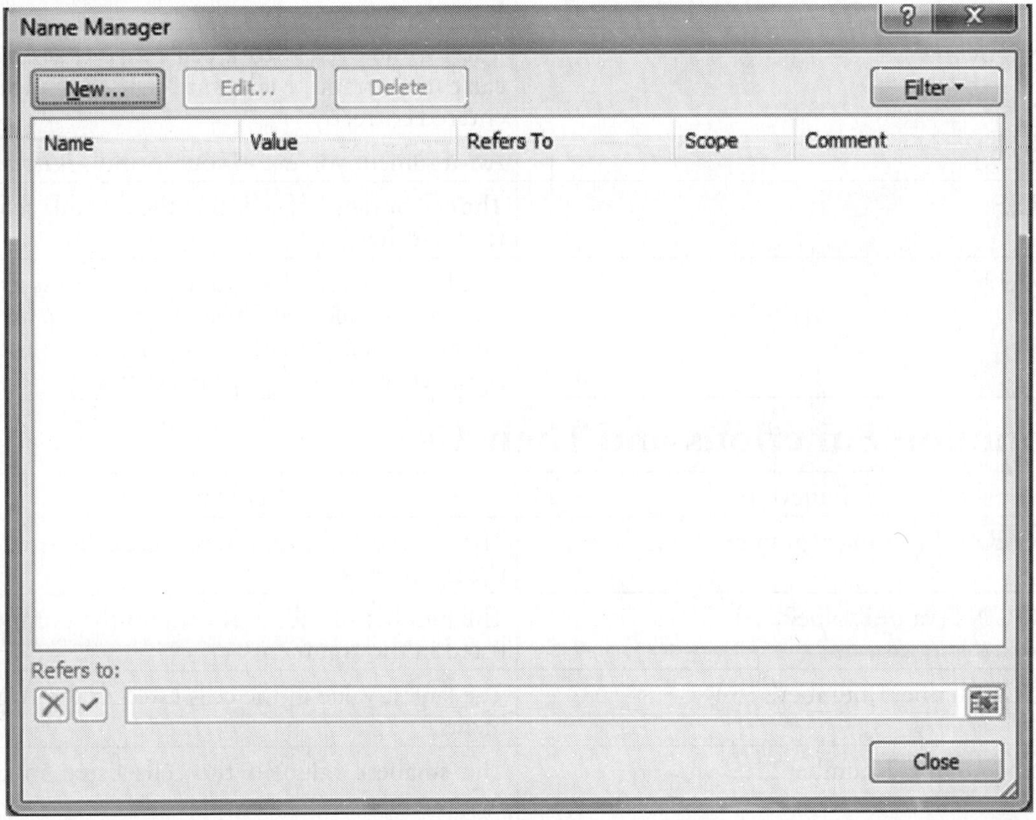

Common Formula Error Messages

Message	Mistake
#DIV/0!	You tried to divide a number by a zero (0) or an empty cell.
#NAME	You used a cell range name in the formula, but the name isn't defined.

Message	Mistake
#N/A	The formula refers to an empty cell, so no data is available for computing the formula. Sometimes people enter N/A in a cell as a place holder to signal the fact that data isn't entered yet. Revise the formula or enter a number or formula in the empty cells.
#NULL	The formula refers to a cell range that Excel can't understand. Make sure that the range is entered correctly.
#NUM	An argument you use in your formula is invalid
#REF	The cell or range of cells that the formula refers to aren't there.
#VALUE	The formula includes a function that was used incorrectly, takes an invalid argument, or is misspelt. Make sure that the function uses the right argument and is spelled correctly.

Common Functions and Their Use

Function	Returns
AVERAGE(number1,number2,. . .)	The average of the numbers in the cells listed in the arguments.
COUNT(value1,value2,. . .)	The number of cells that contain the numbers listed in the arguments.
MAX(number1,number2,. . .)	The largest value in the cells listed in the Arguments.
MIN(number1,number2,. . .)	The smallest value in the cells listed in the Arguments.
PRODUCT(number1,number2,. . .)	The product of multiplying the cells listed in the arguments.
STDEV(number1,number2,. . .)	An estimate of standard deviation based on the sample cells listed in the argument.
STDEVP(number1,number2,. . .)	An estimate of standard deviation based on the entire sample cells listed in the arguments.
SUM(number1,number2,. . .)	The total of the numbers in the arguments.
VAR(number1,number2,. . .)	An estimate of the variance based on the sample cells listed in the arguments.

Function	Returns
VARP(number1,number2,. . .)	A variance calculation based on all cells listed in the arguments.

Entering a function in a formula

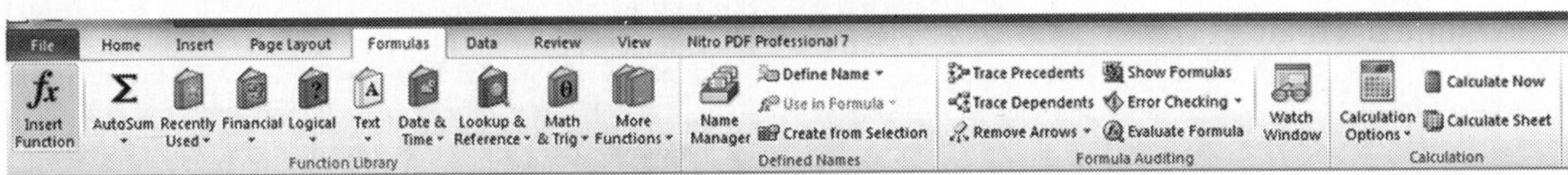

To enter a function in a formula, you can enter the function name by typingit in the Formula bar, or you can rely on Excel to enter it for you. Enter function names yourself if you're well acquainted with a function and comfortable using it.

No matter how you want to enter a function as part of a formula, start this way:

✓ Select the cell where you want to enter the formula.

✓ In the Formula bar, type an equals sign (=). Be sure to start every formula by entering an equals sign (=). Without it, Excel thinks you're entering text or a numbering the cell.

✓ Start constructing your formula, and when you come to the place where you want to enter the function, type the function's name.

Excel's help in entering a function as part of a formula:

On the Formulas tab, tell Excel which function you want to use.

You can do that with one of these techniques:

❑ **Click a Function Library button:** Click the button whose name describes what kind of function you want and choose the function's name on the drop-down list. You can click the Financial, Logical, Text, Date & Time, Lookup & Reference, Math & Trig, or More Functions buttons.

❑ **Click the Recently Used button: Click** this button and choose the name of a function you used recently.

❑ **Click the Insert Function button:** Clicking this button opens the Insert Function dialog box. Find and choose the name of a function. You can search for functions or choose a category and then scroll the names until you find the function you want.

❑ Enter arguments in the spaces provided by the Function Arguments dialog box. To enter cell references or ranges, you can click or select cells in your worksheet. If necessary, click the Range Selector button (you can find it to the right of an argument text box) to shrink the Function

Arguments dialog box and get a better look at your worksheet.

- ❑ Click OK when you finish entering arguments for your function. I hope you didn't have to argue too strenuously with the Function Arguments dialog box.

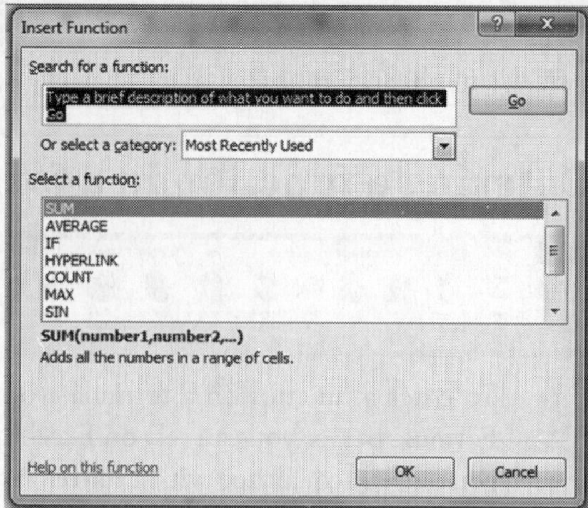

Function argeements dialog box

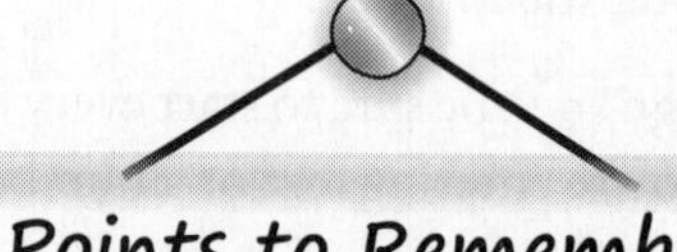

Points to Remember

- Use correct formula operators & methods to ensure the genuine data.
- Use correct Functions
- Use correct syntaxes & arguments while formation the text.

Microsoft Publisher 2010

Welcome to MS Publisher

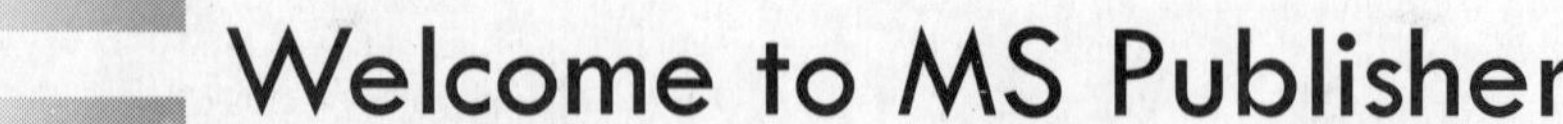

In this chapter you will learn

- Getting started with Publisher
- Creating a Publisher document

Creating a Publication

Microsoft Publisher 2010 is a program designed to help you create publications, or documents that you can print and distribute. Here you will learn about the advantages and disadvantages of using publisher 2010. You will also learn about the publisher interface, including the Ribbon, rules and guides, and backstage view.

Use one of these methods in the Available Templates window to create a publication:

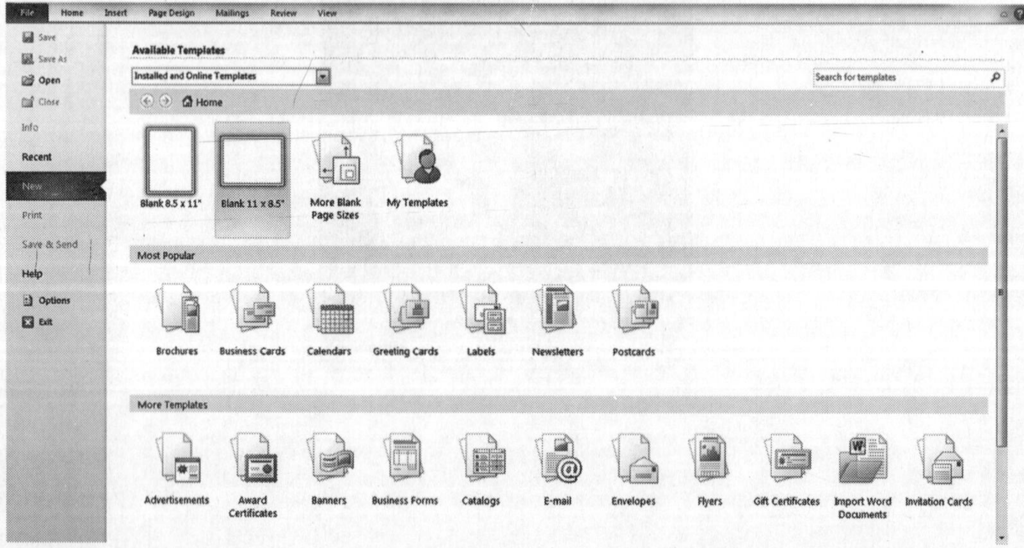

- ❑ **Start from a template category:** Select the icon representing a category (Brochures, Business Cards, and so on). You see a dozen or more templates. Scroll through the list and select a template.
- ❑ **Search for a template:** In the Search for Templates text box, enter the name of a publication type and click the Search button (or press Enter). Then select a template.

- ❑ **Use a template you created:** Click the My Templates icon and then select your template.

Setting up your pages

On the Page Design tab, visit the Page Setup group to determine the marginsize, orientation, and page size of your publication:

- ❑ **Margins:** Click the Margins button and choose an option on the dropdown list or click Custom Margins to enter margin measurements in the Layout Guides dialog box.
- ❑ **Orientation:** Click the Orientation button and choose Portrait or Landscape on the drop-down list to stand your publication upright or turn it on its side.
- ❑ **Size:** Click the Size button and select a page size on the drop-down list. You can choose Create New Page Size on the menu to declare a page size of your own for your publication in the Create New Page Size dialog box. Decide right away which page size to use for your publication. How large or small the page is determines how the headings, graphics, and text fit on the pages.

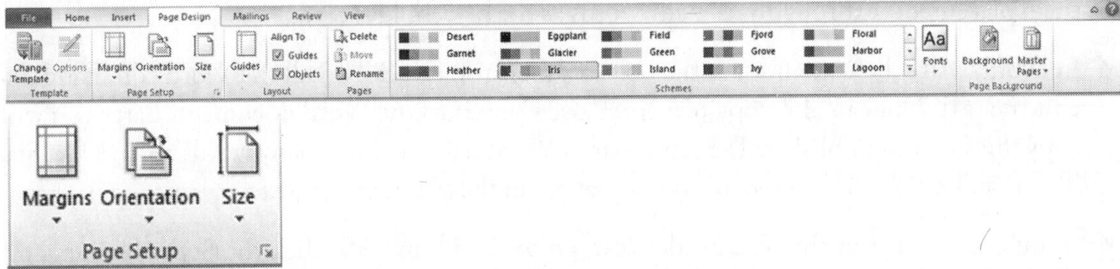

A Screen Shot of a Template

Entering Text on the Pages

The placeholder text that appears in publication designs has to go, of course. One of your first tasks is to replace the placeholder text with your own words. In the case of a story, you have a lot of writing and replacing to do (story is Publisher's term for an article that reaches across several textframes). If you're putting together a sign or greeting card, you have only a handful of words to write. If you have to replace more than two dozen words, follow these steps to replace the placeholder text in a text frame with text of your own:

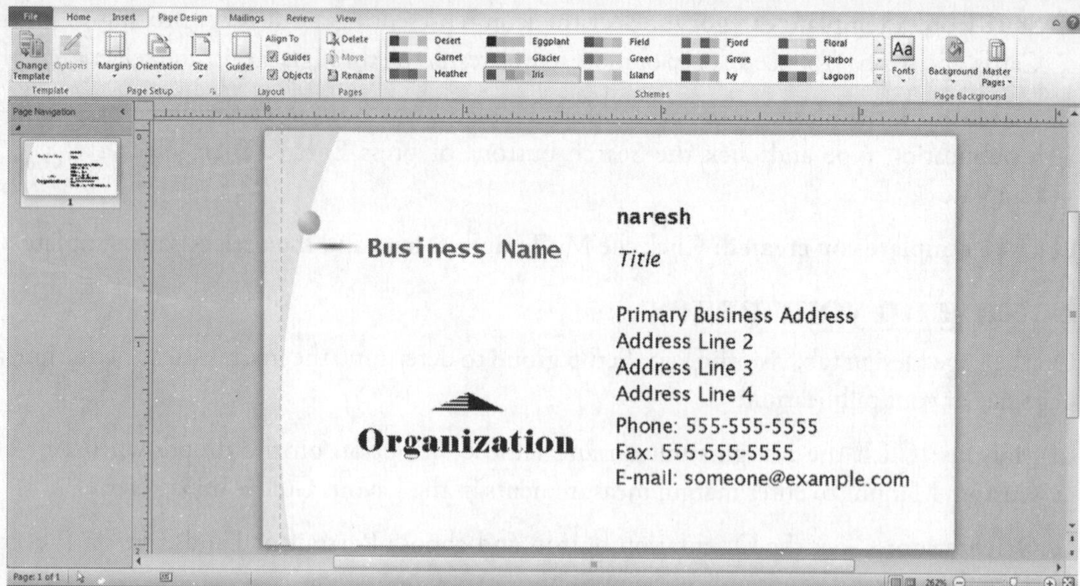

Entering text on a page

- ✓ Read the first paragraph of the placeholder text to see how many words can fit in the text frames that hold the story. Each placeholder story starts with a sentence describing roughly how many words are in the story. You can spare yourself a lot of time and trouble by making the replacement text roughly as many words as the placeholder text.
- ✓ In Word, write the text and save the text in a file. You can call on all the Word commands to edit the text. You can also copy text from elsewhere into the Word document. Later you will copy this file into Publisher. The status bar in Word tells you how many words are in a file. See if you can keep to the number of words that are in the place holder text.
- ✓ In Publisher, click in the placeholder text, go to the Home tab, click the Styles button, and note on the Styles drop-down list which style has been assigned to the place holder text. You can tell which style has been assigned to the text because it is selected on the Styles drop-down list. You will assign the style that is currently applied to the text to the replacement text you insert into the text frame.
- ✓ If necessary, press Ctrl+A to select the text in the story, and with the text selected, right-click and choose Change Text → Text File. You see the Insert Text dialog box. You can also open this dialog box by going to the Insert tab and clicking the Insert File button.
- ✓ Select the Word file with the replacement text and click the OK button.

Replacement text from the Word file "flows" into the text frame or frames. If the replacement text doesn't fit in the text frames allotted to the story, you see the Autoflow dialog box. You can click the Yes button to tell Publisher to flow the text into different text frames in the publication, but I recommend clicking No in the Autoflow dialog box. Later in this chapter, "Making text flow from frame to frame" explains how to decide on your own where to put overflow text from a story. The replacement text maintains the styles assigned to it in the Word document. In the next step, you reassign a style to the text.

✓ Press Ctrl+A to select the text in the story, go to the Home tab, click the Styles button, and choose the style that was assigned to the placeholder text.

Making Text Fit in Text Frames

Fitting overflow text in a single frame

To fit a heading or paragraph into a single text frame, try one of these methods:

- ❑ **Shrink the text automatically:** On the (Text Box Tools) Format tab, click the Text Fit button and choose Shrink Text On Overflow on the dropdown list. This command shrinks the point size of text so that all text fits in the frame. Sometimes, however, shrinking the text this way makes the heading or paragraph hard to read.

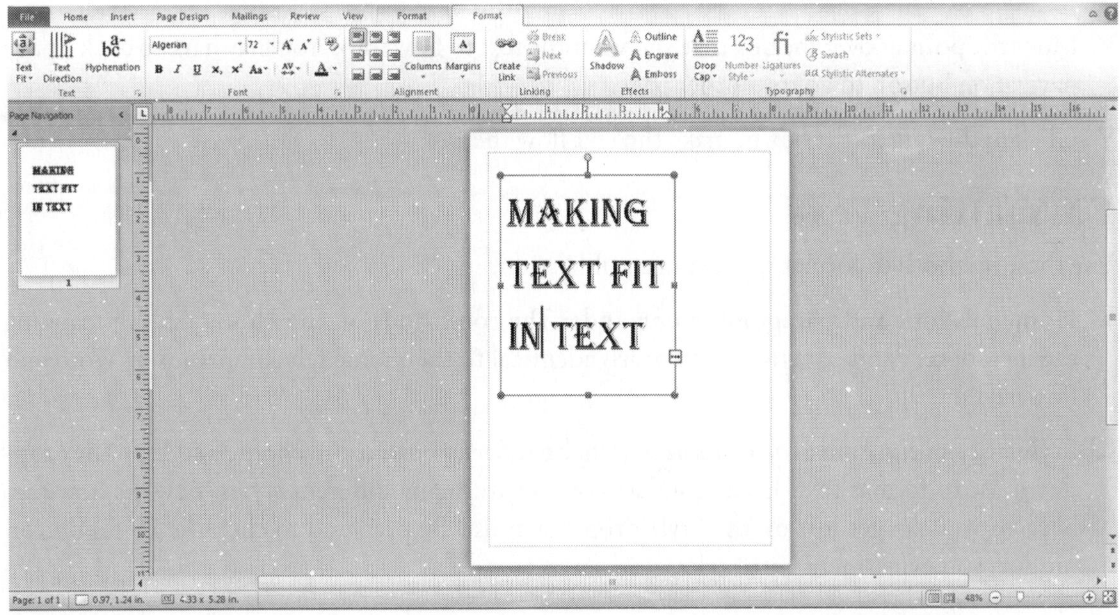

- ❑ **Edit the text:** Snip out a word or sentence here and there to make the text fit. Have you ever wondered why magazine articles always fill the page and never end in the middle? That's because skillful editors and typesetters remove and add words here and there to make the story fit the page.

Making Text Fit in Text Frames

Make the text frame margins smaller: Like a page, text frames have internal margins to keep text from getting too close to the frame border. To shrink these margins and make more room for text, go to the (TextBox Tools) Format tab, click the Margins button, and choose Narrow onthe drop-down list. You can also choose Custom Margins, and on the Text Box tab of the Format Text Box dialog box, enter smaller measurements for the text box margins.

Making text flow from frame to frame

Create a new text box for the overflow text and follow these steps to direct text from one frame to another in your publication:

- ✓ Select the text frame with overflowing text. You can tell when text is overflowing because the Text in Overflow icon appears in the lower-right corner of the frame
- ✓ On the (Text Box) Formatting tab, click the Create Link button. The pointer turns into an overflowing pitcher after you click the button.
- ✓ Move the pointer over the box that you want the text to flow into. You may have to click a page navigation button to go to another page.
- ✓ Click in the target text box to make the text flow there.

Formatting Text

Use these methods to format the text in a publication:

- ❑ **Home tab font and paragraph commands:** The commands on the Home tab for changing the look of text and paragraphs are nearly identical to the Home tab commands in Word and PowerPoint.
- ❑ **Styles:** Select text, and on the Home tab, click the Styles button and choose a style on the drop-down list to format text. Each template comes with many different styles. Beware, however, because you can get lost on the Style drop-down list. Be prepared to click the Undo button often as you experiment with styles.

Wrapping Text

✓ Select the item that text is to wrap around.

✓ On the Format tab, click the Wrap Text button and choose a wrapping option on the drop-down list.

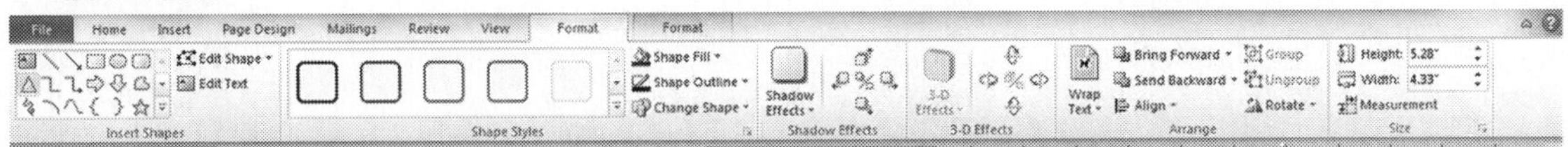

Inserting, Removing, and Moving Pages

Suppose that you have too many pages or you need to add a page or two. On the Page Navigation pane (select the Page Navigation check box on the View tab), click a thumbnail to select the page where you want to insert, remove, or move pages. Then follow these instructions:

- ❑ **Inserting a new page:** On the Insert tab, click the Page button and choose an option on the drop-down list:
- ❑ **Insert Blank Page:** Inserts an empty page.
- ❑ **Insert Duplicate Page:** Inserts a page identical to the thumbnail page you selected.
- ❑ **Insert Page:** Opens the Insert Page dialog box, where you can enter the number of pages you want to insert and click an option button to put the new pages before or after the page you selected. You can also tell Publisher what to put on the new page or pages.
- ❑ **Removing a page:** On the Page Design tab, click the Delete button. You can also right-click a page thumbnail and choose Delete.
- ❑ **Moving a page:** On the Page Design tab, click the Move button. Give instructions for moving the page in the Move Page dialog box and click OK.

- ☞ Make custom frames to place different objects
- ☞ Use different types of frames as per your need
- ☞ Keep in mind that you do everything in the frame, since on printing & publishing the material in frame will appear

Microsoft Access 2010

Welcome to MS Access

In this chapter you will learn

- Getting started with MS Access
- Creating an Access document

What is a database?

A database is defined as an organized collection of data (information) on people or things. In raw form, a sheet of paper divided into columns and rows or a table in Microsoft Word or Excel is considered a simple database. Single table databases are very limited in their uses and would not be considered as a business solution.

In Access information is stored in tables. Information can be seen in tables or through forms and reports. A database will be able to store data in a structured manner across multiple tables, use queries to locate specific information according to given criteria, produce detailed (on-screen or printed) reports, perform calculations and much more.

An example of a multi-table database is a database of classes, which might consist of tables showing information on several of these: classes, instructors, students, and rooms.

Note....

Access 2010 saves database files with an .accdb file name extension. The data in the database is saved automatically when you enter it. However, changes to an object such as a table, form or report need to be saved. When necessary, Access will prompt for objects to be saved when switching views.

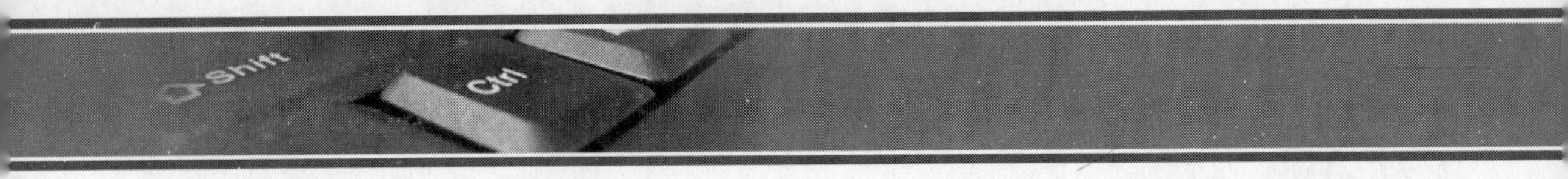

What is a table?

Tables are used to store the data in a structured and organized format. As previously mentioned, tables are similar to those of Word and Excel, in that they contain rows (*records*) and columns (*fields*).

Students

	Student I	First Name	Last Name	Address	City	Stat	Zip Code	Phone Numbe
	25	Richard	Christian	2568 Trinity Mills	Carrollton	TX	75234-2345	(972) 418-8906
	26	Mackenzie	Smith	6200 Macarthur	Irving	TX	75038-3456	(972) 929-3556
	27	Hugh	McGeary	100 Belt Line Rd.	Grand Prairie	TX	75051-2235	(972) 641-2333
	28	Zach	Roberts	Lettermen 301	Dallas	TX	75275-0000	(214) 768-0987
	29	Miguel	Gonzales	4567 Barnes Bridge	Mesquite	TX	75149-0258	(972) 279-1245
	30	Kayla	Roberson	890 Camp Wisdom	Duncanville	TX	75116-1002	(972) 283-5569
*	(New)					TX		

Record: 1 of 30 No Filter Search

What is a record (row)?

A record applies to data entered into a **single row** of a table. All data in that row would belong to an individual or item. A record would normally include a unique ID number, name, description, plus other relevant information. With each new record, a new row is created. For example, the figure above has all the information on Peter in the row beginning with "1".

What is a field (column)?

Each column (or field) is used to define what **specific information** is to be entered into that particular column or "field". A column titled "**Class**", for example, would signify this to be the place in a record to enter the Class name when creating each new record. For example, the figure above has an email address for each row in the column headed "Email".

What is data?

Data is the information entered into tables within the database. Databases are used in businesses and in education, often without people realizing they are using a database. Something as simple as entering contact details into the "Contact" or "Address Book" section of an email client, involves entering data into a database.

Data entered will generally be alphabetical (names, addresses) or numerical (dates, currency), however Access is also able to store other forms of data, such as links to websites, documents created in other programs such as files and images.

Data can be entered into the database manually, via the keyboard, imported from or linked to external sources or even collected through email or an internet form.

Data types

Data types define what type of data will be entered into each "field" (column) in a table. If you create a table by typing in the data in new fields, Access will determine the data type for you based on what you type. If you type a name, it sets the type for that field to "Text". If you type a date either as "12/09/2010" or "December 9, 2010" it will set the type to "Date/Time". If you type a digit or digits it will set the type to "Number". If you also type $ as in $49.95 or a specific number of decimal places "5.00" that will be included as the format for a numeric field.

Although you can enter data without setting up the fields first, you should create the table and specify the data types for each field before entering data. You should also set defaults, limits, and use **Input Masks** as needed. **Text** – holds up to 255 characters; can be numbers, letters, or symbols.

- ❑ **Memo** – holds over 255 characters; can be numbers, letters, or symbols
- ❑ **Number** – numbers only
- ❑ **Date/Time** – valid dates or times
- ❑ **Currency** – numbers displayed as currency
- ❑ **AutoNumber** – a number is automatically input; you cannot type in this field
- ❑ **Yes/No** – only two answers: yes or no [true or false] [on or off]
- ❑ **OLE Object** – you can attach one document to the record
- ❑ **Hyperlink** – you can put in a hyperlink
- ❑ **Attachment** – attach multiple files to one record including digital photos
- ❑ **Look Up Wizard** – allows you to input a list of choices for a text field
- ❑ **Calculated** – displays a value calculated from other data in the table

Field Properties

Field Properties should be set in order to: format numbers and dates; to limit data entry to specific characters; to validate entries; to provide a mask for input; to require data in a specific field; and/or to set default data. You can see the **Field Properties** that have been set by viewing the table in **Design View.** Some of the **Field Properties** are only available for specific **Data Types.** Below is a brief description of some of the more popular Field Properties.

Field Properties

General | Lookup

Field Size	255
Format	
Input Mask	
Caption	
Default Value	
Validation Rule	
Validation Text	
Required	No
Allow Zero Length	Yes
Indexed	No
Unicode Compression	Yes
IME Mode	No Control
IME Sentence Mode	None
Smart Tags	

Field Size allows the setting of the maximum number of characters that can be entered.

Format allows you to specify a "format" or appearance of a date, time, or number. It has choices such as: short date, medium time, long date, currency, etc.

Input Mask uses a particular format of the data entered. Such as a phone number (xxx) xxx-xxxx or social security number xxx-xx-xxxx. The **Input Mask** puts in the parenthesis, dashes, slashes while the user just types the data.

Caption displays at the top of a column in a table. [It does not replace the field name.]

Default Value is a value that is common, for example, for a database with names and addresses, the State field could have a Default Value of: TX

Validation Rule & Validation Text allows you to set limits, for example on a Number or a Date field you could specify the number be less than or greater than a specific number or that a Date between specific dates.

Required can either be Yes or No. Required Yes means that it will not allow the field to be empty.

Indexed has three choices: No, Yes (Duplicates OK), and Yes (No Duplicates). Indexed Yes means that searches and sorts work faster.

Text Format (Memo fields)has two choices: Plain Text and Rich Text. (Rich Text allows the person entering data to use bold, italic, underline and a few other features.)

Text Align is used to set the alignment of text in the field.

Show Date Picker is available for **Date** fields. The **Date Picker** looks like a tiny calendar (small figure right). When you click the **Date Picker**, the current month calendar pops up (larger figure right).

A First Look at Access 2010

Opening Access 2010

Click the Start button (bottom left of screen), then select All Programs. Scroll up to locate the Microsoft Office folder button, click it. Click Microsoft Office Access 2010. Open the Sample2011 database.

Exploring the Access 2010 window

Similar to other Microsoft Office 2010 applications, Access 2010 uses tabs which display a ribbon. The Ribbon is designed to display the most appropriate tools / functions according to the task at hand. Each ribbon is divided into Groups.

✓ The "biggest" change is the new (1) File tab in place of the Office Button.

✓ The Quick Access Toolbar in the top left corner of the screen has not changed from Access 2010.

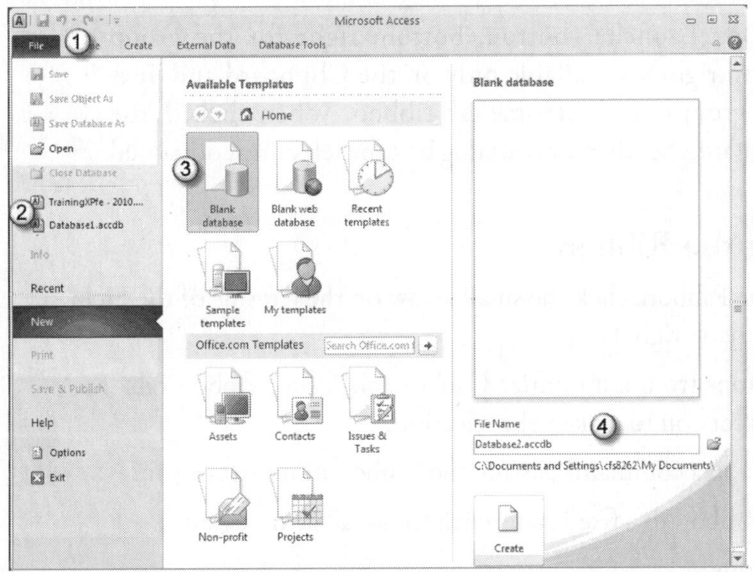

✓ Recent Documents are listed on the **File** tab.

✓ New Blank database is easy to access.

✓ Type the New database name and select the folder it will be stored in.

✓ Under the File tab in the top left corner is the Views group. There are also two tiny View buttons in the bottom right corner of the screen.

✓ At the bottom, near the center are the Record Navigation buttons. Use the navigation buttons to display the records in a table. In the "1 of 1" box the first number represents the current record and the second number is the total number of records.

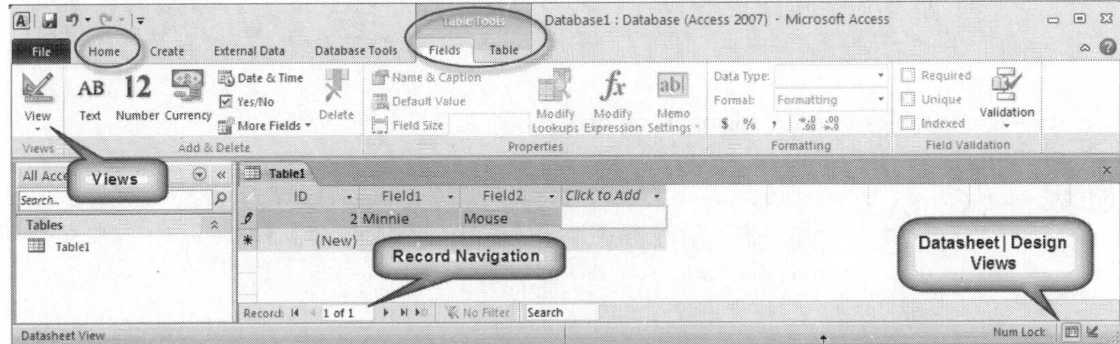

✓ All commands are organized into groups on the various Ribbons. Groups were designed to help identify tools quickly.

✓ A Dialog Box Launcher button, bottom right for the group (see figure on right) is available only on the Clipboard and Text Formatting groups on the Home tab ribbon. When clicked, the Dialog Box Launcher displays a dialog box for selecting additional features.

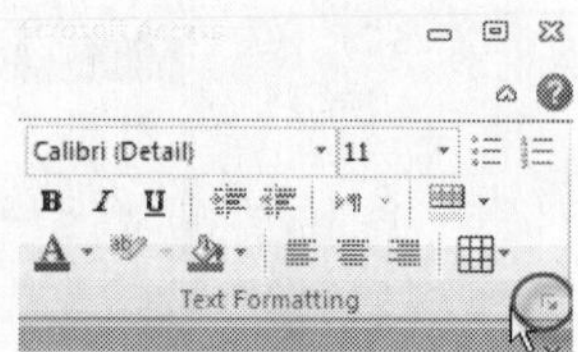

Minimizing the Ribbon

To minimize the Ribbon, click the small arrow on the left side of the Help button (see figure on right).

Click to Minimize

To make selections from a minimized ribbon, click on a ribbon tab. The ribbon expands for you to make your selection.

Click to un-Minimize

When you click on a command button, the Ribbon minimizes again.

To restore the Ribbon to a fixed state, click the small arrow again.

Tabs and Ribbons

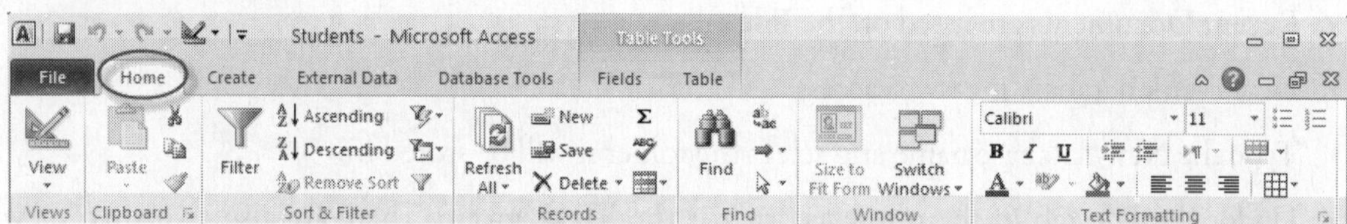

Home – font formatting, record commands, sorting, filtering, & find

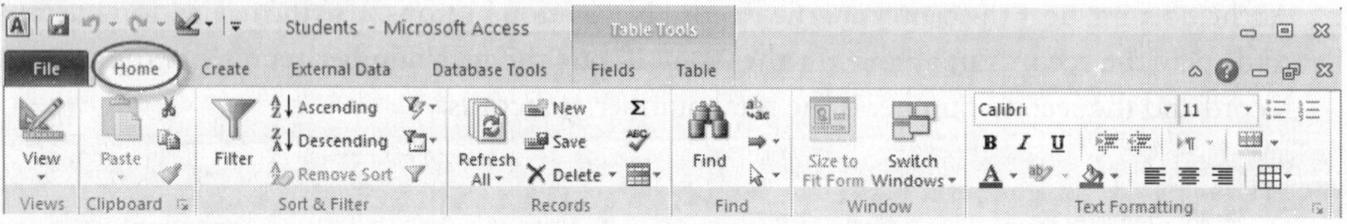

Create – create tables, queries, forms, & reports

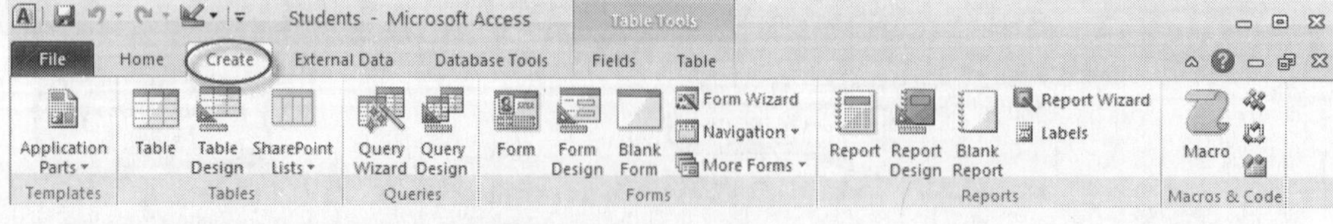

External Data – import & export records from/to Excel and various other file types

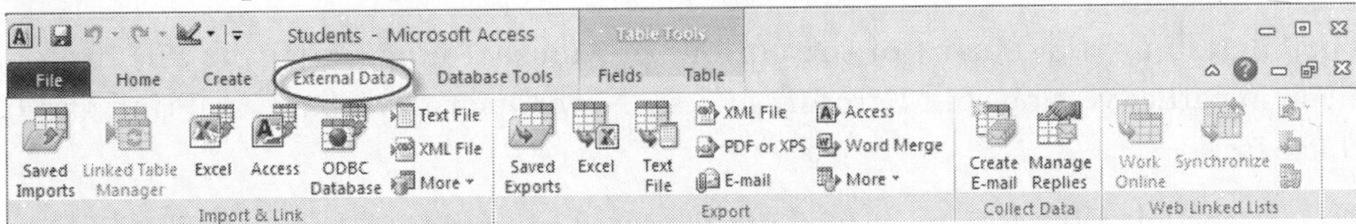

Database Tools – relationships and compact & repair database

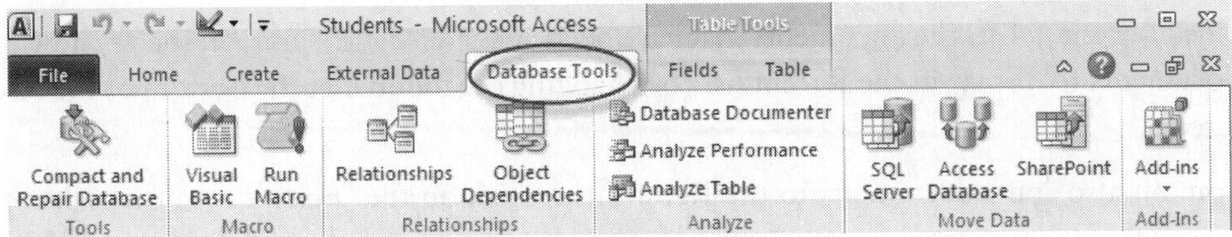

Table Tools Fields – views, insert, delete, or rename fields; set properties & data formatting

Table Tools Table – (not shown) is for working with macros and programming steps to run

Customizing Access 2010

Quick Access Toolbar

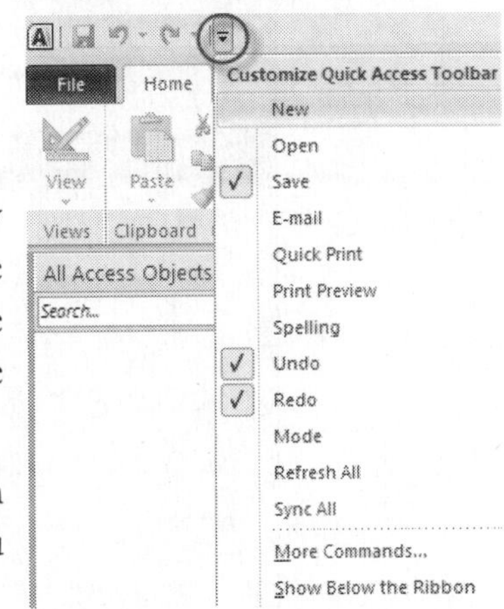

The Quick Access Toolbar offers an easy way to access frequently used command buttons, such as Save, Undo and Redo that are already on the Quick Access Toolbar. Other functions may be added to the toolbar by selecting them from the Customize Quick Access Toolbar drop down list.

To customize the Quick Access Toolbar, click the drop-down arrow to the right of the Toolbar. The list has commands that you may easily turn on or off. (A checkmark means they are on.)

You may also click More Commands and add additional commands to your Quick Access Toolbar. Any command may be added to the Quick Access Toolbar.

The File Tab & Access Options

- ✓ The File tab provides many of the options previously found under the File drop down menu in earlier versions of Microsoft Access: New, Open, Save, Save As, Print, and Close Database.
- ✓ Also, on the File tab is Recent documents, Password protection, Compact & Repair Database and Access Options.
- ✓ Click Recent. It lists the documents that have been opened recently. You can specify how many documents to display in the Recent list (by changing the number at the bottom of the Recent screen).
- ✓ You can also "pin" documents to the Recent list. Click on the "pushpin" to the right of the Filename. The document is now "pinned" to the Recent list. Click the "pin" again to "unpin" the file.

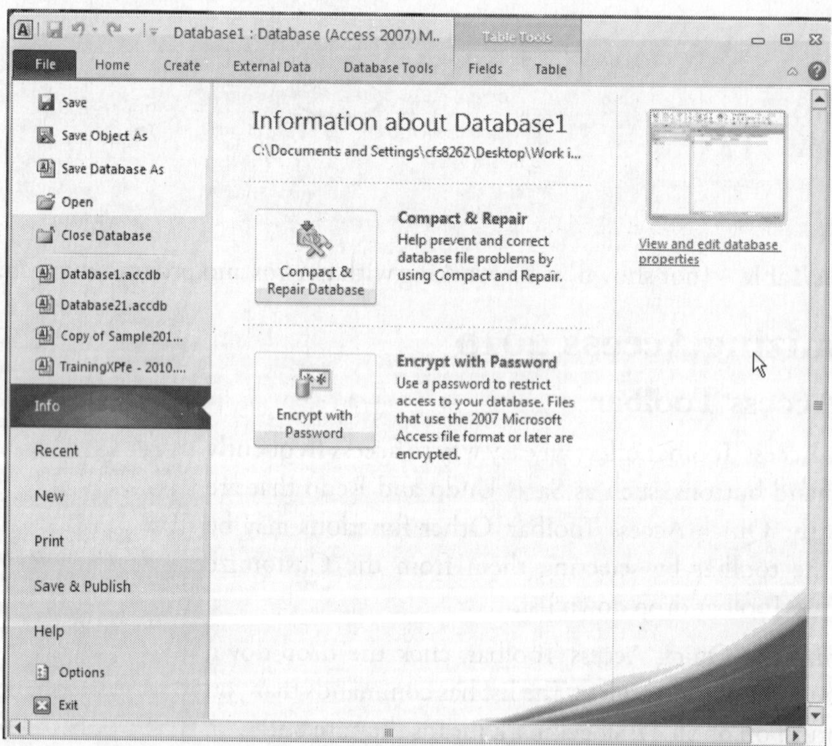

File tab and Access options

- ✓ Click the File tab, then Options.

✓ On the General screen, you may want to change the Default file format (see the figure). If that is the only change click OK at the bottom of the Options window.

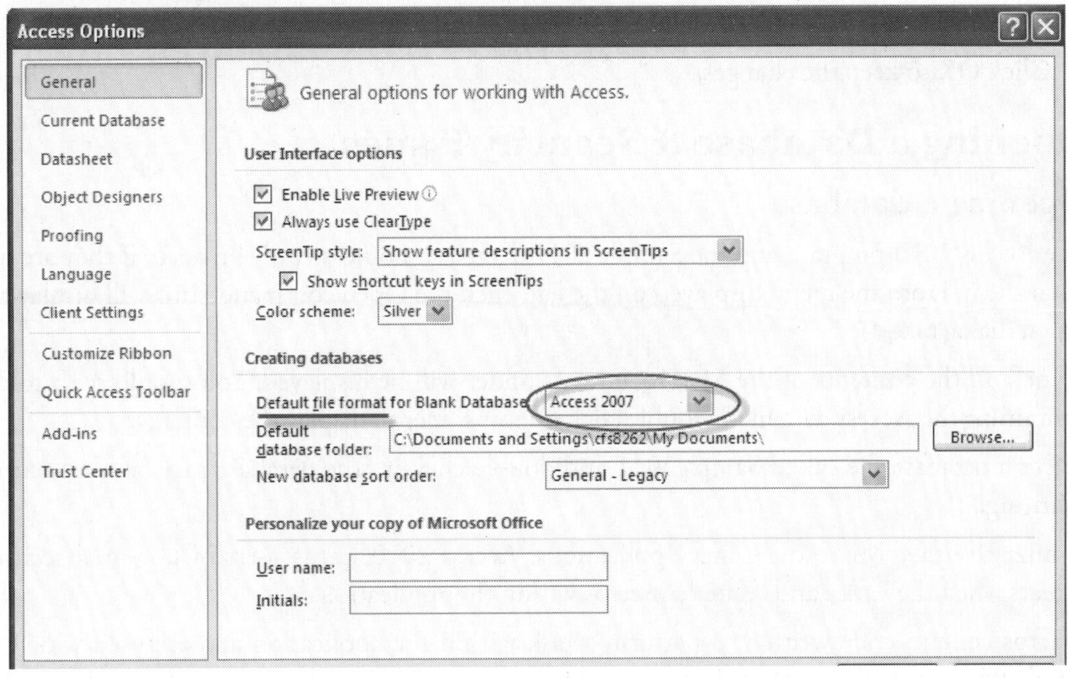

Access options

✓ Still on the Options screen, click Current Database on the left. Locate Document Window Options (across from Quick Access Toolbar).

✓ Click Tabbed Documents to select it. This will enable having tabs across the top of open files within Access, as shown in the figure below.

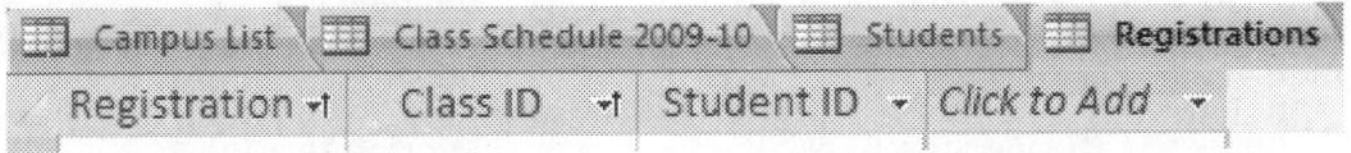

✓ Click Object Designers, the fourth item in the Options menu. If you would like to change the Default text field size, select 255 and type the number you want. 50 is suggested unless you think that is too low. Click OK if finished with Options.

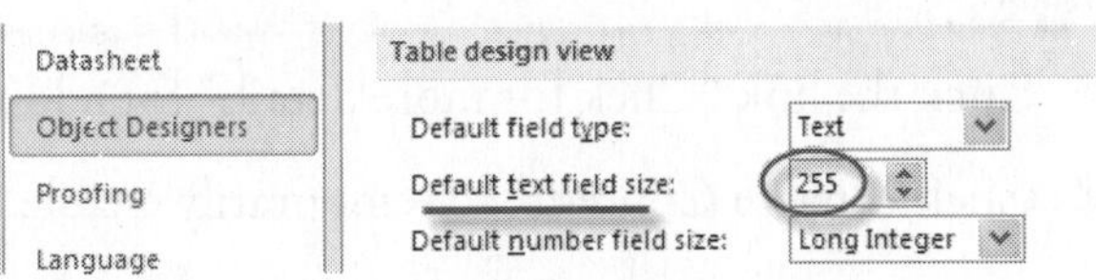

✓ You can also make changes to the Quick Access Toolbar, select the Quick Access

Toolbar in the menu on the left. To add buttons to your toolbar, select a command in the list on the left, click the Add button and the command is added to the Toolbar on the right side of the screen. Add as many commands as desired.

✓ Click OK to keep the changes.

Opening a Database & Security Issues

Opening a database

The Access 2010 program and the Sample 2011 database should already be open, if they are not open them. From the menu displayed on the left, click the Open command. This will display the Open dialog box.

By default the contents of the My Documents folder will be displayed. You should see a folder containing the Access data files. Double click on this folder to display the contents.

Select a database file called Sample2011 and double click it. The database may have a Security Warning.

Similar to other Microsoft Office applications, Access 2010 warns users of potential security threats when they arise and relate to macros within the application.

Macros contain code written to perform a task within the application and are used widely in Excel, Word as well as Access. Because macros use code designed to allow advanced users the opportunity to create their own functions to enhance the functionality of a database, others can also write malicious code intended to have the opposite effect. For this reason, Microsoft Office applications prevent macros from running and display a warning instead, which is outlined in the figure below.

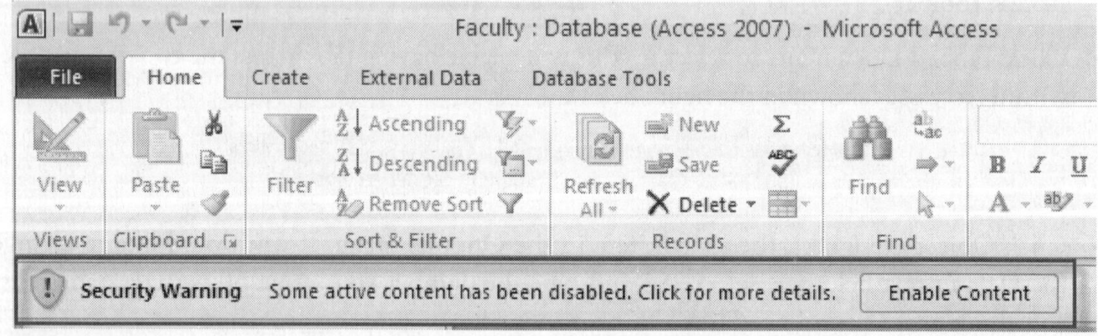

✓ Click the link "Click for more details" for additional information.

✓ Click "Enable Content" to temporarily enable the file (this time only).

✓ "Click for more details", brings up the screen shown below-

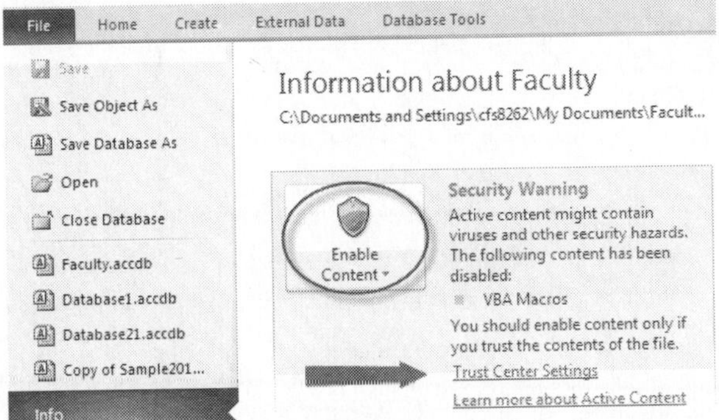

✓ You can also click Enable Content (as a temporary fix).

✓ Click Trust Center Settings to enable the contents of the file permanently.

✓ If you trust the source of this database file and the content, you can select Enable content, to allow the macro to run, then click OK.

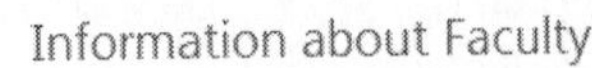

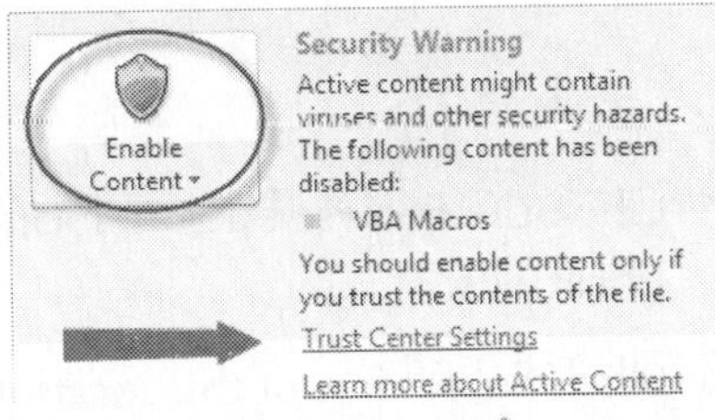

NOTE: Selecting Enable content is a temporary enabling of macros and warnings will be displayed again the next time this database is opened.

Add a Trusted Location

✓ You can add a trusted location so you do not get the security warning each time you open a database.

✓ Click Trust Center Settings.

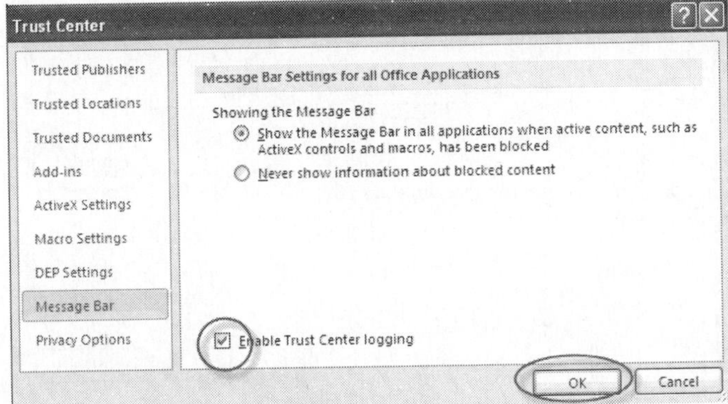

Access trust centre

- ✓ Click the Enable Trust Center logging checkbox (to turn it on).
- ✓ Click Trusted Locations.
- ✓ Click Add New Location.

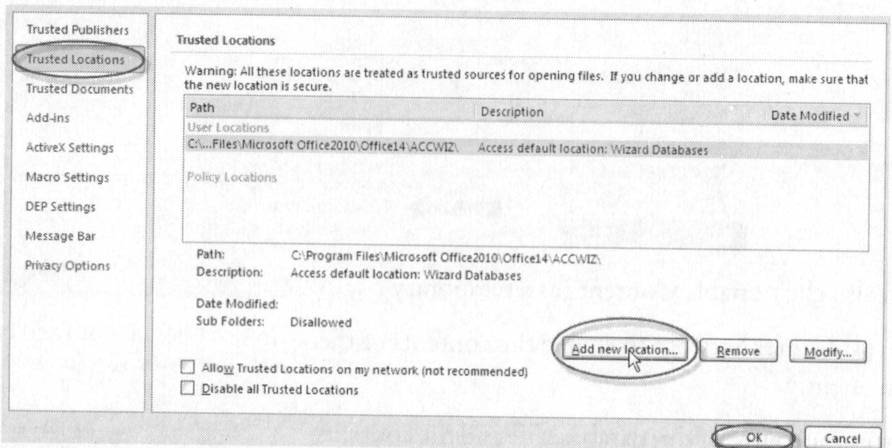

Trusted location is Access

- ✓ Click the Browse button, locate and click on the folder that you wish to add to the Trusted Locations.
- ✓ Click Subfolders of this location are also trusted.
- ✓ Click OK
- ✓ The "new" location should be in the list of Trusted Locations.
- ✓ Next time you open the database, you should not receive the security warning.

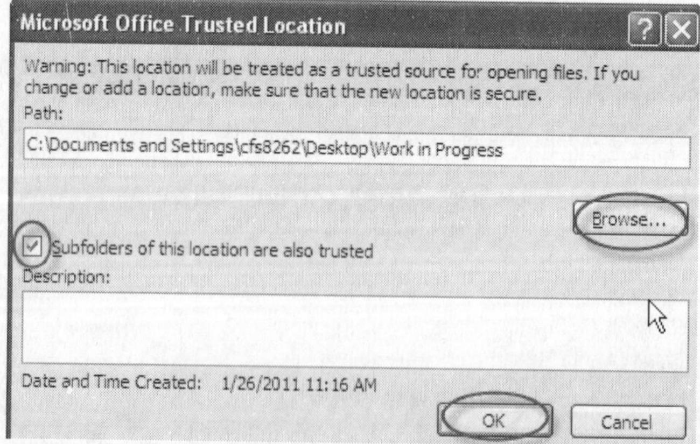

Security warning in trusted location

Navigating an existing database

✓ Still using the Sample2011 database (it should be open).

✓ Open the Students table in the Sample2011 database file. Scroll through the records using the record navigation buttons at the bottom of the table window. You can also scroll through fields with the Tab or arrow keys.

Student I	First Name	Last Name	Address	City	Stat	Zip Code	Phone Numb
28	Zach	Roberts	Lettermen 301	Dallas	TX	75275-0000	(214) 768-0987
	Micah	Parker	4567 Barnes Bridge	Mesquite	TX	75149-0258	(972) 279-1245
	Kayla	Roberson	890 Camp Wisdom	Duncanville	TX	75116-1002	(972) 283-5569
	Krista	Roberson	890 Camp Wisdom	Duncanville	TX	75116-1002	(214) 123-4567
(New)					TX		

Navigation buttons

Record: 31 of 31 No Filter Search

Navigating through records within a table

✓ The record navigation bar is located at the bottom of the object window. When a table is open, you will see these buttons. (see figure on right)

First Next New

Record: 2 of 9

Previous Last

✓ To use the specific record option, click within the box and enter a record number, then press the Enter key.

✓ Click below the last record

Add a New Record

✓ Click under Kayla at the bottom of the list. Type Krista in the First name field [once you type the name, 31 (or the next number) will show in the first (Student ID) column] press Tab. [Press Ctrl and Quote to copy from the record above.]

✓ For the Last name press "Ctrl" press Tab;

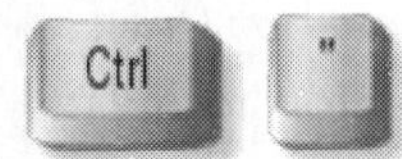

✓ For the Address press "Ctrl" press Tab;

✓ For City press "Ctrl" and "Tab" twice to accept the State and in the Zip Code field press Ctrl then press Tab;

✓ Type the Phone Number shown – just type the digits 214 1234567 and the Input Mask (already set up) will put in the parenthesis, space, and dash in the correct places.

Closing a database

✓ Click the File tab to display the menu.

✓ Select the Close Database command. (This will close Sample2011, the open database.)

✓ The database closes and returns to the Access 2010 "Available Templates" screen. The database name is listed on the left of the screen with the Recent Databases.

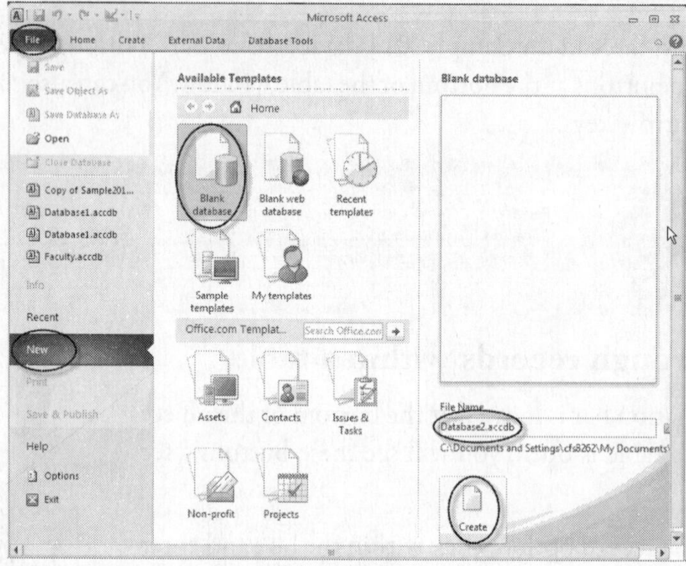

Colsing database

Creating a new blank database

✓ Start the Access 2010 program if it is not already open.

✓ Select the Blank Database icon, or if you are in Access, click the File tab and select New then click the Blank Database button.

✓ Type Faculty in the File Name box (lower right). Set the folder location for storing it in My Documents\Training (or wherever your instructor tells you to store it).

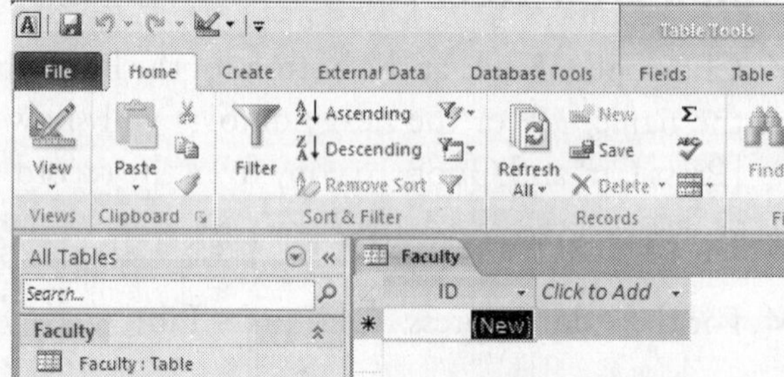

Creating new blank database

✓ Click the Create button at the bottom of the screen.

✓ A screen similar (and much larger) to the one below is displayed:

Saving a table

✓ Before adding information to an Access database, the fields should be added to a table. The fields should be named, given the correct Data Type and formatted appropriately. Field

Properties should be selected as needed. If necessary you can put validations in the fields as well as defaults.

✓ Fields are used to organize data into specific fields or columns, for example a First Name field would store the first name for every individual record entered, as would the Last Name, Birth Date, and other fields, etc.

✓ Click the Save button in the Quick Access Toolbar. The Save As dialog box is displayed. Type the name Faculty. Click the OK button. [Each object: Form, Query, Report, and Table has its own name]

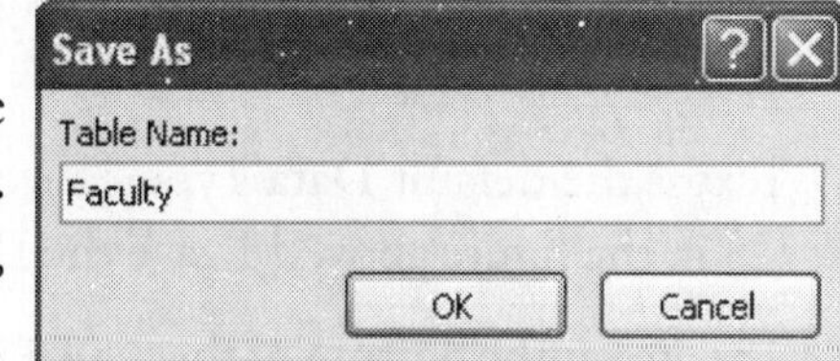

Creating a Table & Setting Field Properties

✓ Follow these steps to create the fields in a table.

✓ Type the Field Name (has to be unique in the table).

✓ Select the Field Type from the drop-down menu or by typing the first letter. Text is the default Field Type.

✓ Set any Field Properties necessary

✓ Click the Design View button – top left to add to our table. See figure below to locate the Design View button.

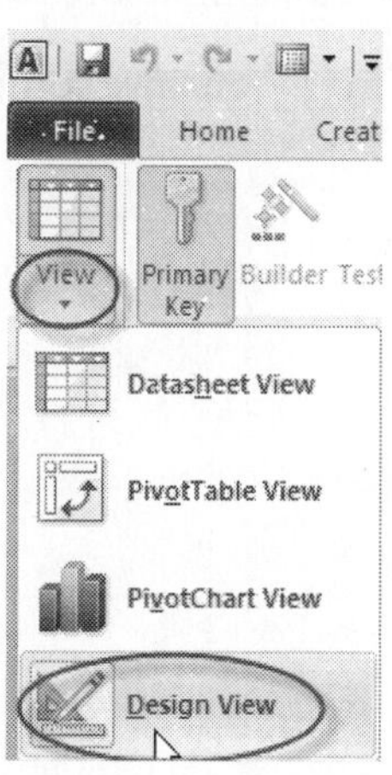

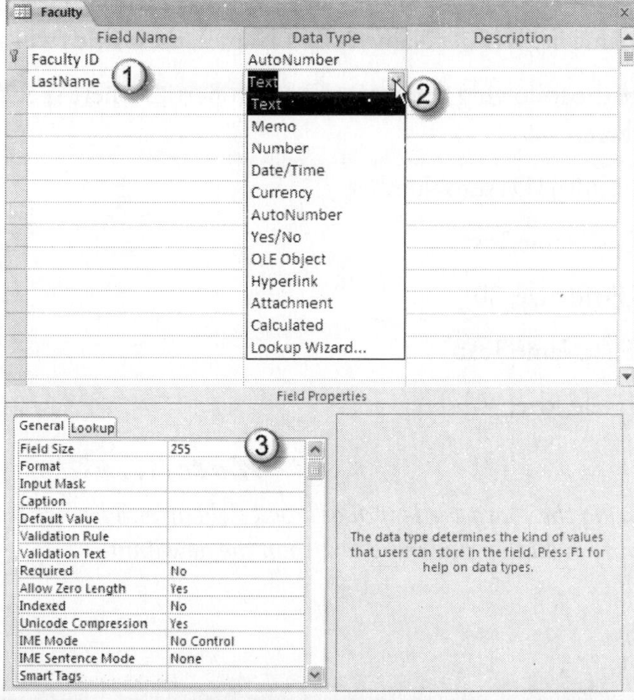

Creating table and setting field properties

✓ The first field is automatically created and is called ID and it is an AutoNumber Data Type. It is the Primary Key. Setting the field as the Primary Key causes entries in the field to be unique. Change the Field Name to: Faculty ID

✓ Type the Field Name (1): LastName press the down-arrow key to go to the next field. The third field should be FirstName, press the down arrow. (It will automatically make the Data Type Text.)

✓ Text is the default Data Type. [If you want a different Data Type, click the drop down arrow (2) in the figure above.] Leave the Data Type as Text for both name fields.

✓ The area at the bottom of the screen is titled Field Properties (3). Set the Field Size to 30 for both name fields (First Name & Last Name); these fields will allow a maximum of 30 characters.

✓ The first field is automatically created and is called ID and it is an Auto Number Data Type. It is the Primary Key. Setting the field as the Primary Key causes entries in the field to be unique. Change the Field Name to: Faculty ID

✓ Type the Field Name (1): Last Name press the down-arrow key to go to the next field. The third field should be FirstName, press the down arrow. (It will automatically make the Data Type Text.)

✓ Text is the default Data Type. [If you want a different Data Type, click the drop down arrow (2) in the figure above.] Leave the Data Type as Text for both name fields.

✓ The area at the bottom of the screen is titled Field Properties (3). Set the Field Size to 30 for both name fields (First Name & Last Name); these fields will allow a maximum of 30 characters.

✓ Create the following fields, give Field Properties where specified in []. You have completed the first three.

- ❑ Faculty ID AutoNumber
- ❑ LastName Text
- ❑ [Field Size, 30]
- ❑ FirstName Text
- ❑ [Field Size, 30]

Note.... ✍

Reducing the character length of a text field after data has been entered can result in loss of data in a field that had more text than the new limit.

- ❑ Birthdate Date/Time
- ❑ [Format, Short Date]
- ❑ [Required, Yes] (Required will not allow blank fields)
- ❑ Graduate Hrs Number
- ❑ [Validation Rule, >=18]
- ❑ [Validation Text, Must be equal to or greater than 18] (this Validation Rule says it must be 18 or more)
- ❑ PhD Yes/No
- ❑ Campus Text
- ❑ Comments Memo
- ❑ [Text Format, Rich Text] (Turning on Rich Text means you can use bold, italic & underline among other features)
- ❑ Phone Text
- ❑ Insert two new rows below First Name.
- ❑ Put the mouse on the left edge of Birthdate, click once and drag down to select both (1) Birthdate and Graduate Hrs (see figure right).
- ❑ Click (2) Insert Rows in the Tools group.

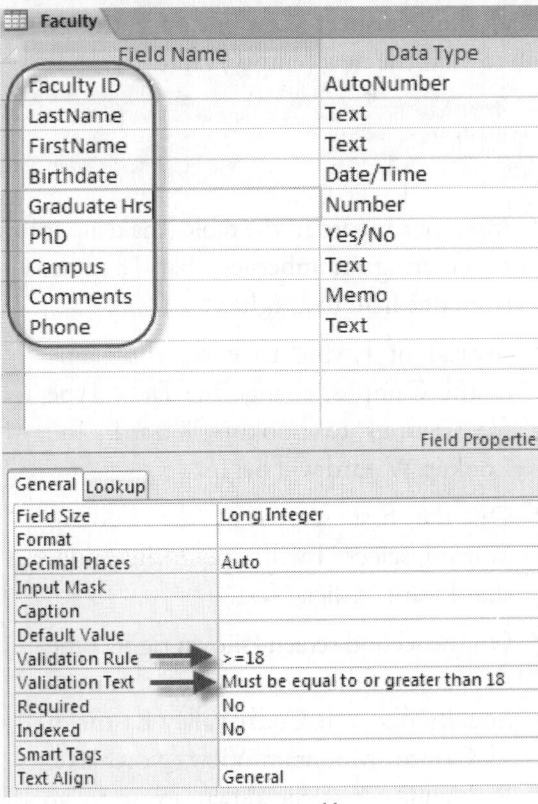

Creating a table

Add the following two fields (on the new blank rows) below First Name: County Text

[Default value, Dallas]

State Text

[Default Value, TX]

Save the Faculty table again.

Move the Comments field to the bottom, below Phone: click the selection box on the far left to select it, then drag it to the bottom of the fields and let go]

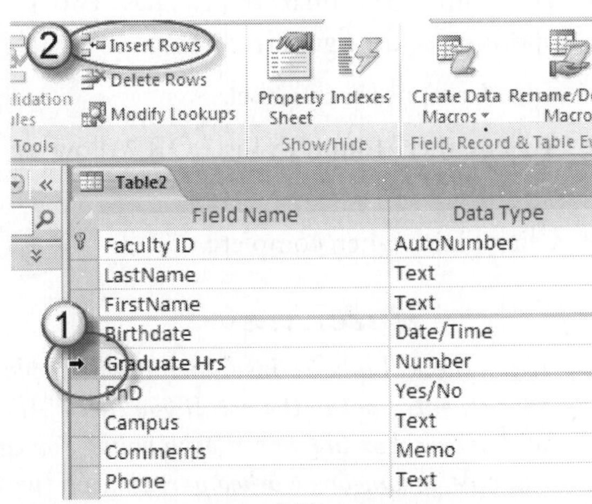

Setting field properties

Click the Datasheet View button in the Views group on the left edge of the Table Tools Design tab to view the new (empty) table.

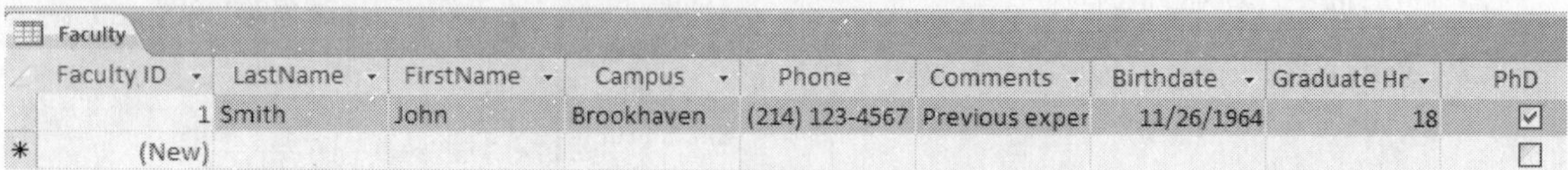

Faculty

Faculty ID	LastName	FirstName	Campus	Phone	Comments	Birthdate	Graduate Hr	PhD
1	Smith	John	Brookhaven	(214) 123-4567	Previous exper	11/26/1964	18	☑
(New)								☐

- ✓ Input one record in the table (make up information; try leaving the Birthdate field blank. Also try entering a number less than 18 in the Graduate Hrs field), use the Tab key to move across from one field to another.
- ✓ Instead of having to enter the name of the Campus, change the Data Type for Campus to Lookup Wizard. The Lookup Wizard will begin.
- ✓ On the first screen of the Lookup Wizard, select "I will type in the values that I want." Click Next.
- ✓ On the second screen (shown right) type the names of the seven campuses, one per line: Brookhaven, Cedar Valley, Eastfield, El Centro, Mountain View, Northlake, Richland. (Press the down arrow to go down one line for each campus.)
- ✓ Click Next.
- ✓ The third and final screen has two options. See the figure (right).
- ✓ Type Campus for the label.
- ✓ Select either "Limit To List" OR "Allow Multiple Values".
- ✓ Click Finish when complete.

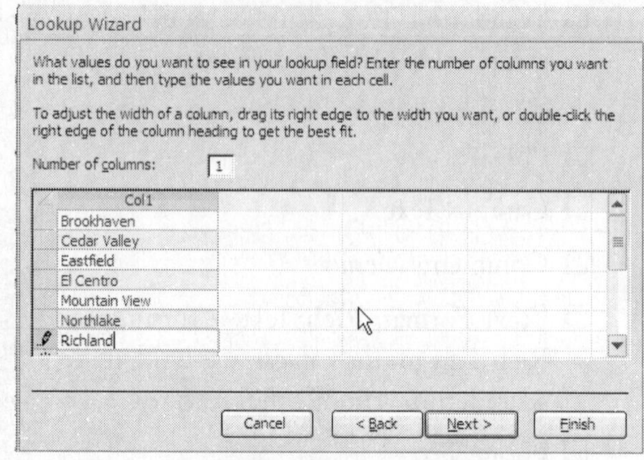

Screen of lookup wizard

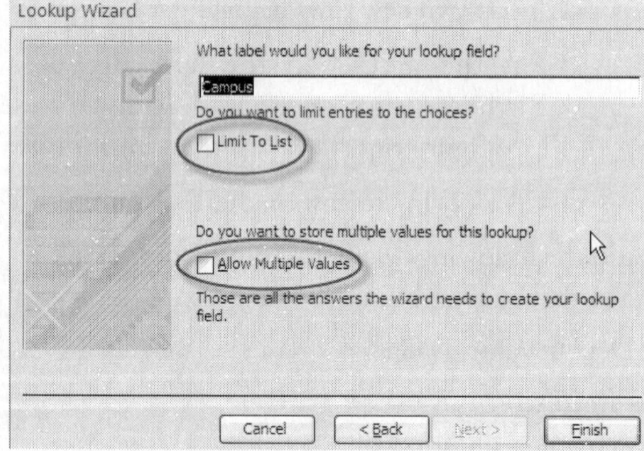

Working on lookup wizard

Note....

If you check "Limit To List" then it will display a drop-down list, but it will not allow you to type an entry not in the list. If you check "Allow Multiple Values" then it will display the list with a checkbox in front of each value. You can check the box for more than one value. (For example, if someone worked part time on two campuses.)

- ✓ In Design View; add a field at the bottom (below Comments) called Documentation and select Attachment as the data type. Save the Table again. (There are twelve fields in the table.)
- ✓ In Datasheet View, the Documentation column displays a paper clip symbol at the top instead of the field name.
- ✓ In the figure on the right, the top paperclip is in place of a field name. The paperclip (2) means there are 2 attachments in the first record. (0) means there are no attachments in the second record.

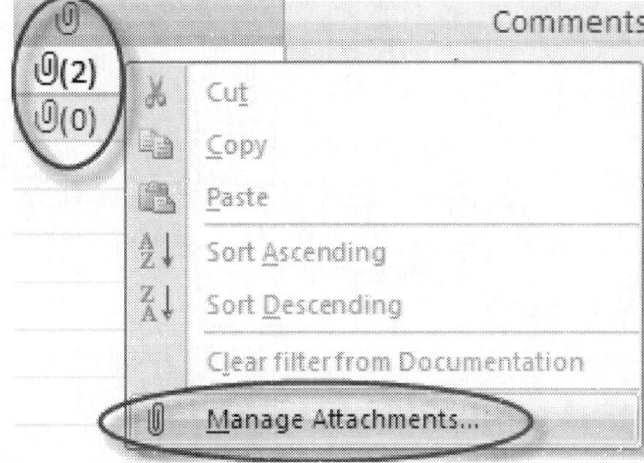

Adding documentation & attachment

- ✓ In Design View, look at the Documentation Field Properties. For the Caption, type Resume & Other Documents. The Caption displays at the top of the field (column). Save the Faculty Table.
- ✓ The Attachment data type is useful for attaching images, resumes, descriptions and other file types, etc.
- ✓ To attach documents and images, either double click on the cell containing the paper clip image, or with the cell active, right-click on the Attachment field and select Manage Attachments from the pop-up menu.
- ✓ In the Manage Attachments box, shown on the right, all the attachments for a specific field are listed. Click Add to attach a file.
- ✓ Click Remove to remove a file already attached.
- ✓ Use Open to see the contents of an attached file.
- ✓ Click OK when finished with the Manage Attachments window.
- ✓ Save and Close the table.

Note....

When viewing the Attachment field of a record (in a form), click once on an attachment and the scroll buttons shown here, are visible.

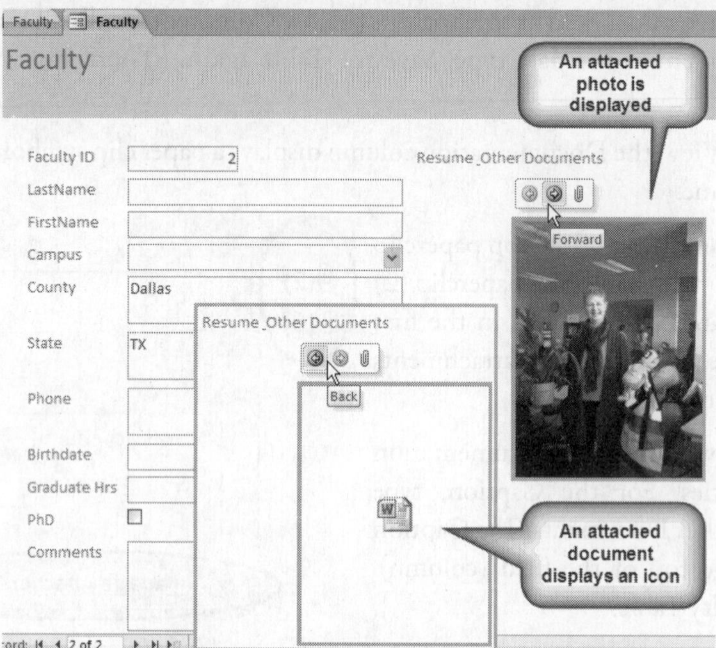

✓ Click Forward or Back to scroll through the attachments. Click the paperclip to bring up the Manage Attachments dialog box.

In a form, attached photos are displayed, other documents are shown as an icon.

Closing a database

✓ Click the File Tab to display the menu.

✓ Select the Close Database command.

✓ Save your changes. The database closes and it returns to the Blank Database screen. The database named Faculty is in the Recent list.

Navigation Pane

The Navigation Pane is located on the left side of the screen and displays all objects contained within the database, including all tables, forms, queries and reports.

✓ Open the database Sample2011

✓ The Navigation Pane can be minimized by clicking on the (left pointing) arrows button, top right of the pane. To restore the Pane to normal view, click the right pointing arrows button at the top right of the pane.

- ✓ Object categories can be minimized/maximized using the upward/downward pointing arrow buttons to the right of the object type.
- ✓ In the figure, All Access Objects are displayed: Tables, Queries, Forms, and/or Reports. Queries are also shown in the figure. It may not be evident which Table goes with each Query, because Tables and Queries can be named anything.

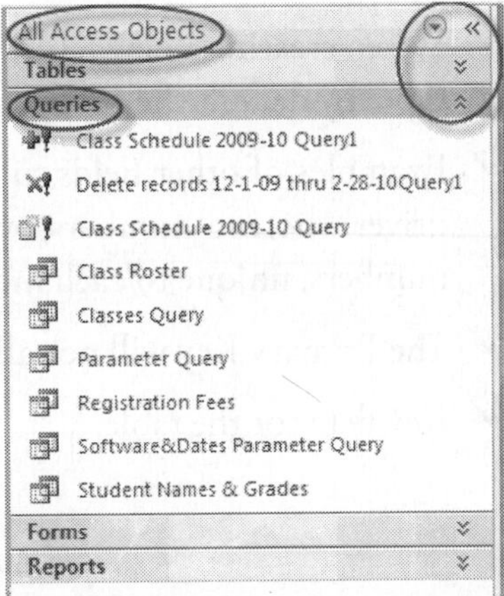

- ✓ A preferable way to view the Objects is by All Tables set to Tables and Related Views. This view shows the Table and its Objects together.
- ✓ To select the way you would like to view the objects, click the (1) Menu button which is the down pointing arrow in the top right corner of the Navigation Pane (see figure on right).
- ✓ Select Tables then Tables and Related Views. In this way tables will be listed with all their individual Forms, Queries, and Reports. [Each object type has its own icon in front of the name. See the figure right.] ➡
- ✓ Experiment with the views. Leave it displayed by All Tables and Tables and Related views. (See the figure.) ➘
- ✓ The objects are shown listed with the Table. In the example, the Class Schedule 2009-10 group shows one Table and four related objects. The related objects include two Queries, one Form, and one Report. This makes it easy to know which table it is pulling information from.

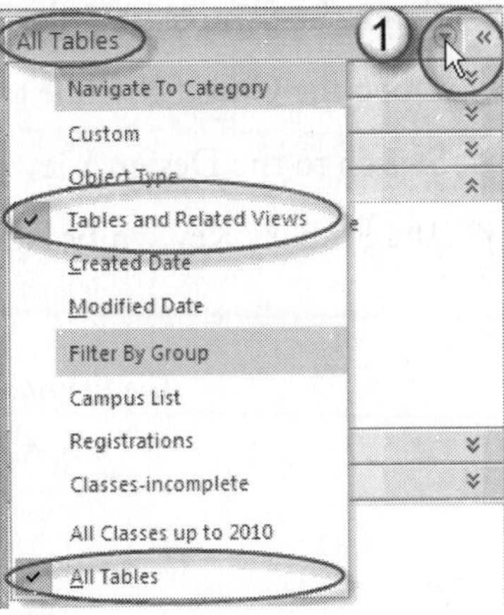

Navigation pane

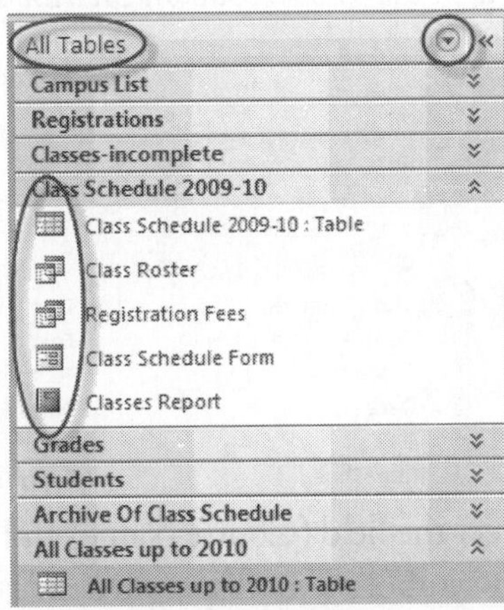

Object shown in a table

Primary Key

- ✓ A **Primary Key** is used as a unique identifier for each record in a table and is essential when working with relational tables.
- ✓ To be effective, a **Primary Key** cannot have duplicate entries and must be set on a field with a unique identifier.
- ✓ When creating a new table, Access automatically adds the ID field with an Auto Number data type. By default the ID field is also the Primary Key.
- ✓ Examples of other fields suitable to be set as a Primary Key are: passport, social security and driver's license numbers, military identification, tax, workplace or personal identification numbers, unique to each individual.
- ✓ The Primary Key will not allow duplicate entries in the Primary
- ✓ Key field for the table.

Note....

A Primary Key field can never be empty.

- ✓ Open the Sample2011 database.
- ✓ Open the Class Schedule table.
- ✓ Switch to the Design View, by clicking on the View button.
- ✓ The Primary Key symbol identifies the Class Number field as being the Primary Key.

Note....

The Primary Key button is in the Tools group on the ribbon.

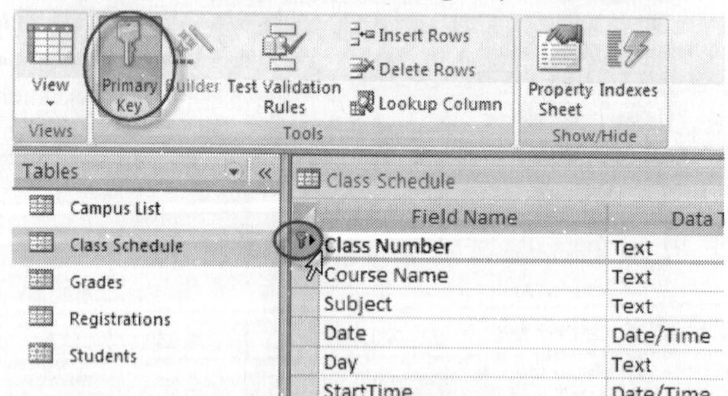

- ✓ To use another field as the primary key, select the field (Course Name) and then click the Primary Key button on the ribbon. The Primary Key symbol is now displayed beside the Course Name field.

Note....

The Course Name field is NOT a suitable data type to become a primary key, as data within this field is unlikely to be unique.

- ✓ Reset the Primary Key to the Class Number, before continuing.
- ✓ Close the Sample2011 database.
- ✓ Open the Faculty database again.

Input Mask Wizard

Input Masks are used to restrict how data is entered. By forcing users of the database to enter data in a fixed format it greatly reduces the chances of data input errors. There is usually less typing with an **Input Mask** because parenthesis and dashes are put in for you.

Note....

Input Masks only work with Text and Date data types. When creating a field with information such as phone numbers, social security numbers, id numbers, etc. it needs to be a Text field if you want to type parenthesis, dashes, or spaces in the field. (A Number field will only allow digits, decimal points, or negative signs to be typed.)

- ✓ Open the Faculty Table in Design View.
- ✓ Click in the Phone field in the Field Properties. Notice the ... button (circled in the figure above) on the right end of the line for Input Mask.
- ✓ Click the ... button. This will start the Input Mask Wizard.

[If prompted to save the table, click Yes.]

- ✓ The Input Mask Wizard dialog box is displayed. (see figure on right)

General | Lookup

Field Size	25
Format	
Input Mask	...
Caption	
Default Value	
Validation Rule	
Validation Text	
Required	No
Allow Zero Length	Yes
Indexed	No
Unicode Compression	Yes
IME Mode	No Control
IME Sentence Mode	None
Smart Tags	

Faculty table

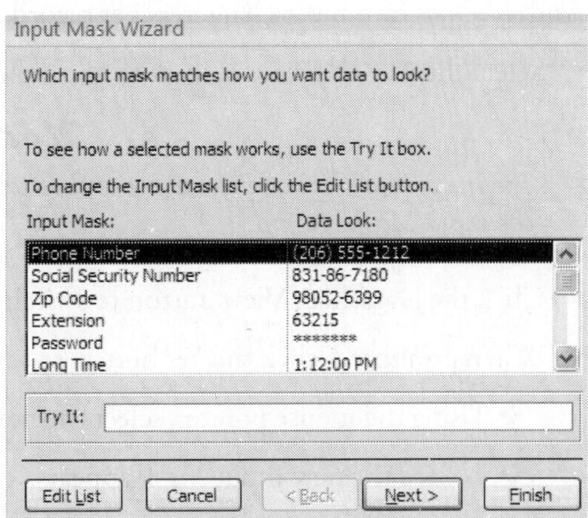

Input mark wizard dialog box

- ✓ Select Phone Number under Input Mask.
- ✓ In the Try It: box, type 10 digits and see how it fills in the parenthesis, space and dash.
- ✓ Click the Next button.
- ✓ The second screen allows you to change the Placeholder character. For example, you could change from using underline _ to using a pound sign #. (It is easier to see how many characters you can type with # because the _ run together as a line.)
- ✓ Change the Placeholder character and then click in Try It: and type 10 digits to see how it works. Click the Next button.
- ✓ The last screen of the Input Mask Wizard asks if you wish to store the data with or without the symbols in the Input Mask. In other words, store a phone number like this: (972) 495-1234 or 9724951234 ? (with or without the symbols, as ten digits or fourteen characters)

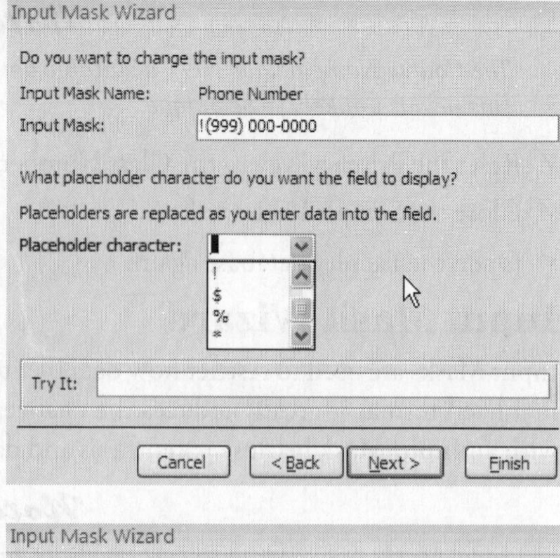

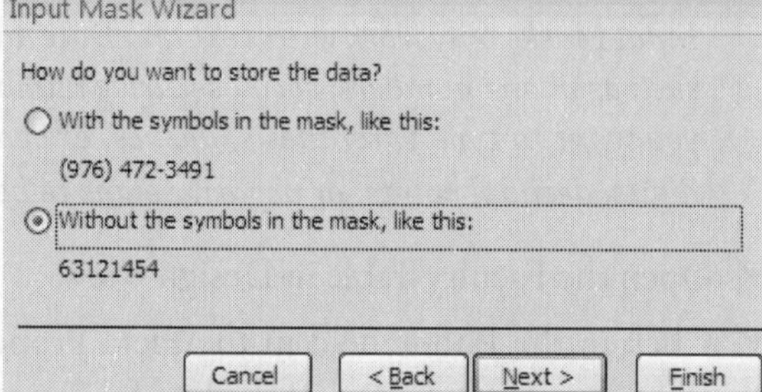

Working on input mark wizard dialog box

There are two questions you should ask yourself –
If I export this to a text file will it matter whether the parenthesis, space, & dash are there or not?
And/or Does four more characters per record make that much difference in storage space?

- ✓ Select the way you want it to store, then click the Finish button.

Note....

The Input Mask has additional codes that can be used to create an Input Mask without using the Input Mask Wizard.

- ✓ Click the Datasheet View button to switch to Datasheet View.
- ✓ When prompted, click the Yes button to save the changes.
  - ❖ Using the mouse pointer, select the next blank cell at the bottom of the Phone column.
  - ❖ Notice the new Input Mask appears. Type in a phone number.

Note....

If at any stage incomplete data has been entered into the field using an input mask, you will not be able to move out of the field or select another function until the data is either removed or completed.

Input Mask Details

- ✓ An Input Mask can be typed instead of using the Wizard. It is divided into three sections separated by semi-colons (;).
- ✓ The first section is mandatory. The sample consists of characters with special meaning such as 9 means it is optional – you can leave it blank or type a digit, but it will only accept digits. The character 0 means it is mandatory to type a digit.
- ✓ The second section will either be a 1(to store only what is typed) or a 0 (to store all characters such as parenthesis or dash along with the typed data.)
- ✓ The # at the end indicates the chosen placeholder. Anything in quotes or preceded by a backslash \ will appear as shown. The ! at the beginning means if there are optional characters, it will fill from right to left.

Manipulating Records

Using the Undo command

Like other Microsoft Office applications, the Undo button is located on the Quick Access Toolbar. The Undo command (CTRL-Z) allows the user to undo some actions. You can Undo deleting or editing the contents of a field. However, it will Undo all of the actions in the same record at one time.

Unlike other Office applications, however, when working with tables, the Undo function will only undo the actions on one record. You cannot UNDO the deleting of an entire record. (It warns you accordingly.)

- ✓ Open the Faculty table (in the Faculty database). Experiment with creating a new record, making changes and then try clicking the Undo button. Access will Undo sorting and some other changes.
- ✓ Deleting data within a record
- ✓ Deleting data in a record is similar to editing data in a record; however, there are a number of considerations to take into account.

Note....

Data cannot be deleted from fields where the required field property is set to Yes, as this prevents the field from being left blank.

- ✓ To remove data from a record, select the information in the field, press the F2 key to activate editing mode, then use either the Delete or the Backspace key to delete the entry. Press the Enter key to commit the changes.
- ✓ The pointer moves to the next column, leaving the field empty.

Deleting a single record

- ✓ Occasionally you may need to remove a record from a table. There are several ways to do this.
- ✓ First select the record: move to the selection box to the left of the first field, click to select the whole row (record).
- ✓ Click the Delete button in the Records group of the Home ribbon, (see figure) or click Delete Record in the drop-down list

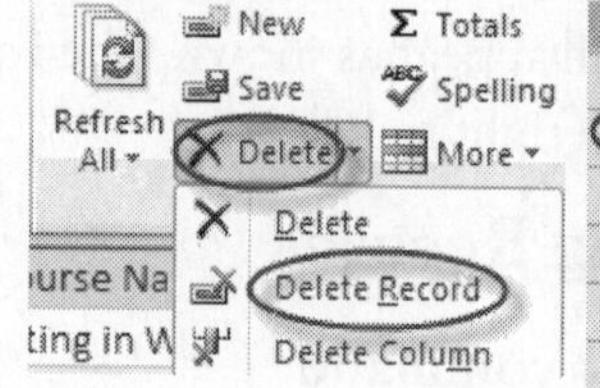

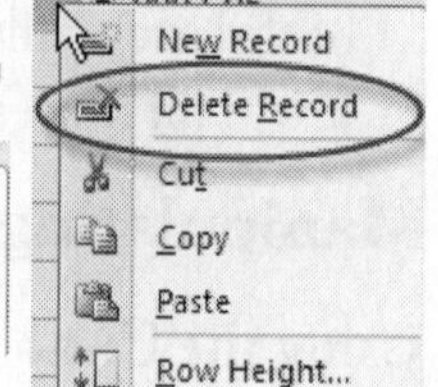

- ✓ Press the Delete key on the keyboard, or Right-click the mouse, click Delete Record in the popup menu displayed (bottom right figure).
- ✓ A warning is displayed. Click Yes to confirm deletion.

Note....

As mentioned previously, Undo is not available when deleting records, therefore any record deletions will be final. When deleting records from a table, the unique number in an ID (AutoNumber) field is also deleted and will not be reused.

Deleting multiple records

- ✓ If a group of records needs to be deleted the records must be together in the table. There are two ways to select the records:
- ✓ Move the pointer to the selection box to the left of the first record, click and drag down to highlight the block of records to be deleted, or
- ✓ Click in the selection box of the first record to delete, move the pointer down (do NOT DRAG); while pointing to the last record to select, hold the SHIFT key down and click.
- ✓ Once the records are selected, click Delete and respond Yes to the warning.

In a small table it is easy to find a specific record. However, if your table has hundreds or thousands of records you need help from Access.

- ✓ Open the Sample2011 database and Open the Class Schedule 2009-10 table.
- ✓ Click in the field you will be searching, for example click in Course Name if you will be searching for a class with a specific name.
- ✓ Click in Course Name.
- ✓ Click the Find button, it is in the Find group in the center of the Home ribbon.
- ✓ A dialog box like the one shown in the figure below.
- ✓ **Find What:** (type the text you want to find)
- ✓ **Look In:** has Current Field (which means it is important to click IN the field that you are searching first). The other choice is Current Document, in a Table that means all fields are searched.
- ✓ **Match:** chose from Any Part of Field, Whole Field, or Start of Field; any part of field means what you are searching for could be anywhere in the field, whole field means it can only have what you're searching for; and start of field means it will only be searching the beginning of the field for the text you typed.
- ✓ **Search:** chose from All, Down, Up; All will search all records no matter where you start the search, Down will start on the current record and search Down (stopping on the last record), Up will search from the current record to the top and then stop searching.
- ✓ **Match Case** if checked it will only search for the exact case that you typed in the Find What box. If it is unchecked it does not look at the "case" only the text typed

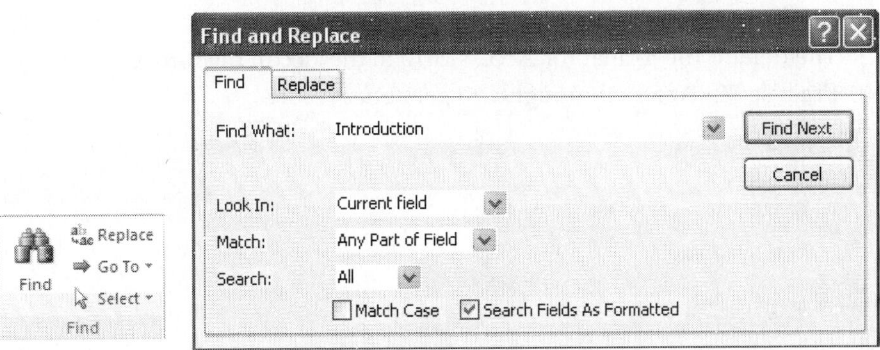

Search Fields As Formatted if checked will only look for data entered in the same format.

For example, if a Time field is formatted like this: 4:30:00 PM it will NOT find 4:30 PM if Search Fields As Formatted is checked.

Find What: Introduction

Look In: Current field

Match: Any Part of Field

Search: All

Click the Find Next button on the right.

When it has searched all the records, it will display the message shown on the right. Click OK and it will end the Find.

Close the Class Schedule table.

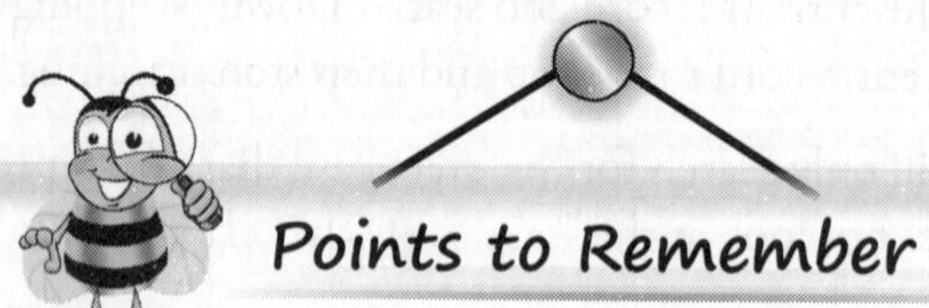

- The default file format for Access 2010 in the .accdb file format.
- Practise MS Access thoroughly to get better results.

Microsoft Outlook

Welcome to Ms Outlook

In this chapter you will learn

- Get started with MS Outlook
- Check inbox
- Sending and receiving mails
- Print Emails

What is Microsoft Outlook

Microsoft Outlook 2010 offers premium business and personal e-mail management tools to more than 500 million Microsoft Office users worldwide. With the release of Outlook 2010, you get a richer set of experiences to meet your communication needs at work, home, and school.

From a redesigned look to advanced e-mail organization, search, communication and social networking features, Outlook 2010 provides you with a world-class experience to stay productive and in touch with your personal and business networks.

Add an e-mail account

Before you can send and receive e-mail messages using Outlook 2010, you must add and configure an e-mail account. If you have used an earlier version of Microsoft Outlook on the same computer where you have installed Outlook 2010, your account settings are automatically imported.

If you are new to Outlook or are installing Outlook 2010 on a new computer, the Auto Account Setup feature automatically starts and helps you configure account settings for your e-mail accounts. This setup requires only your name, e-mail address, and password. If your e-mail account cannot be automatically configured, you must enter the required additional information manually.

✓ Click the File tab.

✓ Under Account Information, and click Add Account.

Create a new e-mail message

Outlook 2010 enables you to communicate with one or more recipients with a rich set of features and customizations.

✓ In Mail, on the Home tab, in the New group, click New E-mail.

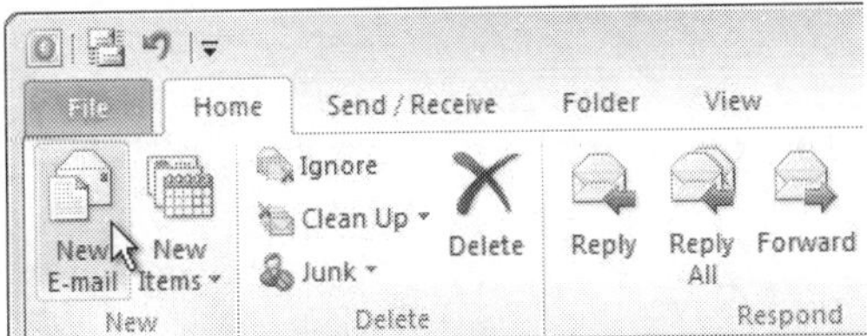

Creating new e-mail message

Keyboard shortcut To create an e-mail message, press CTRL+SHIFT+M.

Forward or reply to an e-mail message

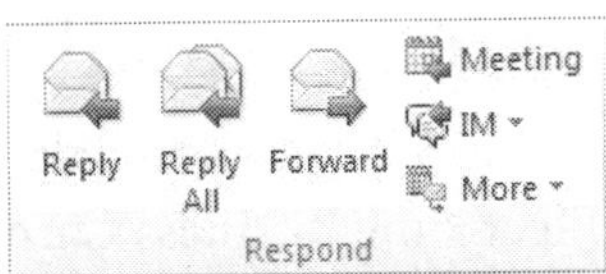

✓ On the Home or Message tab, in the Respond group, click Reply, Reply All, or Forward.

Note....

The name of the tab depends on whether the message is selected in the message list or opened in its own window.

To remove a name from the To and Cc lines, click the name and then press DELETE. To add a recipient, click in the To, Cc or Bcc box and enter the recipient.

Add an attachment to an e-mail message

Files can be attached to an e-mail message. Also, other Outlook items, such as messages, contacts, or tasks can be included with messages that you send.

Attaching a file

✓ Create a message, or for an existing message, click Reply, Reply All, or Forward.

✓ In the message window, on the Message tab, in the Include group, click Attach File.

Open or save an e-mail message attachment

You can open an attachment from the Reading Pane, or from an open message. After opening and viewing an attachment, you may choose to save it to a disk drive. If a message has more than one attachment, you can save multiple attachments as a group or one at a time.

Open an attachment

✓ Double-click the attachment.

Save an attachment

✓ Click the attachment in the Reading Pane or the open message.

✓ On the Attachments tab, in the Actions group, click Save As. You can also right-click the attachment, and then click Save As.

Saving an attachment

Add an e-mail signature to messages

You can create personalized signatures for your e-mail messages that include text, images, your **Electronic Business Card**, a logo, or even an image of your handwritten signature.

Create a signature

✓ Open a new message. On the Message tab, in the Include group, click Signature, and then click Signatures.

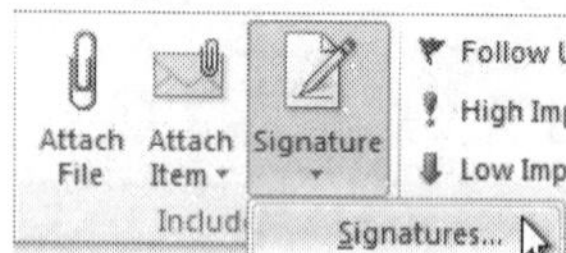

Creating a signature

✓ On the E-mail Signature tab, click New.

Add a signature

✓ In a new message, on the Message tab, in the Include group, click Signature, and then click the signature that you want.

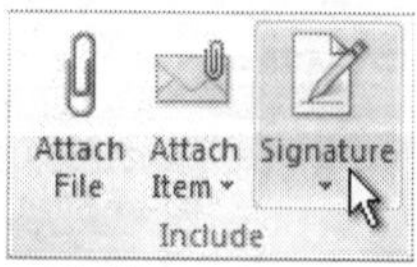

Adding a signature

Create a calendar appointment

Appointments are activities that you schedule in your calendar that do not involve inviting other people or reserving resources.

Creating calendar appointment

✓ In Calendar, on the Home tab, in the New group, click New Appointment. Alternately, you can right-click a time block in your calendar grid, and then click New Appointment.

Keyboard shortcut To create an appointment, press CTRL+SHIFT+A.

Schedule a meeting with other people

A meeting is an appointment that includes other people and can include resources such as conference rooms. Responses to your meeting requests appear in your **Inbox.**

✓ In Calendar, on the Home tab, in the New group, click New Meeting.

Keyboard shortcut To create a new meeting request from any folder in Outlook, press CTRL+SHIFT+Q.

Creating new meeting

Set a reminder

You can set or remove reminders for a variety of items, including e-mail messages, appointments, and contacts.

For appointments or meetings

In an open item, on the Appointment or Meeting tab, in the Options group, in the Reminder drop-down list, select the amount of time before the appointment or meeting when you want the reminder to appear. To turn a reminder off, select None.

For e-mail messages, contacts, and tasks

✓ On the Home tab, in the Tags group, click Follow Up, and then click Add Reminder.

Creating new meeting

TIP

You can quickly flag e-mail messages as to-do items by using reminders. Right-click the Flag Status column in the message list. Or if you have the message open, on the Message tab, in the Tracking group, click Follow Up, and then click Add Reminder.

Create a contact

Contacts can be as simple as a name and e-mail address, or include additional detailed information such as street address, multiple phone numbers, a picture, birthdays, and any other information that relates to the contact.

✓ In Contacts, on the Home tab, in the New group, click New Contact.

Creating new contact

Keyboard shortcut To create a contact from any folder in Outlook, press CTRL+SHIFT+C.

Create a task

Many people keep a list of things to do — on paper, in a spreadsheet, or with a combination of paper and electronic methods. In Microsoft Outlook you can combine various lists into one, get reminders and track task progress.

✓ In Tasks, on the Home tab, in the New group, click New Task.

Keyboard shortcut To create a new task, press CTRL+SHIFT+K.

Creating new task

Create a note

Notes are the electronic equivalent of paper sticky notes. Use notes to jot down questions, ideas, reminders, and anything you would write on paper.

✓ In Notes, in the New group, and click New Note.

Keyboard shortcut To create a note, press CTRL+SHIFT+N.

Creating new note

Print an e-mail message, contact, calendar item, or task

You can print individual items, such as e-mail messages, contacts, or calendar items, or larger views, such as calendars, address books, or content lists of Mail folders.

The procedure for printing is the same in Mail, Calendar, or any other folders in Microsoft Outlook — all printing settings and functions are found in the Backstage view. Click the File tab to open the Backstage view.

✓ Click an item or folder in Outlook that you want to print.

✓ Click the File tab.

- Always write the right email id of the person you want to send an email to.
- Check attachment if any before you click the send button.

Audio Tutorials on Youtube

The book comes with a Audio containing 23 Video Tutorials for better understanding of some useful applications discussed in the book. For convenience of the reader the videos are divided section wise, such as MS Word, MS Excel, MS PowerPoint, MS Publisher and MS Access.

MS Word:

Youtube Link: https://www.youtube.com/watch?v=6IVmxqm7HJk

1. **New Features:** This video tutorial guides you through the new features Word 2010 has added its domain, such as Ribbon Improvements, Photo Editing and Smart Art, Editing & Productivity and many more.
2. **Word Environment:** This video tutorial familiarizes you with the basics of word environments and teaches you how to use and customize various features of Word 2010 before you start working on a word document.
3. **Creating Documents:** In this video you will get to know how to open a new document, and open an existing document that is already saved in your computer.
4. **Formatting Text:** In this video tutorial you will learn the various methods of formatting text so that you can communicate your message to readers better.
5. **Working with Text:** This video tutorial guides you on the basics of working with text that includes cut, copy and paste; drag and drop; find and replace.
6. **Working with Tables:** This video will teach you how to work on tables in Word using various features to organize text in tabular format and make things comprehensible and organized.
7. **Printing Documents:** This video will takes you through a short tutorial on how to print a finished document, view print preview and adjust margins of a document before clicking the print command.
8. **Saving Documents:** This video tutorial guides you on how to save a document for the first time, how to open an auto saved document, how to save a document in previous versions like word 2003, 2007, and how to save a document in PDF format and other formats.

MS Excel:

Youtube Link: https://www.youtube.com/watch?v=outTdeoFUSM

1. **New Features:** This video tutorial covers improvements and new features of MS Excel 2010 over the previous versions, such as Ribbon Improvements, Spark lines & Conditional formatting, Slicers, etc.
2. **Excel environment:** This video tutorial guides you on how to explore the Excel environment and customize its various features.
3. **Creating workbooks:** This tutorial teaches you how to open a new file in Excel and open an existing file that is already saved in your computer.
4. **Simple formulas:** This video tutorial guides you on using simple formulas to work with numerical data such as Auto Sum, Average, Etc.
5. **Pivot tables part1:** This important video tutorial shows you how to manage large volume of data using Excel's special feature called pivot table.
6. **Pivot tables part 2:** This video tutorial teaches you how to make report vouchers, slicers, etc., using pivot table.

MS PowerPoint:

Youtube Link: https://www.youtube.com/watch?v=fEZvfboz4kM

1. **PowerPoint Environment:** This video tutorial guides you on how to explore the PowerPoint environment and customize various features of PowerPoint.
2. **Creating Presentations:** In this tutorial you will learn how to open a new file in PowerPoint and open an existing file that is already saved in your computer, selecting templates, etc.
3. **Slide Basics:** This video covers how to work in PowerPoint using placeholders, layouts and PowerPoint slides and templates and backgrounds, etc.
4. **Working with text:** This video tutorial guides you on the basics of working with text such as formatting, adding text boxes to your slides and modifying text boxes to change the size and location.
5. **Presenting a slide show:** This video takes you through a tutorial covering how to present a smooth professional PowerPoint presentation using various presentation tools.

MS Publisher:

Youtube Link: https://www.youtube.com/watch?v=YuaovSq83do

1. **Know it:** This video will guide you on how to create publications such as name badges, business card, brochures, menus, etc., using MS publisher 2010.

2. **Printing and Publishing:** This video will show you several different ways of printing and publishing a document created in MS Publisher.

MS Access:

Youtube Link: https://www.youtube.com/watch?v=umryWJzbzQo

1. **Database Introduction:** This video covers how you can manage your own database to meet the needs of your business or the company you work for.
2. **Working with database:** In this video tutorial you will get to know how to open and save databases and objects in MS Access 2010. This video also teaches step by step different methods of working in MS Access.

Comprehensive Computer Learning

Windows 8

What You Need to Know About Windows 8

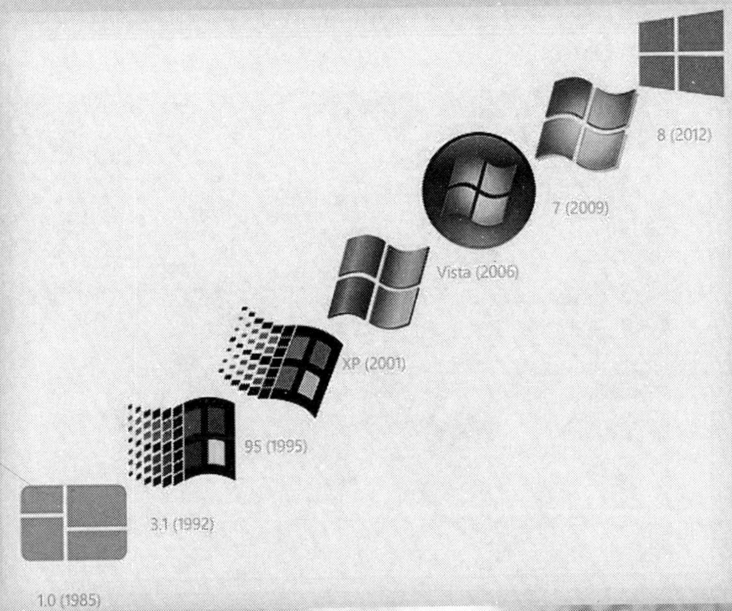

Back in 1991, Microsoft released their first version of Windows, a mouse-driven graphical user interface that revolutionised the way we use computers, both at home and at workplace.

Now, in 2012, they hope to stage a new revolution with Windows 8, perhaps Microsoft's most daring release yet. Featuring an unusual **Tile-Based Start Screen** that's optimized for touchscreen devices, Windows 8 will be available on new computers, laptops, ultrabooks, hybrid tablets and even a new range of Microsoft-branded, iPad-style tablet called **Microsoft Surface** and mobile phones also.

Whichever device you end up running Windows 8 on, you'll need to know a few things. First, how are you going to get the data from your current operating System to the new one? Second, you'll probably be wondering where the famous Microsoft desktop has gone. Finally, you might be wondering just what is going on? Why did Microsoft discard the Start menu?

Upgrading from Windows XP or Windows Vista or Windows 7

If you're upgrading, and you're already using Windows Vista or Windows 7, the new version of Windows offers an Upgrade option. This enables you to manage the transfer of data with little or no trouble – Windows 8 will effectively upgrade the existing OS without damaging your data – although you should backup your vital files anyway, just in case.

If you're upgrading from Windows XP, the process is a little different. Windows 8 cannot upgrade Windows XP in the same way in which it can Windows Vista and 7, in which case you will need to use a more detailed and drawn out process for saving your data and migrating it to the new operating system.

Where's the Desktop Gone?

So you've installed Windows 8. At least, you thought you installed Windows, but what you see doesn't look at all familiar.

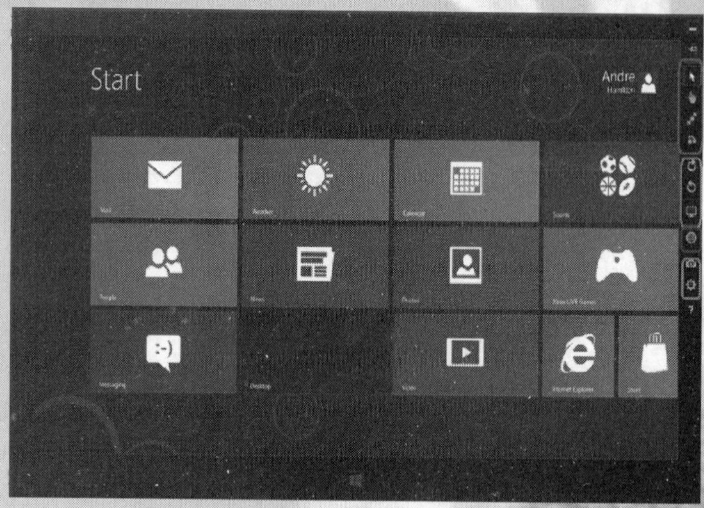

One of the most striking developments in the new version of Windows is the way in which the desktop – the area hosting the Start button, taskbar and icons in previous releases – has been demoted in favour of a new Start screen, Complete with tiles that can be clicked or tapped (depending on your hardware) to launch apps and adjust settings.

Have no fear, however – the old Desktop is still available. Indeed, it can be reached by tapping one of the tiles. While viewing the Desktop feels and looks like classic Windows, note that there is no Start button – all tasks related to this feature will need to be performed via the Start screen or by setting up some shortcuts on the Desktop.

Windows 8 Devices

There are many types of computer hardware capable of running Windows 8. First and foremost is the standard desktop computer. If your PC is capable of running Windows Vista, chances are it will run Windows 8. There are even some older computers stuck on Windows XP that can run Windows 8 effectively!

Similarly, existing laptop computers and ultrabooks will also be able to run Windows 8 – thanks to useful touchpad gesture apps, Windows 8 might actually be better for smaller systems than Vista or Windows 7 were. Despite this, Windows 8 is really intended for new devices. The reason for this is simple: the change in focus for the Start screen means that fingers are recommended, if not required. As a result new PCs shipping with Windows 8 will come with touchscreens and/or mice with gesture recognition tools, new Mac OS X-style touchpads will become available and laptops will almost all become hybrid devices, with pivoting touchscreen displays.

Microsoft aren't entirely playing nice with their traditional partners, the hardware makers – they've announced the release of a new tablet, Microsoft Surface, which will come in two flavours.

That's a big step for a company that doesn't usually make hardware. Windows 8 is designed to work on devices powered by a low-power ARM processor (found in typical Android and Apple tablets) as well as typical Intel x86 based processors (which is what most desktop, laptops and ultrabooks today use). Surface is seen as a competitor to Android and iOS tablets, and Windows 8's app store and tile–based interface are a big part of that.

With this in mind, there will be no shortage of suitable computers and tablets to run the new operating system! It should also be noted that a Windows 8 device powered by an ARM processor will be unable to run legacy Windows software, such as games and older versions of Microsoft Office. That software is Intel-only.

The Windows 8 User Interface

The major difference between Windows 8 and previous releases – the tile-based UI – means that you will need to spend a bit of time getting used to the Start screen. No longer will you need to click a Start button and browse the Programs list, or use the search function – at least not the way you're used to. Instead you will need to find a new way in which to perform tasks that have become ingrained, hard wired into your brain.

Understanding Metro

Probably the best route to understanding how to use Windows 8 is to forget that you're using Windows at all. There are various ways in which you can interact with the system, but few of them require you to click and drag, open properties or make any adjustments to the layout of the Start screen (although this is possible). Gaining familiarity with the tiles and the navigation is important, as is being aware of the **"charms"** – a hidden array of menu items. You'll need to move your mouse pointer to (or tap) the top or bottom right of your Windows 8 display to reveal the **Charm Bar**. If you are using a device with a keyboard, pressing WIN+C will also open the Charm Bar.

Appearing on the right-hand side of the screen, the Charm Bar provides other features and functions:

- **Search** – like the Windows 7 Start menu, simply type to find what you're looking for. When an app is open, Search will focus on that software rather than the computer itself. For a full computer search, use the tool from the Start screen. Note also that you can commence a search from the Start screen by simply typing – the Search tool will open as a result. Also note that Search can be used to find Desktop-based Windows items.
- **Share** – apps with sharing permissions can be used to share information such as links. Note that this cannot be used in desktop mode, only via the Metro browser.
- **Start** – this is yet another option to open the Start screen, along with the menu in the lower-left corner, or by pressing the Windows key on a hardware keyboard.
- **Devices** – settings for peripherals such as second/external monitors can be adjusted.
- **Settings** – Audio, Brightness, Wi-Fi, Power, Notifications and Language are all accessed from here. The **More PC Settings** link will enable you to access more options in the control panel. The Settings option will display settings for individual apps while they are active.

These options are displayed **Metro-style**. On the left side of your display, the date, time and battery and wireless networking information will also be displayed.

Note that many apps (native and third party) will have their own context menus. These menus can be accessed by right-clicking with the mouse.

Launch and Install Apps, Multitasking

One of the strengths of Windows 8's tile-based user interface is that the applications that are installed can be easily accessed. Another is that adding new apps is a case of tapping the Store tile and finding what you need to use. Multitasking remains a key element of Windows, although in the new-look Windows you'll notice that things have changed somewhat.

Meanwhile, any *legacy software* – applications and utilities designed initially for older versions of Windows – can be installed via the Desktop.

Launching Apps

You'll be stuck running applications in Windows 8 without knowing where your favourite applications can be loaded from. To find your applications, open the **Charm Bar** and click or tap **Search**. This will display the search pane on the right with the Apps list taking up most of the screen to the left of this. You'll be able to scroll left and right through the Apps list, while the search function will help you to quickly find the app you're looking for. You'll be able to open an app by tapping or left clicking.

The Apps List can also be opened from the Start screen by right-clicking or long-tapping and selecting **All Apps**.

Switching Between Applications

As ever, switching between running apps is possible by holding **ALT+TAB** on your keyboard. This will display the task switcher window in the center of the screen, enabling you to select the open app you wish to use. You might also use the **WIN+TAB** keyboard combination, which displays a list of open apps to switch between.

If you're not using a mouse and keyboard – that is, you're using a tablet or other touchscreen computer – you'll find that switching between application is done by swiping left across the display in order to find the app you wish to use. Tapping the top left corner of the display is also an alternative. A quicker way is often to head back to the Apps List and select the desired application again.

Closing Apps

One of the difficulties of Windows 8 is that the method used for closing apps isn't obvious. It is very effective, however. To close an app you will need to use your finger (or mouse pointer) to drag the app down, and discard it. This is done by placing your finger at the top of the display where you should see a small hand icon appear; drag your finger from the top edge of the display to the bottom, where the app will shrink and fade away! The same action can be performed with a mouse.

If you run into problems, you can call on the redesigned Task Manager to get you out of trouble. This will open in Desktop mode, however, but can be used to quickly close unresponsive apps. Note that it isn't optimised for fingers!

The Windows 8 Store

Available via the appropriately labelled tile, the Store will enable you to install apps, games and utilities for the Metro side of Windows 8. Although software can be installed through the desktop, the main way to install a new app in Windows 8 is to head to the Store, one of the first icons you will see on the Start screen. Launching the Store will provide access to a range of free and premium apps and games, similar to the Apple App Store or Google Play on Android. These apps and games have all been designed specifically to work under Windows 8, which means that they will be unavailable via the Desktop mode.

Use Your Windows Account

Key to your ability to access the Windows 8 Store is your Windows account. This might be a Hotmail account, a Windows Live Messenger account, even an MSDN or Xbox Live account. Either way, you will need to use this to access the store, whether you have setup Windows 8 to use this account as your login or not. There is a simple reason for this: some apps are free, others are not. If you wish to purchase an app, you will need to have a credit card attached to your Windows Live account. A credit or debit card can be added to your account via **Settings > PC Settings > Users > More account settings online > Billing**. Note that if you already have a payment card associated with your account, this will be used unless a new one is added.

Finding, Reviewing and Buying an App

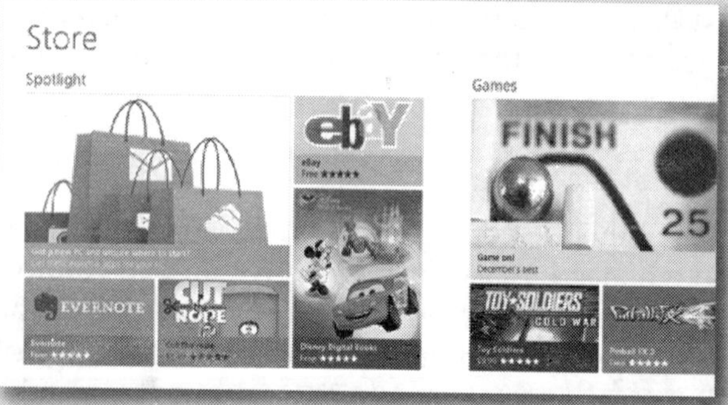

There are different ways of finding new apps in Windows 8. First, you might select the Store tile, and take a look at what is on offer in Spotlight. This lists the most interesting new apps, free and paid, while scrolling right will display interesting options from other categories, such as Games, Social apps, Music and Video, Sport, and many more. Each of these options can be opened and browsed, while the search tool will help you find what you're looking for.

Once you tap into the app or game itself, you will find a list of details about the app, such as its reviews star rating, the permissions it requires and recommended minimum age of the user (useful for video games). The Overview screen will provide a summary of the app; Details provides more information, such as detailed permissions and features, while Reviews provides a record of the thoughts of other users of the app. Images from the app are also displayed, which can be scrolled through. If you have downloaded an app, you will be able to return to its Store screen and leave your opinions and rating via the Write a Review link. Doing so is important – this is a new software ecosystem and other Windows 8 users may benefit from your thoughts when choosing an app or game. Adding a free app to Windows 8 will require you to tap Install on the app's description page. If the app in question has a price listed, tap **Buy** instead to proceed with the purchase. Note that some paid apps will offer a **Try** option, with a short trial period for you to use the software.

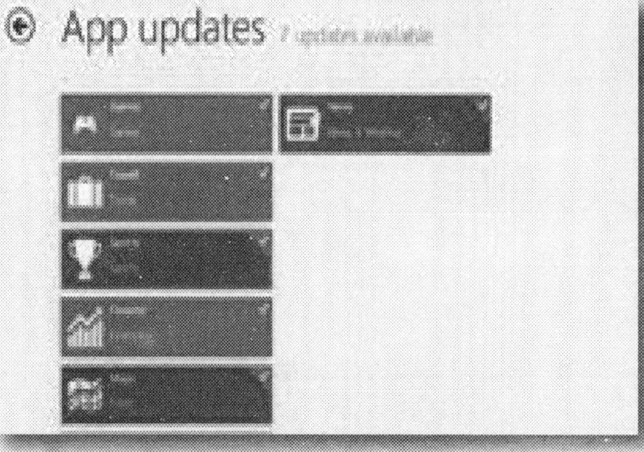

Updating Apps

You'll also notice that the Store will display a notification in the top-right of the screen informing you that apps can be updated. This can be done by right-clicking and selecting **Update > Install**, ensuring that the apps you want updating are selected.

Windows 8 system requirements

If you want to run Windows 8 on your PC, here's what it takes:

- Processor: 1 gigahertz (GHz) or faster with support for PAE, NX, and SSE2
- RAM: 1 gigabyte (GB) (32-bit) or 2 GB (64-bit)
- Hard disk space: 16 GB (32-bit) or 20 GB (64-bit)
- Graphics card: Microsoft DirectX 9 graphics device with WDDM driver

Additional requirements to use certain features:

- To use touch, you need a tablet or a monitor that supports multitouch
- To access the Windows Store and to download and run apps, you need an active Internet connection and a screen resolution of at least 1024 x 768
- To snap apps, you need a screen resolution of at least 1366 x 768
- Internet access (ISP fees might apply)
- Secure boot requires firmware that supports UEFI v2.3.1 Errata B and has the Microsoft Windows Certification Authority in the UEFI signature database
- Some games and programs might require a graphics card compatible with DirectX 10 or higher for optimal performance
- Microsoft account required for some features
- Windows Media Center license sold separately
- BitLocker To Go requires a USB flash drive (Windows 8 Pro only)
- BitLocker requires either Trusted Platform Module (TPM) 1.2 or a USB flash drive (Windows 8 Pro only)
- Client Hyper-V requires a 64-bit system with second level address translation (SLAT) capabilities and additional 2 GB of RAM (Windows 8 Pro only)
- A TV tuner is required to play and record live TV in Windows Media Center (Windows 8 Pro Pack and Windows 8 Media Center Pack only)
- Free Internet TV content varies by geography, some content might require additional fees (Windows 8 Pro Pack and Windows 8 Media Center Pack only)